CONFLICT AND AGREEMENT IN THE CHURCH
Volume Two

CONFLICT AND AGREEMENT
IN THE CHURCH

by
T. F. TORRANCE

Volume Two
THE MINISTRY AND THE SACRAMENTS
OF THE GOSPEL

LUTTERWORTH PRESS
LONDON

To
ANDERS NYGREN
and
EDMUND SCHLINK

Made and printed in Great Britain by
William Clowes and Sons, Limited, London and Beccles

CONTENTS

ACKNOWLEDGMENTS

Acknowledgment is made to the S.C.M. Press for permission to reproduce the essay on *Eschatology and the Eucharist* written for the volume on *Intercommunion* (edited by D. M. Baillie and John Marsh) in preparation for the Third World Conference on Faith and Order held at Lund; and to the editors of *Theologische Zeitschrift* (Basel), *Revue d'Histoire et de Philosophie Religieuses* (Strasburg), *The Church Quarterly Review* (London), *The Canadian Journal of Theology* (Toronto), *The Expository Times* (Aberdeen), *The Scottish Journal of Theology* (Edinburgh), and *Verbum Caro* (Taizé), for permission to reproduce articles printed in their Journals.

INTRODUCTION

IT is increasingly evident to-day that the lines of conflict and agreement in the Church coincide less and less with the frontiers of the historic Communions. That appears to be due in considerable measure to the resurgence of biblical theology and Christology in all the Churches, and may well be taken as an indication of the way ecumenical advance will take in the future. Thus new alignments are cutting through the membership of the existing Churches in a way that is bound to undermine denominational barriers and to bear positive fruit in growing reunion.

On the other hand, it still remains true that the conflict is most acute and agreement is most difficult in regard to what is called "the means of Grace".[1] The reason for that probably goes back to a distinctively Western habit of mind that grew up in the Dark and Middle Ages when undue prominence was given to practical and institutional questions and Latin pragmatism and Christian Gospel came to be compounded together in the daily life and mission of the Church. Thus the traditional Faith tended to be codified in the rational structures of the Church and Grace tended to be institutionalized in canonical forms for its easy ministration to the multitudes. In this highly pragmatic consciousness the Church was regarded as the Ark of Salvation equipped with the means of Grace for the salvation of souls, and in it the ancient Roman genius for organization, administration and deployment of resources found new scope for expression and development.

It was thus that the Roman Church grew up, but it grew up in such a way that the content of the faith was permanently tied to modes of thought deriving from the ancient world, and

---

[1] The very expression "means of Grace" is difficult and misleading, for it brings Grace into the realm of *means and ends* where some object is to be attained or some result achieved, and so it opens up the thought of its administration. In the New Testament Grace is never related to Baptism or the Lord's Supper, and is only once associated with the Spirit (Heb. 10:29).

the evangelical ministrations of the Church were channelled in dogmatically defined ways and means in accordance with unchangeable patterns in the institutional structure of the Church. Thus when the Church came under pressure from within for the renewal of its life and faith in the Gospel, the tension was most severe wherever the renewed life and faith broke through its encasement in the dogmatized and canonized patterns of thought and ministry. The tragedy that came over the Roman Church was that it failed to realize that the mediaeval modes of thought and patterns of life, which had served their purpose for centuries, had only a limited range of applicability, and when absolutized or invested with final authority could quickly become demonic like the principalities and powers or the ἐξουσίαι of which the New Testament warns us, and from which we can be redeemed only by the Blood of Christ.

The Reformers found themselves faced with an extremely difficult situation in their attempt to restore the face of the ancient Catholic Church, for the complete intransigence of Rome, culminating at last in the Council of Trent, left no alternative to a break in which each side found itself forced to barricade itself behind a total exclusion of the other. The fact that the Reformers had to do battle with the Roman Church over the means of Grace, that is, at the point where the Gospel had been tied down in the tradition to inflexible institutional forms, meant that the whole question of the means of Grace was given a place of undue prominence in the Evangelical Churches themselves, so that they were tempted over against the Counter-Reformation and over against one another to seek and claim justification for themselves in their practical manifestations and in the modifications and changes they introduced into the mediaeval institutions they had inherited. Thus the theological issues came to be confused with *post hoc* rationalizations of historical events, and justification by Grace alone was denied in practice by a form of self-justification.

That is what happened in the late sixteenth and in the seventeenth centuries when comparatively peripheral questions, significant though they were, were thrust right into the centre and given a distorted importance in the Evangelical Churches, and they settled down into hardening institutional structures over against one another. What could be more revealing in this

respect, as we look back upon it, than the action of the Westminster Assembly which sought to impose by Parliament a
uniform pattern of faith and ecclesiastical government upon
the Churches of the United Kingdom? Is it any wonder that
the Church of England on its part has barricaded itself behind
institutional structures that have become increasingly adamant,
and that this in turn continues to provoke hardening reaction
on the part of its sister Churches? On all hands we have repeated the failure of the mediaeval Church to see the limited
nature and sanctity of many institutional patterns, and in
claiming to fight for essentials we have often betrayed them by
confounding them with time-conditioned forms that rarely
have historical support from the New Testament or even the
Early Church.

In view of the present state of inter-church relations among
the Evangelical Churches there are three questions, among
others, for which I would like to press for immediate and more
careful consideration.

(1) *Fundamentalist notions of the ministry.* By "fundamentalism"
I do not refer to loyalty to the Gospel and the Word of God as
delivered to us in the Holy Scriptures, but to the binding of
this to fixed forms or set modes of interpretation that in themselves have no essential relation to the Gospel or the Word of
God. There is, for example, a "fundamentalist" interpretation
of Holy Scripture that is tied to rationalist, philosophical forms
of thought deriving from the seventeenth century, but there are
also "fundamentalist" notions of the ministry that are tied to
man-made traditions and time-conditioned notions of the
seventeenth century or earlier. There are Churchmen, for example, who appear to believe in the verbal inspiration of
seventeenth century Presbyterian conceptions of the ministry,
in spite of the fact that they do not stand up well to criticism on
the ground of biblical exegesis or historical evidence now avail-
able from the Early Church. But perhaps nowhere is this
intransigent "fundamentalism" more in evidence than in some
of the champions of Anglicanism, who are prepared to accept
exact, scholarly handling of the Scriptures, but who are not
prepared to extend that treatment to their peculiar notions of
"the historic episcopate".

(2) *Justification by Christ alone.* Justification means that we are

put in the right with God solely through Jesus Christ, that only
in Him are we clothed with righteousness. Therefore it calls in
question and relativizes all else that claims to be righteousness.
Because we believe in justification by Christ alone, we believe
that He and He alone constitutes the Church His Body, that
He alone sanctifies it in Himself, and gives it Truth and Grace,
and that He alone gives it the Ministry of the Gospel. Only in
Him may we look for justification anywhere in the Church's
life and work. Therefore we can never justify ourselves or
demand justification from one another without betraying
Christ or usurping His prerogative. But when one Church
calls in question the orders of another, is it not seeking to
justify itself over against it? and when the other demands
recognition of its orders, is it not renouncing justification by
Christ alone and seeking honour of man rather than of God?
This is the *damnosa inheritas* of Latin Mediaevalism that is still
with us—by tying the ministry of the Gospel to time-conditioned institutions, we give pragmatic questions a dominant
place which distorts and obscures the Gospel. When debate
takes this form, justification by works replaces justification by
Grace, and the whole Gospel is at stake. Justification by
Grace means that pragmatic considerations cannot be put in
the centre, either through insisting on them or through opposing
them unduly, without disastrous betrayal of Grace.

Justification by Christ alone means that in all ecumenical
discussions Jesus Christ must be allowed to occupy the central
place, that we begin only through unreserved committal to
Him and allow ourselves to be guided throughout by what
such committal may involve.

(3) *Intercommunion.* Nothing can be more heart-rending than
the way advocates of so-called "open Communion" or of
"reunion before Communion" seem to be manipulating
division at the Lord's Table in order to achieve their own ends.
On both sides of this issue there is apparent a deep failure to
understand the nature of division at the Sacrament of the Body
and Blood of Christ, and the outrage to Christ it involves. If
we are really ready to seek reconciliation in Christ we cannot
but enter upon Intercommunion as soon as possible, and, in
and through the forgiven and healed relation to Christ which
it mediates, work together towards *fullness* of Communion be-

tween the Churches. How can we sit down at the Lord's Table and then refuse to act out in our body and blood what we have received in communion with the Body and Blood of Christ, that is, refuse to act out reconciliation in the whole of our physical life and work in the Church? Therefore how can Churches sit down separately at the Lord's Table to proclaim the death of Christ till He come, when by their very separation they are acting a lie to reconciliation through the Blood of Christ?

On the other hand, the argument given by so many of our Anglican brethren seems equally to indicate failure to feel deeply enough the outrage of schism in the Eucharist. Thus it is argued against engaging in Intercommunion as part of the way to unity that "since the Eucharist is an offering in history of the memorial of redemption, it can only be offered by those who are historically at one". But does that not mean (except perhaps to the wilfully blind) that no Church which is separated from another Church can offer the memorial of redemption in its separation? To use such an argument against Intercommunion, while not using it against Communion, can only be a form of sinful pretence, while to insist on this argument and yet to hold separated Communion is only to eat and drink judgment. Surely we must recognize frankly that on both sides of this question we are deeply involved in sin, and that arguments advanced from out of that sinful separation are inextricably intertwined with self-justification and with rationalization of disunity.

What is absolutely imperative is that we repent, without waiting for repentance on the part of the other, and resolve together, without laying down conditions for the other, to seek reconciliation in Christ, and so take into our hands the holy means He has provided for repentance, forgiveness, healing, reconciliation, and unity; and then and ever after resolve to work out, in obedience to reconciliation in the Body and Blood of Christ, all that it entails for those incorporated into Him. Anglicans and Presbyterians alike might do well to study the illuminating work on unity in Communion, called *Brotherly Reconcilement*, written by Egeon Askew in 1605 and presented to James I as a contribution toward healing division—that in the seamless coat of Christ schism may be sewed up, men in orders brought into order, that God may be served in verity by His Church, and the Church be preserved in unity until the coming of His Son Christ Jesus unto judgment.

It is with the same prayer that the essays collected in this volume are offered to the Church, and with the desire on my part to learn more and more from my brethren through their criticism of these pages. These essays are not controversial, but are meant to be irenic and constructive, in the hope that they may help to clear some ground for agreement. Nothing like a systematic account is given in them of the Ministry or the Sacraments, so that perhaps I may be permitted to direct any who are interested to the new edition of *A Manual of Church Doctrine* by Wotherspoon and Kirkpatrick for an interpretation of Church, Ministry and Sacraments, as held in the Church of Scotland.

1

THE MINISTRY

(a) *The Meaning of Order*[1]

ORDER is the co-ordinating of the life of the Church in its fellowship, worship, and mission in the service of the glory of God. The order of the Church's ministry is the ordering of its life and work through participation in the obedience of Christ. Let us elucidate that in a number of paragraphs.

(1) In the biblical revelation the whole concept of order is viewed over against disorder and chaos. Apart from the ordering of God's creative Word the world is without form or void, but into the ordered cosmos there has broken the disorder of sin. It belongs to the very nature of sin to divide, to disrupt, to be anarchic—sin is lawlessness, *anomia*. The opposite of all that is order, harmony, communion. When God made the world He made it in order and everything was set in its due proportion. But through the lawlessness of sin the world fell out of proportion, out of order, and was threatened with sheer chaos. Were it not for the persistent fact of God's purpose of love the world would destroy itself; but in His Covenant mercy God holds the world together in spite of its chaos, and to that end He has promulgated His law which restrains and contains disorder and chaos, and reduces it to a measure of proportion, even while it is in the grip of *anomia*, or lawlessness. But God's Covenant contains the promise of a new order, of a new creation when all things will be restored to their obedience and perfection in the divine Will. Meantime wherever there is *anomia* it is met by the divine *nomos*, and there is conflict between disorder and order.

(2) The biblical revelation does not work with a concept of natural law, that is, of an order immanent in natural processes capable of being brought to its self-expression. There is an order of creation (*ordo creationis*) but that is not discernible by observing the creation (*cursus naturae*) but only by observing the

[1] Reprinted from *The Church Quarterly Review*, vol. CLX, Jan. 1959, pp. 21–36; French text in *Revue d'Histoire et de Philosophie Religieuses*, No. 2, pp. 129–142.

creative Will of God. This creative Will of God will restore to creation its lost order, and restore to creation its true form and harmony in the Word of God. That is shadowed forth in the divine law promulgated in the Old Testament, the revealed law of God, but as yet that law set over against the lawlessness of the world is revealed mainly in its negative aspect of judgment upon disorder, and of restraint upon lawlessness. It is through the judgment of disorder that order is maintained, and laws are formed to make life in the disordered world possible at all. But the ultimate function of that law is to point beyond itself to the new law, the new order of the new Covenant. Under the old Covenant there was a divine form of administration or economy given in the law of Moses; but that points ahead to the new Covenant when the Covenant Will of God will bring and manifest a new form of administration or economy. This will be inserted into the world and written into its inner being—the new law to be inscribed upon the heart through the Spirit. As such it is a new order that comes from without and is planted within.

(3) That new order, the new economy, or rather the eternal Economy of God for His creation, came into the world in Jesus Christ. In the Incarnation the Word of God entered into His own disordered world; the Light shone into the darkness; the divine economy entered within historical and creaturely existence. In other words, the Covenant Will of God broke into our world and is completely fulfilled in Jesus Christ both from the side of God and from the side of man. That is the economy of which St. Paul speaks, when he describes its work as that of gathering up all things into Christ the Head, things visible and invisible, and their ordering in the eternal purpose of the divine love and fellowship. *OIKONOMIA* describes literally the ordering of a house, household administration. God is the great Householder who has come to take control of His own house and family and order it according to His Love. He does that in and through the Incarnation, in which His *OIKONOMIA* is not imposed upon the world from without but enters into it and operates from within it. *OIKONOMIA* represents the great condescension of the divine Will to work out His purpose of love without violence within the alienated will of man, to work out His divine economy within the disordered existence of the world. Now the *mode of that economic condescension* is the way of

Jesus Christ the Servant, the way of obedience even to the death of the Cross, and it is through that mode of economic condescension that He is exalted to be the Head of all things, and especially the Head of the Church, His Body.

(4) In Jesus Christ, therefore, in His Incarnation and in the whole course of His obedience, there has taken place in the divine economy a restoration of alienated man to fellowship with God, a conversion of rebellious humanity to the obedience and love of God. In other words, in the whole human life of Jesus the order of creation has been restored; in the midst of our disordered, sin-disrupted existence, there has been lived a human life in perfect order and proportion to the Will of God. The Covenant purpose of God in creation has been fulfilled and more than fulfilled. Here we have the divine economy entering into our creaturely and human existence and ordering it from within *against* our human nature, that is, against the consequences of sin in all its disorder, chaos, and lawlessness entrenched in fallen human nature. This is the order of redemption which reaches back to the original order of creation and far transcends it in the amazing purpose of the divine love, as the order, of the new creation. Here in the new Humanity in Jesus Christ nothing is out of order, or out of proportion. Everything has its proper order, proper time, proper place, proper sequence, and proper end. From beginning to end the whole life of Jesus in obedience to the Father is directed to His praise and glory, so that the new order of creation established and revealed in the Humanity of Christ can be spoken of as the praise of creation for the Creator.

(5) Order in the new creation is to be regarded as a third dimension. We are not concerned here simply with the Will of God and the obedience of man, with the Law of God, and the conformity of man to that divine law, but with a *third dimension*, with a divinely provided fulfilment of the divine Law. In the Old Testament we have a situation in which God gathers His children into Covenant relation with Himself, and within that Covenant He declares: "I will be your God, and you will be my children. . . . I am holy, therefore be ye holy. I am God, walk before me and be perfect." But God knows that His children are unable to be holy or obedient or perfect before Him; they are unable to fulfil the requirements of His Covenant Will, so that within the Covenant and as part of its Covenant

mercies He graciously provides a way of response to His Will, a way of obedient conformity to His Covenant which He is pleased to accept as from His people in the Covenant. That was provided in Israel's Cult or *leitourgia*. But that cultic pattern of response had to be acted out in obedience, while it pointed beyond itself to God's promise of a way of obedient fulfilment of it in the actual existence and life of His people. That was the theme in the Servant Songs, which was fulfilled at last in Jesus Christ, who in His obedient Humanity is our God-given way of response to the divine Will. God's Covenant Will is fulfilled for us, on our behalf, and in our stead, and through our participation in the obedient Humanity of Christ we are given to share in the fulfilled economy of the new Covenant, indeed of the new creation. That then is the third dimension. We are not simply concerned even in the Christian Church with the Will of God in love and grace, and then with the obedience of man in love and fellowship. We are concerned with these two, but with the two as fulfilled and completed in Jesus Christ, in the obedient ordering and perfection of His human life as an oblation of all praise and thanksgiving to God the Creator and Father, and therefore of our sharing in His obedience through the power of the Spirit. Thus *order* in the New Testament refers to the concrete ordering of our human life and being in the obedient Humanity of Jesus Christ. All order in the Christian Church is a participation in His obedient Humanity—whether that order be an ordering of its daily life, daily worship, or daily fellowship, or daily mission. The whole of the Church's life is ordered through participation in the ordered life of Jesus Christ, the New Adam, the Head of the New Creation.

(6) The form which this re-ordering in Jesus Christ takes is the form of a Servant. It was through His obedience within our disobedient humanity that He restored us to order and peace in God. But in that He the obedient Servant is given to be the Head of all creation, all creation is now re-ordered in obedience to Him, for He gives it to share in His obedience to God. Because Christ is the Head of creation, chaotic, lawless creation is restored to order in Him, and because He restored order through obedience to the Father, He restores order to the creation through bringing creation into obedience to Himself, by granting it through the Spirit to share in His own obedience.

Thus as Jesus was obedient in the Father, who sent Him to fulfil His Will, so the Church is ordered in its obedience to Christ who sent it to fulfil His Will. The obedience of the Church to Christ is not simply an imitation of His obedience but a fulfilling of God's Will through participation in Christ's obedience.

(7) It is through the Spirit that the Church is given to share in Christ's obedience, and so to be ordered in and by and through His obedient Humanity. Christ is the Law of the Church's life, the Law according to which its life and work are to be ordered, but that Law is fulfilled not simply by external obedience and conformity but by inner and outer sharing in His Life, so that *through the SPIRIT* the Church is in-the-law to Christ (*ennomos Christou*), conformable to Him through communion with Him. It is the Spirit who is the Law of the Church's ordered life; not the Spirit as a new law of nature, not the Spirit as the soul of the Church, not the Spirit as a new immanent norm in the development of the Church through history, but the Spirit who gives the Church to share in the obedience of Christ the Head of the Body and who is other than the Church, its Lord and King but who in economic condescension has come to be obedient to the Father from within the Church, that the Church may share in an obedience not its own, and in an order that is new to it, indeed against its own nature; an order from beyond the Church's own being but in which it is given to participate by the Spirit.

(8) This being so, *actual order* as we see and have it in the historical Church on earth is essentially ambiguous. Its basic order is the obedient new humanity in Christ. The Church shares in that through the Spirit, so that its life is ordered through the Communion of the Spirit. But the Church that shares in that order of the New Creation is the Church that is sent by Christ out into history, to live its life in the physical and temporal existence that awaits redemption in the second advent of Christ. The Church in the midst of the old creation and all its disorder shares in the new creation and its new order. By sheer participation in the empirical life of this fallen world which comes under the divine judgment, and therefore the divine law, the Church participates in worldly forms and laws and cannot escape from them. It is sent to have its mission right there under law, but under law to share in the new order in-the-law to

2—C.A.C.

Christ through the Spirit. Just as the Son of God Himself condescended to be made under the law and through obedience to
fulfil the Will of God, and as such was exalted above all, so the
Church which is given to share through the Spirit in the new
Humanity of Christ is sent into history to live out its new life in
the form of a servant under the law—not to be fettered by the
law, not to be schematized according to the forms and patterns
of this age, that is, not to be legalized in its life, but to use the
patterns and forms of the law of this age in the service of its new
life in the risen and ascended Lord. Thus all order in the
historical Church is essentially ambiguous because it is order in
the overlap of the two ages, this present age that passes away
and the new age which through the Spirit already overlaps it in
Christ.

Another way of putting that is to say that all order in the
historical Church is essentially eschatological. By "eschatological" here two things are meant: (a) that order carries within
it the tension between the new and the old; and (b) the tension
between the present (including the past) and the future. True
order in the Church of Christ is order that points above and
beyond its historical forms to its new order in the risen Christ,
and points beyond its present forms to the future manifestation
of its order in the new creation. All order in the Church is thus
ambivalent and provisional: it is order that visibly reflects its
life hid with Christ in God, and order that exercises a provisional service in time, until Christ comes again. The outward
order is like the scaffolding of a building which is to be torn
down and cast away when the building itself is complete. In
history God has given the Church its historical order and structure which participates in the forms of this passing world, but
when the building of the Church as an habitation of God is
complete, and its new order is revealed in the advent of Christ,
the historical forms of order and structure will be cast away.
Or to put it another way: all order is at once juridical and
spiritual. It is at once participant in *nomos* and participant in
Pneuma, that is, in Christ through the *Pneuma*. The validity of
orders in the Church partakes of that ambivalence. Validity is
at once a juridical term relative to the particular nomistic
structure of a Church, relative to the law of a Church, but
validity is also a spiritual term referring to the sharing of the

Church in the authority of Christ through His Spirit, a sharing in the *exousia* of the Son of Man. It is that essential ambiguity in validity that makes it such a difficult term, and forgetfulness of it that causes persistent confusion.

Now in the light of all these eight paragraphs we have to think of the *order* of the Church's ministry with reference to its actual life in the space and time of this world. The ordering of the Church's life through sharing in, and therefore according to, the obedient Humanity of Christ, is an ordering within the physical and temporal life of this world. Order has therefore to be thought out in terms of *space* and *time*.

(1) *Order in regard to Space*

Because the Church is the Body of Christ, it has a physical and spiritual life in which the physical and the spiritual are not to be separated, though they may be distinguished, from one another. The Church as Body of Christ in history has therefore space. It has its place in this world, the place which it has been given by Christ, and into which He has sent it. It is in its place in the physical world that its life is to be ordered. Let us look at that in this way. Jesus Christ, the Man Jesus, is the place in this physical world where God and man meet and where they have communion with one another. The Temple in the Old Testament was the place where God put His Name, where He kept tryst with His covenanted people, and where they kept covenant with Him. Jesus Christ is that Temple on earth and among men where God has put His Name, and where He has appointed us to meet Him. It is the place where heaven and earth meet, the place of reconciliation. Jesus Christ is Himself God's mercy-seat, God's place in this world where He is really present to us in our place. But Jesus Christ ascended and He is in heaven—that is, He has a heavenly place far beyond anything that we can understand and far beyond our reach, but Jesus Christ through His Spirit has also bestowed His presence upon us in the Church, so that the Church on earth is the place of Christ.

The place of the Church in history is the place where Christ's presence is to be found. That is His real presence. It is of course above all in the Sacrament of the Lord's Supper, in the midst of the Church on earth, that we are given the real presence of

Christ. That is the place of Christ in the place of the Church on earth. That is the place where heaven bends down to earth, and where man on earth is made to sit in heavenly places in Christ. Here we are concerned with two places, as it were: the heavenly place of Christ and the spatial place of the Church. The place of the Church is to be defined with regard to that heavenly place of real presence of Christ on the one hand, and with regard to its participation in the spatial context of the physical world on the other. The Church's life, worship, fellowship, and ministry are all ordered in regard to that twofold place, heavenly and earthly place. No adequate understanding of the order of the Church can neglect that twofold involvement in space enshrined so clearly in the Sacrament. Order will concern the indicating or defining of the place on earth where the heavenly place of Christ makes contact with it, but that earthly place cannot be so delimited and defined as thereby to define and delimit also the heavenly place of Christ. Christ the risen and ascended Lord is in a place that is beyond definition and delimitation. It is through the Sovereign Spirit that He graciously condescends to be really present in the appointed space of the Church and to make that His place on earth. But He does not thereby bind Himself to that place on earth; rather does He bind us through that place to His own real Presence, to His heavenly place, and so from that appointed place on earth He exalts us to sit with Him in heavenly places. All this means that the Church's *order* in space is concerned with the ordering of its physical fellowship and worship in the Spirit. Order serves the proclamation of the Word and the Eucharistic fellowship on earth, but orders it in such a way that it makes room in it all, makes a place in it all, for the Sovereign presence of the Spirit, for the heavenly place of Christ—that is, for His real presence. The Christian Church as the Body of Christ on earth knows nothing of a spaceless ordering of its life.

(2) *Order in regard to Time*

Because the Church is the Body of Christ, it has a temporal and eternal life in which the temporal and the eternal are not to be separated, although they may be distinguished, from one another. The Church as the Body of Christ in history therefore has time as an essential ingredient of its reality. It has its time in this world, the time which it has been given by Christ, and into which He has sent it. It is in the time-form of this world, in historical existence that its life is to be ordered—to be ordered as Christ's Body in time. Now Jesus Christ in His historical life is the area in the time of this creaturely world where God and man, eternity and time, meet and have communion with each other. Israel through its history was the area within world-history into which God intervened with His redeeming purpose, in order to work into our time and from within our time toward that area in the fullness of time when God would become man and gather man into the life of God, when the Eternal would come into the passage of time, and gather time into union with the eternal. In Israel God bound our time into Covenant-relation with Himself, but all that is completely fulfilled in Jesus Christ where time is not only the sphere of the eternal event, but time is sanctified, redeemed, reconciled, and given new reality in union with Eternity, once and for all.

In Jesus Christ, therefore, the Eternal Son of God has lived His life within our time; He became time, and has in Himself elevated time into abiding communion with the eternal God. In Jesus Christ God has recreated time, redeemed it from its vanity, from its guilt and irreversibility, its decay and corruption, and given it a new reality in the new Humanity of the incarnate Son. But Jesus Christ has ascended and He is in heaven, in Eternity—that is, He has an eternal time far beyond anything that we can understand, or can measure by the kind of time we have in this passing age. It is not a timeless time, or a timeless eternity, but eternal time in which our time, redeemed new time, is eternally real in union with Eternity itself. That is the new time of the Kingdom manifested in the forty days of the risen Jesus Christ upon the earth, and within the lapses of our temporal history; but now that Jesus Christ has ascended, He has withdrawn that new time of His New Humanity from sight, from the visible succession of passing time on the plane of history.

And yet Jesus Christ bestows Himself upon us in time, and in such a way that our faith and worship are not timeless, any more than they are spaceless. It is within our passing time that He has time for us, that He makes time for us, makes time for

communion, for faith, for worship, for growth, for development, for advance. It is in the Church in history that Christ
has time for us, for by the very act of His ascension He waits
for us and makes time for us, in which we can hear the
Gospel, time in which we can repent, time for decision
and faith, time in which we can preach the Gospel to all
nations.

This was a frequent element in the teaching of the historical
Jesus, in His parables of the householder or the king who went
into the far country and waited till the right time to return, but
in that period of waiting he gave his servants time, and then
returned to call them to account for the time he had given them
—the word sometimes used to describe that is *chronizein*, but it
has also associated with it the word *chorein*, to make room, that
is room for freedom to believe, freedom to decide, and freedom
to be obedient (within time) until the return of the householder
or king. It is in that light that we are to understand Christ's
ascension, and the fact that by the very act of ascension, and His
heavenly waiting until the right time for Him to return, Jesus
Christ establishes the Church in history with temporal form
within the passage of time where it has time to work, and time
to obey Him. It is in that time that the Church has time to exist
and carry out its mission, within the succession of history where
there is time between revelation and decision, time between
decision and act, time between present and future, time for the
Gospel. Thus the existence of the Church as bound up with
its mission is inseparable from time. The Church as the
Body of Christ in history is the area within the time-form of
this world where God and man meet in the Gospel, and
where man is reconciled to God and united to Him in Jesus
Christ.

But it is *IN Jesus Christ* that God gives the Church that time,
and that place in time—and that means in the historical Jesus,
and in the risen and ascended Jesus. Just as Jesus Christ is the
place where heaven and earth meet, and God and man are
reconciled, and the only place where that takes place, so Jesus
Christ is the one place within time and the only place within
time where God has provided time for the reconciliation of
man, and man finds time for forgiveness and redemption. Jesus
Christ is Himself the fullness of time. Therefore the order of the

Church in time means the ordering of the Church's life and mission in relation to the time of Jesus Christ, the historical Christ, and the risen and ascended Christ. In all Church order we are concerned with *the time of Jesus on earth* when God's Son condescended to enter within our fallen time in order to redeem it, but also with *the time of Jesus ascended into Eternity* who yet bestows Himself upon us in time through His Spirit. The time of the Church will therefore be defined by the relation of the Church in history to the historical Jesus Christ, and to the ascended and advent Jesus Christ; the Church's life, worship, fellowship, and ministry are all ordered with regard to that twofold time, heavenly and earthly, historical and eternal time. No adequate understanding of the order of the Church can overlook that twofold involvement in time.

Look at it like this. On the one hand, Christ by His ascension has withdrawn Himself from the visible passage of time on the plane of this earth in order to send us back to the one time in all history where in the fullness of time the Son of God became incarnate—that is the time of the whole historical life of Jesus, culminating in the "hour" of His death and breaking out into the new time of the resurrection. The Church is for ever bound to the historical Jesus, for the Truth and the Life of God have become historical fact in Jesus and are now historically communicated and transmitted. The Church exists in that history stemming from the historical Jesus, and lives by the Word historically communicated through the apostles. Therefore all the life and ministry of the Church has to be ordered in time, according to the nature of that divine event in time, the time of the historical Jesus. By withdrawing Himself from the visible succession of history, and by refusing to abrogate our existence in time by sheer immediacy, Jesus Christ gives us time, enables us to take time with the historical Jesus and the historical Word communicated by and from Jesus. Thus, far from abrogating our existence in the on-going time of this world, by His ascension Jesus Christ sends us into the time of this empirical world, and commands us within it to focus our attention on the time of the historical Jesus, to be bound by it, and to be obedient to it; for it is by that time and through it that Jesus continues to rule the Church and order it according to His Word in actual history. Hence throughout all its life on earth, throughout all its continuity in history, the Church lives its life in historical attachment to the fullness of time in Jesus, and in historical continuity with it. It is out of that one time in Jesus that the Church lives from age to age, and from it that the Church derives its own time in history. It cannot in any circumstances detach itself from the historical Jesus, or depreciate its historical attachment to Him in the fullness of time, for it is precisely by its being bound and obedient to the historical Jesus Christ in the tradition of the apostolic Church that Christ continues to rule over the Church by His Word and Spirit, making it His own Body and Servant in history.

Church order is therefore the ordering of the Church's life in history in relation to that one time in all history, the time of Jesus; for that is the only place in time where eternity and time have really met, and where they are for ever joined, and it is in and through that union of eternity and time in Jesus that the Church lives its life on the plane of history. On the other hand it is in that time of the historical Jesus that the Church, from age to age, still meets with the eternal God and is gathered up "into" eternal time. It is only within the time of the historical Jesus that the new time of the risen Jesus breaks in upon the Church in history, and gives it to share and abide in the new time of the new creation. It is in the historical Jesus that the new time overlaps with the old time in our history, and only there, so that it is as the Church lives there in that overlap of the two times, that it is given to share in new time above and beyond the time of this passing age on the mere plane of earthly history. The Church continues to live within the time of this on-going world, but it finds its life above and beyond it in the risen and ascended Lord, not in some timeless eternity, but in One who has Himself descended into our time, redeemed it and gathered it up in Himself into union with Eternity. The Church is therefore bound to the succession of time by relation to the historical Jesus, but it is precisely in the historical Jesus that it knows its true life to be hid with Christ in God, and to be found beyond the passing and successive forms of this age. This does not mean the abrogation of the Church's historical existence, but it does mean that the historical existence of the Church, its continuity within the succession of time on earth, is determined by relation to the new time of the risen Lord. Hence the Church within the succession of time on earth is given a new orientation within the limitations of time; so that instead of being fettered by the bonds of time, bound by the sheer irreversibility of time that is laden with guilt, instead of being determined by the temporal processes of this world, the Church within time has freedom to meet with eternity, to rise above its past and to live a new life from age to age in Christ.

It may help us to understand that by thinking a little naïvely of the "two times" of the Church, as *horizontal time* on the plane of history in which it is bound to, and ordered in relation to, the time of the historical Jesus, and as *vertical time* in the Spirit in which the Church shares with Christ the time of His new Humanity. If the Church had only horizontal time, then the Church would only be a construct of historical succession, having only its temporal origin in Jesus but actually being fettered and determined by its place within the temporal process. Then the Church would not be free to have real meeting with the risen Lord; it would be enslaved to history, enslaved to its own past and all the errors and sins of its past; it would not be free from all the limitations and determinisms of history. But the Church within history is the Church of Jesus Christ in whom the Eternal has broken into our sin-determined and guilt-fettered time, and brought freedom and redemption from bondage. Jesus Christ is the area in our fallen time where the Eternal has broken through the limitations of this passing age to which we are in bondage, and where God acts freely upon men through His Word and Spirit, confronting them with His own Person and enabling them to respond freely in spite of all the downward drag of sin, in spite of all the piled-up determinisms of our guilty past, in spite of our bondage in the time of this world. The Church is therefore the place within time where that free meeting with the Eternal is possible, where within time men are delivered from the tyrant forces of bondage and are made free for God, so that real meeting in faith and love is not only possible but actual.

In the light of all that, then, the order of the Church's ministry in time is to be regarded as the ordering of its life within the on-going time of history and its succession which makes time for meeting with the risen and ascended Lord. It is an ordering of the historical and temporal life of the Church that

binds it to that one place in history and time in the historical
Jesus, but because in Jesus the Eternal breaks into our history
and time giving us, through the Spirit, freedom to meet with the
living God within time and history, it is also an ordering that
will not allow the life of the Church to be tied down to the
temporal framework of mere succession on the stage of this
world. The ordering of the Church's life and ministry in time
means giving it such a new orientation within on-going time
and all its limitations, that the time-forms of the Church's
historical existence become the signs of the new divine order
that already breaks in upon the Church in history. Thus for
example the historical succession in the ordering of the ministry,
far from involving the Church in bondage to the past, attests the
binding of the Church to the historical Jesus and so becomes the
sign of the new ordering of the Church's life in Jesus Christ.
Historical succession does not secure or guarantee the binding
of the Church in Christ, for He, the risen and ascended Lord, is
not bound by the forms of fallen time; for by His resurrection
He has triumphed over them. Historical succession, however,
binds the Church to that one time within our fallen history
where the risen and ascended Lord keeps tryst with us as the
Lord of all time and history, and where alone we may freely
meet Him. It attests the fact that, through relation to the historical Jesus, Christ binds us to Himself on the ground of the
historical incarnation, atonement and resurrection, and declares that we cannot find any life or salvation in detachment
from the historical Jesus.

All this is wonderfully enshrined in the Lord's Supper. "This
do in remembrance of Me. As often as ye do this, ye do proclaim
the Lord's death till He come." In the Supper the Church's life
and ministry is so ordered that it is bound to the historical Jesus,
to His death on the Cross, but at that very point in time the
Church is given to have communion with the risen and ascended
Lord and to share in His New Humanity, and from the Supper
it is sent out to proclaim that until He comes again. Thus the
ordering of the Church's life and ministry should follow the
pattern enshrined in the Lord's Supper. "For I have received
that which I also delivered unto you. . . ." It is celebrated in
that succession or tradition, and it is ordered within that continuity, but within that continuity it is the risen Christ, the Lord

of the Supper, who comes through closed doors, through all the limitations of our fallen time and sinful history, and gives us to eat and drink with Him in the new time of the Kingdom of God. While the Supper is to be ordered therefore within the historical continuity of the Church, it is such an ordering that room is left within it for the new time of the Kingdom, and in the presence of that new time all the historical time-forms of the Church are relativized and given new orientation—they are taken under the command of the risen and ascended Lord, are made obedient to His real presence, so that instead of being mere limitations to the Church's life and ministry they are the signs pointing beyond to the reality of the new time of the new creation. In so doing they are themselves transcended, and made subordinate to communion with Christ in the time of His New Humanity.

(3) *Order in regard to Space and Time*

Space and time cannot be separated in the Church. The Church on earth and in history is inescapably involved in space and time and in all the machinery of physical existence, for it is sent out to minister the Gospel in space and time. It is in that involvement with space and time that lies the significance of its order. The Church's very bodily and historical existence and mission require spatial and temporal order if it is to perform its divine purpose in space and time, but it can only live its life and fulfil its work in space and time, if its place on earth is ordered in obedience to its share in Christ's heavenly place, and if its time on earth is made obedient to its share in Christ's heavenly time. Church order concerns the ordering of the Church's life and ministry in the meeting of heaven and earth in the place of the Church, and in the intersection of historical continuity and immediate unity with the risen and ascended Christ. The place that the Church has in the space-time form of this world is not abrogated, but in that place the Church is given to share in the real presence of the New Man and real time of the New Creation. Until Christ comes again to change the space-time form of this fallen world (not to eliminate it but to change and renew it) the Church shares in the real presence of the New Man and the real time of the New Creation, under the form of space and time as we know it in this on-going world, as under a veil, as in a mystery. The actual space of the Church, its physical place in this world, has to be regarded as the trysting place of Christ on earth; and the time of the Church, its historical actuality, has to be regarded as the time appointed by Christ for meeting with Him. This space and this time have to be used therefore in obedience to His appointment, in subordination to the space and the time of the historical Jesus, that is, the actual founding of the Church upon the rock of the apostles, and to the actual tradition of the historical Jesus which we have received from the apostles, for it is in that obedience within the space-time form of the Church on earth to the historical Jesus that the Church goes into history as His servant, the obedient Body of which He is the Head. Only as that Body is it His Church. Therefore the ordering of the Church in space and time is concerned with its obedience to Christ, to the risen Lord in the space and time of the historical Jesus alone. Then it is, however, that through the Spirit Christ keeps tryst with His Church in history and bestows upon it His real presence, so that the time and place of the Church become Christ's own time and place among men. Then it is that the Church lives and works as the earthly and historical form of Christ's Body (as Karl Barth has called it), obedient to Him, its risen Head and Lord, and as such it is the instrument He is pleased to use to proclaim His Word to all nations and to manifest Himself to all who believe.

In all this the Church looks upon itself as covenanted with Christ, and as gathered into union and communion with Him as His covenant-partner. Just as its historical succession in time and space does not secure or guarantee its unity with Christ, but only serves to attest its binding to Him in the time and space of the historical Jesus, so the Church's obedience to the time and space of its foundation in the apostles and to the apostolic tradition does not secure or guarantee that it is the Body of Christ. Throughout all its succession in the relativities and contingencies of our sinful history, throughout all its life of faith and obedience, in which the Church cannot but acknowledge its unfaithfulness and disobedience, the Church relies upon the New Covenant which Christ has made with it in His Body and Blood. It is only in that Covenant undergirding all its historical relativity and all its unfaithfulness that the Church's security rests. In obedience the Church relies not upon its own obedience but upon the obedience of Christ, and acknowledges that it is given a ground of faith and reliance beyond all the changes and chances of this passing world and all its own unworthiness. The Church can never justify itself, therefore, by claiming historical succession or doctrinal faithfulness, by reference to its own place and time on earth and in history, but must cast itself upon the justification of Christ's grace alone, and rely upon His covenant-mercies who promised that the gates of hell would not prevail against His Church, and that He would be in its midst until the end of the world. The ordering of the Church can never be allowed to assume a role of independence and authority, as if the duly ordered Church, even in its obedience to Christ, could be anything more than an unprofitable servant. Order must always be maintained in ever renewed amazement at the grace of God, and in ever renewed thankfulness for His undeserved grace and justification.

To sum up. The Church is ordered in its life and ministry on earth:

(a) By being obedient to the historical Jesus Christ in space and time in the tradition of the apostolic Church, in which He, the risen and ascended Christ, comes to rule and order the Church by His Word and Spirit, making it His Body and Servant in history;

(b) By sharing in the obedience of Jesus Christ in space and time through the communion of the Spirit in which He, the New Man, gives it to share in His New humanity as He, the Lord, undergirds it in all its frailty and weakness by His New Covenant, so that already it is given to abide in the life and time and order of the New Creation;

(c) By looking beyond the historical and institutional forms of its ordering in space and time to the fullness of its life in Christ, who comes to meet it in mercy and judgment, and who at His Parousia will unveil the full reality of the Church in the glory of the Son of Man.

In this threefold way the Church looks upon its ordering in the space and time of this on-going world as the required form of its obedience to Christ, or the attestation of its reliance upon the new Covenant founded for ever in the historical Jesus, as the sign that points to the new divine order of the Church's life communicated to it even now through Word and Sacrament in the Spirit, and as the provisional form given to it, until the redemption of the body, of the order of the new creation which will be revealed only at the final advent of Christ.

(b) *Consecration and Ordination*[1]

In order to understand the New Testament teaching about consecration and ordination we have to examine the rites and language of the Old Testament tradition. The rites were not carried over as such into the Christian Church, for they were fulfilled in Christ and abrogated; but the New Testament does use the language of the rites to speak both of Christ and His Church, and it does adapt some of the Old Testament rites for its own use, but with entire freedom and with quite new significance. The basic line we have to consider is the consecration of the priest, and king, and prophet in the Old Testament, and see how they are fulfilled in Christ, and then see how *in this Christ* the New Testament thinks of the ministry as consecrated and ordained.

The Consecration and Ordination of the Priest

The main passages that concern us are Exod. 28 and 29; Lev. 6, 7, 8, 9; and Num. 8. It is worth remembering right away that the Leviticus passages fell in the Jewish Lectionary for the Passover week, and are clearly reflected in the Gospels, especially in John 13–17.

To get the proper perspective we have to remember that Israel was consecrated in the Covenant to be a holy people, a kingdom of priests to God (Exod. 19: 6; Lev. 20: 26; Deut. 7: 6 f.; 14: 21; 26: 19; 28: 9; cf. Is. 62: 12). As such, too, Israel was God's "first-born son"; that is, it occupied among the human family the part of "the head of the house" (the *ben-bayith*, the householder or steward of God's holy purposes, reflected in several of Jesus' parables). Within Israel it would appear that the primitive priests were the first-born sons, the heads of the house which is preserved in the Passover rite where the ceremony is conducted by the head of the house. But the first-born

---

[1] Prepared for the use of the *Aids to Devotion Committee* of the Church of Scotland, November, 1957, and reprinted from *S.J.T.*, vol. 11/3, 1958, pp. 225 ff.

were "redeemed back" for life among the people and their place was taken by the tribe of Levi (Num. 3: 12 f., etc.). Thus within Israel as a priestly nation, one tribe is set aside for priestly functions instead of the first-born, and within the tribe of Levi the "sons of Aaron" are set apart for special functions as liturgical priests. The Old Testament priesthood has thus an interim institutional character, and its importance lies in its functions and in obedience to the divine ordinances. It was the business of the Levites and priests to teach the Law to Israel, and so they lived scattered through the twelve Tribes. The sons of Aaron came to be divided into twenty-four courses, twelve functioning in the Temple and twelve in Israel, although all twenty-four came up to Jerusalem for the great festivals.

How then were *the priests* consecrated and ordained? This is very fully described. The whole congregation (*ekklesia*) assembled at the door of the Tabernacle where they were addressed by Moses and told they were about to act in accordance with God's ordinance. Then he "brought forward" or "brought near" or "presented" Aaron and his sons. They were solemnly washed at the Laver, and clothed with priestly garments. Aaron was anointed with oil by pouring, but his sons were only sprinkled with his anointing oil. Aaron only was called "the anointed", the *christos*. Then there followed sacrifices, the most significant of which was the "consecration offering" or "fill-offering". Some of this along with unleavened bread was offered for the consecration of Aaron and his sons, some of it was broken up into portions, and portions of flesh and bread were put into the hands of Aaron and his sons who offered them as "peace-offerings". Then Aaron and his sons repaired to the door of the Tabernacle and in the presence of the congregation partook of a sacred meal of what remained of the flesh of the fill-offering and bread of the consecration offering—that was called "a sacrifice of praise and thanksgiving". This was repeated for seven days, during which they stayed within the Tabernacle.

It is to be noted that in this rite the chief and proper subject is Aaron the high priest, although his sons are consecrated through association with him, and have their hands filled too and share with him in the sacred meal of consecration. But Aaron alone is the *christos*. (In an extended sense of cause all Israel is spoken of as *messiah* = anointed, Ps. 84: 9; Hab. 3: 13; Ps. 89: 38, 51.)

That act takes place only once and does not need to be repeated. The *Minhah* that Aaron offers avails for himself and the sons of his house. On his death, his eldest son was clothed with his high-priestly garments and was consecrated with his priests in the same way—but the anointing was apparently not repeated, except to recover a break in the priestly line (2 Chron. 13: 9). It has also to be noted that although the priests were consecrated only once, every time they went in and out of the Tabernacle or Temple they renewed their consecration through washing their hands and feet, while the high priest renewed his consecration through solemn and total baptismal ablution once a year in preparation for the renewal of the Covenant on the Day of Atonement. It should also be noted that the consecration of Aaron and the sons of his house to the priesthood was called *"the covenant of salt"*.

What about *the Levites*? In Num. 8 we are told that all the Levites were cleansed and "separated" within Israel, cleansed by the sprinkling of the water of expiation (used at circumcision and in cleansing the leper to restore him to membership in the priestly race) and then they were "presented" to God with the same offerings as Aaron and his sons; but in addition all the Levites *had hands laid on them* by the Children of Israel (doubtless acting through their elders) gathered at the door of the Tabernacle, who offered them up to their holy use as their representatives. Then Aaron took the Levites and offered them before the Lord as an oblation on behalf of the people that they might do the service of the Lord. Here the laying on of hands indicates the representative part played by the Levites, but as such they are offered unto God. Thus in their case ordination is twofold: laying on of hands and commissioning by the whole priestly people, and offering to God as consecration for His service.

What about *Moses* in all this? As Augustine pointed out long ago, Moses stands above all this without any ceremonial consecration. It is he who offers the sacrifices for Aaron and his sons, offers them to the Lord, and consecrates them. He himself had no other consecration than that of his supreme relation to the Word of God alone. Moses did not therefore pass on a consecration he had himself received; he acted only as "the servant of the Lord", and the entire validity of the consecration of the priesthood depended on God's command and grace alone—not on any "priestly grace". The priesthood is represented as God's "gift" (Num. 18: 7) and rests on its "givenness". Hence the Hebrew word to give, *nathan*, is frequently employed for ordaining to the priesthood; it is an appointment of grace.

The Language of Consecration and Ordination in the Old Testament

The general term used for consecration and/or ordination in the Septuagint is *hagiazo*, meaning "sanctify" or make holy. The emphasis here is always upon the fundamental fact that God will be sanctified or hallowed in the midst of His people (Exod. 31: 13; Lev. 20: 8—cf. also the incident of Nadab and Abihu in Lev. 10: 1, 2, etc.). All consecration or hallowing is a sharing in God's hallowing of Himself in the midst of His people, and has its significance only within the Covenant in which He is Holy and requires His people to be holy too.

Three distinctive terms are used, however, to describe this sanctification or consecration of the priest in holy things:

(a) To clothe with priestly garments—"to put on" (including baptismal ablution, etc.);

(b) To anoint with holy oil (the preparation of which was a secret) given along with sprinkling of blood;

(c) "to fill the hands", which was accompanied by a special sacrifice of consecration.

Of these three it is the third that is the distinctive term for consecration or ordination—the priest has his hands filled: *mille' yadh* (מִלֵּא יָד Exod. 28: 41; 29: 29; 35: 35; Lev. 8: 33; 16: 32; 21: 10; Num. 3: 3; Judges 17: 5,12; 1 Kings 13:33; 2 Chron. 13: 9; cf. 2 Chron. 29: 31; Is. 43: 26). The offering of consecration was called "filling" (*millu'im*).

What "filling the hands" means exactly is not clear. Generally it means that the priest has the priesthood committed to him; he receives it as a gift. Specifically it means that the act of consecration is brought to its fulfilment or completion when his hands are filled with the holy oblations. It can also be applied in an extended sense to the consecration of the altar through having the oblations laid on it. Its meaning is thus twofold, which comes out very well in the Greek of the LXX in its twofold translation of *mille' yadh*:

(a) *pleroun tas cheiras* (πληροῦν τὰς χεῖρας). Cf. Lev. 7: 29;
    Exod. 32: 29.
(b) *teleioun tas cheiras* (τελειοῦν τὰς χεῖρας) or simply *teleioun*
    as applied to the priest as object or in the passive with the
    priest as subject. It is almost equivalent to *hagiazein.* Cf.
    Exod. 28: 41; 29: 33.

These words are used, then, to describe the act of the consecration of the high priest in whose self-consecration the sons of his
house are also consecrated; that consecration is brought to its
completion in the filling of the hands with the oblations and in
the sacrificial meal of flesh and bread, "the sacrifice of praise
and thanksgiving".

The Language of Consecration in the New Testament

Although in the Old Testament "to fill the hands" was the
more technical term, it does not make very good Greek when
translated literally. It is natural therefore that in the Greek the
word *teleioun* should be preferred to *pleroun tas cheiras.* The latter
expression is, perhaps, to be detected lying behind John 3:35,
which has reference to Christ's baptismal consecration in the
Jordan and His anointing of the Spirit. If so, the underlying
Aramaic has been turned into smooth Greek, and the "filling of
the hands" is not very recognizable except to one familiar with
the Old Testament rite. Along with this should be compared
John 17: 2-4; cf. also John 4: 34; 5: 36. Possibly the Pauline
pleroma hints of this too sometimes, cf. Eph. 1: 23 ff.; 3: 19.

It is, however, the word *teleioun* that is prominent in the New
Testament especially in the Fourth Gospel and in the Epistle to
the Hebrews. The verb *teleioun* is of course often used in the New
Testament with no relation to the conception of priestly consecration, but when it is found in John 17, Christ's high-
priestly prayer, which clearly reflects the reading of Lev. 7–8,
we must see it in a different light. The evangelist also uses the
other word *hagiazein,* e.g. 17: 17–19: "Sanctify them in the
truth. Thy Word is truth. As thou hast sent me into the world,
even so have I sent them into the world, and for their sakes I
sanctify myself, that they also might be sanctified through the
truth." Then in verse 23 Jesus prays that the disciples might be
consecrated in one (*teteleiomenoi eis hen*).

When we turn to the Epistle to the Hebrews there are several instances of *teleioun* which refer to the consecration of the high priest, while the word *hagiazein* is used in a sense parallel to the usage, both in the Old Testament and in John 17. Thus Heb. 2: 11: "For both he who sanctifies (or consecrates) and those who are sanctified are all of one, for which cause he is not ashamed to call them brethren." In Heb. 7: 28 and 9: 9 the other word, *teleioun*, is used of the consecration of Christ the High Priest. In the tenth chapter the writer uses both terms, *hagiazein* and *teleioun*, to describe the fact that through Christ's own self-offering once and for all we are consecrated. By consecration the author of this epistle meant what Paul meant by justification through the blood of Christ and sanctification through His Spirit. It is Christ's own consecration of Himself on our behalf which both justifies us and sanctifies us as His holy servants, giving us to share in His consecration in such a way that through Jesus Christ our High Priest we all, with our bodies washed with clean water and with our consciences sprinkled with His blood, draw near to worship God, that is as priests in the House of God. It is interesting also to note that in this Epistle the institutional priesthood of Aaron is set aside because fulfilled and abrogated in Christ, and that He is High Priest as God's First-Born Son, and therefore we are all first-born sons in Him, while the Church is the Church of the first-born. That is to say, here where the institutional priesthood is done away all God's children are priests after the fashion of the first-born in Israel. Just as we are given to share in Christ's Sonship, so we are given to share in His Priesthood. In Christ sonship and priesthood are the same.

The Consecration of the King

The classical passage about this is found in 2 Kings 11: 12, 17 which describes the consecration of the king by Jehoiada, and which reposes upon Deuteronomy 17:18–20. It is also based on the rites formed under King David and carried out with regard to Solomon (1 Kings 1: 33 ff.; 1 Chron. 29: 22 f.; cf. 2 Chron. 6: 42). The main elements here are as follows:

(a) Anointing, possibly along with washing in the Gihon. David and Saul were the first to be anointed, and the anointing was accompanied by the gift of the Spirit (1 Sam. 10: 1; 16: 13;

cf. 1 Sam. 26: 11; Ps. 2: 2 (Acts 4: 26)). David himself was anointed three times. (Cf. 2 Sam. 2: 4; 5: 3. This was regarded in the Old Testament as indicative of the Messiah; cf. Ps. 45: 7 and Hab. 3: 13.)

(b) The kings were enthroned and crowned—the royal insignia of David were apparently used in later times.

(c) The putting of the "Testimony" into the hands of the king. According to Deuteronomy the king had to copy out the book of the Law with his own hand, so as to remember it and rule by it.

(d) A covenant was made between the king, God and the people. In the case of God's covenant with David it was known as "a covenant of salt", like the covenant made by God with the house of Aaron. In the case of Solomon's consecration we know that there was also prayer and sacrifice—see 1 Chron. 29: 22 f.

Here, then, in the consecration of the king the fundamental pattern of consecration was similar to that of the consecration of the priest, involving: anointing, filling of the hands, and affirmation of the covenant relation. The difference lies chiefly in that to which the king is consecrated, kingship, not sacrifice, and that the king's hands are filled therefore not with oblations but with the Law. He is crowned and enthroned, which does not apply to the priests.

The Consecration of the Prophet

We have even less information about this, but a clear instance of the consecration of Elisha by Elijah is given in 1 Kings 19: 16. It was by anointing followed later by investment with the prophet's mantle. In Ps. 105: 15 "the anointed" and the prophets are synonymous. The anointing of both Saul and David gave them prophetic gifts, and presumably that meant that the anointing of kings was an extension of the anointing of prophets through whose Word proclaimed and enunciated God ruled as King.

In Is. 61: 1 the Servant of the Lord speaks of himself as anointed to preach the Gospel, which Christ claimed to be fulfilled in Himself, Luke 4: 18; John 10: 36.

In addition to this Old Testament tradition, it should be noted that in the Judaean Scrolls the Anointed of the Lord, the Messiah, is regarded apparently as deriving both from the

House of David and from the House of Aaron—the anointed priest-king. The members of the community initiated into the new covenant are spoken of as "anointed ones" and as forming a holy and "priestly" messianic community. That may have some influence on the New Testament, e.g. on 1 Peter.

Summary of the New Testament Teaching

Jesus Christ is the fulfilment of the threefold consecration to the office of priest, king, and prophet in the Old Testament. We have seen something of the fulfilment of priestly consecration in Christ, but kingly and prophetic consecration was also fulfilled in Him (Luke 4: 18; Acts 4: 26; 10: 38; Heb. 1: 9). This was all fulfilled in His anointing by the Spirit, which no doubt referred to His birth of the Spirit as well as to His anointing at His Baptism in the Jordan; it was as the Anointed Son of the Father that He gathered up and fulfilled the threefold anointing of Prophet, Priest, and King. The Church which He has made His own was anointed with Christ's Spirit at Pentecost by the Baptism of the Spirit, so that through Baptism all who come to Christ are not only given the right to be sons of God but are anointed with His anointing, receive the *chrism* of the Spirit (1 John 2: 20, 27; 2 Cor. 1: 21), or are given the *seal* of the Spirit, as St. Paul puts it.

Here, then, in Christ the First-Born Son of God and our High Priest, we are restored to the priestly Kingdom, for He has washed us from our sins in His own blood and made us kings and priests unto God. Every one who is a Son of God through Christ the Son belongs to this royal priesthood, and shares in Christ's self-consecration on our behalf. Christ alone is the *Christos*, the Anointed and Consecrated One (John 10: 36), but we who follow Him in Baptism are given to share in it, putting off the old impurity and putting on Christ as our priestly garment, clothed with His righteousness, His consecration, and His holiness. Here there is no institutional priesthood like that of the Aaronic priesthood. That was an imperfect interim-measure only, necessarily done away when the true priesthood of sonship, the priesthood of the first-born, was restored in Christ. Here priesthood and sonship are the same, but when this is so, it is Baptism, through which we are consecrated as sons of God, which is our consecration to priesthood in Christ.

Consecration and Ordination of the Ministry in the New Testament

When we turn to the consecration and ordination of a special ministry as Christ's gift to His Church we find that this has its place only within the consecration of the whole membership of Christ's Body, and therefore within the ministry of the whole Body, which it has through sharing in Christ's vicarious Self-consecration. But within that there is something else. There are in fact two things: (1) The special consecration of the apostles in Christ's Self-consecration; and (2) The apostolic ordination of others through the laying on of hands and prayer.

(1) *The special consecration of the apostles in Christ.* The accounts of Christ's appointment of the apostles, His "making" of them, of His drawing them into a very private and close relation to Himself and to His teaching and His passion, and above all His special purpose for them in the Last Supper, as reflected in the Fourth Gospel as well as the Synoptics, are of special importance.

Although the Lord's Supper belongs to the whole Church, its first enactment belonged peculiarly to the apostles, who were at that point given a special place in the New Covenant and in the Kingdom of Christ, appointed to sit upon twelve thrones judging the twelve tribes of Israel, as the patriarchs of the New Israel, the Foundation of the Church. Jesus' solemn washing of their feet and His deliberate actions at the Supper clearly designed for the disciples peculiarly, and His high-priestly prayer of consecration in which He prayed above all for the disciples, make it clear that He regarded Himself, in going forth to the Cross, as the High Priest in whose Self-oblation and Self-consecration He was giving the disciples to share in a most intimate way as "the sons of His house". His Self-consecration as the *Christos*, His action as the High Priest on the Great Day of Atonement, was fulfilled once and for all, and can never be repeated. Just as when Aaron acted all Israel acted in him and through him, for he acted for all Israel, but at the same time the sons of his house had a special place in it, being sprinkled with the blood of sacrifice and with the oil of anointing, so when Christ went forth to the Cross all His people were given to share in it, for He acted on their behalf and in their stead; and yet in a special way the Twelve were given to be related to it. They alone went forth to the events of His passion after having shared with Him the consecration meal of the bread and wine of the Last Supper, and they alone, as it were, were sprinkled with His blood in Gethsemane where they were taken to watch and pray with Him in His awful agony; and they alone when He returned from His sacrifice had breathed upon them His Spirit in the Upper Room and so were anointed with His anointing. As such the apostles belonged to the once-and-for-all events of the Founding of the New Covenant in the Body and Blood of Christ; they remain for ever the authoritative witnesses of the New Covenant, the Pillars of the Church, in whom and through whom Jesus Christ made an everlasting Covenant of Salt with His Church making it a royal priesthood in Himself.

The apostle-disciples were appointed to their ministry like Moses directly through the Word, and were given to sit, as it were, in Moses' seat, or rather in Christ's seat, inasmuch as they mediated His Word to the Church and in Christ's Name were appointed to rule and order His Church; but, like the sons of Aaron, the apostles shared peculiarly in the Self-consecration and anointing of their High Priest. All that is something that cannot be repeated, and therefore cannot be extended. The apostleship can have no successors, for the apostles remain under Christ as the permanent authorities over the Church, the foundation upon which all other ministry within the Church depends. And so they were sent out by Christ with His Commission to engage in the mission of reconciliation. It was in the fulfilment of that commission and mission that they came to ordain others to the ministry, giving the sign of the laying on of hands to attest that they were sent to fulfil their ministry within the one Commission of Christ given to His apostles, and within the once and for all Consecration of His Church upon the foundation of the apostles. But in taking an entirely different method of ordination from that which they had received the apostles showed unmistakably that they were in no sense extending their office to others, but ordaining a ministry in dependence upon their unique ministry in Christ.

(2) *The apostolic ordination of others through the laying on of hands and prayer*[1] (Acts 6: 6; 13: 3; 1 Tim. 4: 14; 5: 22; 2 Tim. 1: 6;

[1] In this section I am indebted to the discussion of A. Ehrhardt, *The Apostolic Ministry, S.J.T. Occasional Paper* no. 7, ch. II.

cf. Acts 14: 23; 2 Cor. 8: 19). The laying on of hands is the only ceremony that is taken over from the Old Testament by the New Testament Church for the consecration and ordination of its ministry. The consecration of the Church and of its ministry in the apostles had of course already taken place, and taken place once for all, so that whenever in the history of the Church there is an ordination to the ministry that ordination is grounded upon the once and for all consecration of the Church and its apostolic ministry in Christ; it shares in it, takes place only within it, and is the means whereby that consecration is through prayer related directly and particularly to those set apart for the ministry within the sphere of the apostolic commission and mission.

It does not appear that the early Church took over the rite of laying on of hands from Judaism so much as from the Old Testament. The elders in the Sanhedrin were instituted apparently only by enthronement in Moses' seat, but later on ordination by laying on of hands took the place of this. This rite may have had earlier usage in Judaism which influenced the New Testament Church, but the evidence on the whole suggests that the apostles went back directly to the Old Testament itself for their guidance.

In a recent work (*The New Testament and Rabbinic Judaism*, p. 224 f.) Professor Daube has pointed out that three different words are used in the Old Testament for a rite of blessing or ordination with hands. (1) *Nasa* to describe the priestly blessing when hands are lifted up, e.g. in the Aaronic benediction. This was an act of prayer and blessing in which the Name of God was put upon the people—the act used by Jesus in blessing His disciples at His ascension. (2) *Sim* or *shith* which describes the act of placing hands upon someone for blessing, as in the patriarchal blessing of Joseph's sons by Jacob. It was possibly this act that was used by Jesus in healing, and perhaps by the early Church at Baptism. (3) *Samakh* which describes the solemn act of laying (literally "leaning") on of hands as applied to sacrifices when sins are symbolically transferred to a victim, or used where the transference of guilt or association in responsibility is indicated, e.g. in stoning a blasphemer or in instituting someone to responsible office. (I cannot agree with Professor Daube's psychological interpretation of *Samakh* as "the pouring of personality" from one person to another.) There is no evidence that Jesus ever used this. In Judaism the laying on of hands was not used for the ordaining of "the seven of a city" or local "elders", although their appointment to the local presbytery required the authorization of the Presbytery of the People or the Sanhedrin in Jerusalem. In the second century (and possibly in the first) rabbis were ordained by *samakh*, the solemn laying on of hands, called "the laying on of hands of the elders".

There are two instances of laying on of hands in the Old Testament important for the Christian precedent. (1) The laying on of hands through which the Levites were ordained to their office. This was an act carried out by the people, presumably through their elders, and was a lay-act in which the Levites were inducted into responsible representation of the people, appointed to stand for the first-born of the people in their ministry at the Tabernacle. That act of laying on of hands was completed when they were offered to God by the priests. (2) The other instance is the act of Moses in ordaining Joshua as his successor in the leadership of the people. In doing so Moses was commanded to "put of his honour upon Joshua" (Num. 27: 18, 23; Deut. 34: 9). With this act God bestowed upon Joshua His Spirit to enable him to fulfil his appointed task. Joshua was not of course ordained to take Moses' place either as a priest or as the mediator of the Word of God, but simply in civil and military leadership of the people. He was a lay-governor under the Kingship of God. This was in a different sense an act of *lay ordination*.

Laying On of Hands in the New Testament

The first case of laying on of hands was that of the seven elder-deacons in Acts 6. Here, as we have noted, hands were laid on the seven by the congregation, not by the apostles (except according to Codex Bezae), but they were set before the apostles, to indicate that the apostles had part in the act. It was, however, an act of lay-ordination like that of the Levites in the Old Testament. At the same time the language used in the Old Testament of Joshua's ordination is reflected in Acts, in the choice of seven men in whom there was the Spirit. But again the language also seems to reflect the appointment of the seventy elders in Numbers 11: 16, when, without any laying on of hands,

God put His Spirit upon them to enable them to fulfil their office on appointment to the Presbytery of Israel. The laying on of hands upon the seven elder-deacons in Acts was accompanied by prayer, and these ordained were given the Spirit in fulfilment of their ministry. The fact that the apostles did not lay hands on them suggests that they were not being appointed as their deputies, but only as their assistants (i.e. as Levites!).

The instance of the separation of Paul and Barnabas by the command of the Spirit and their ordination at the hands of a group of prophets and teachers to which they belonged at Antioch seems to be (as Professor Daube suggests) a case of ordination for special embassage, in which they were commissioned to carry out a particular task on behalf of the rest. They were not ordained as "Rabbinic" pupils or disciples, but rather sent out as "apostles" of the community on a limited mission. The language used here, e.g., "separate me Paul and Barnabas", also suggests that used of the Levites in Num. 8: 6 f. It does not seem to refer to ordination in the proper sense. This sort of thing was a common Rabbinic practice in the second century, but may well have been used earlier.

The most important instance of ordination by laying on of hands in the New Testament is that of Timothy, described in two verses, 1 Tim. 4: 14 and 2 Tim. 1: 6, which have to be taken together with the other passages in Timothy and Titus regarding the appointment and ordination of other ministers.

In 1 Timothy 4: 14 we read: "Neglect not the gift that is in thee which was given thee by *prophecy* with the laying on of hands of the presbytery." In 2 Tim. 1: 6, we read: "Stir up the gift of God which is in thee through the laying on of hands." Putting these together, as I think we must, I make the meaning to be as follows: Timothy has been carefully instructed in the faith and trained in the *didaskalia* which he exercises; in that training it was clear that he was called to the ministry, that God had imparted to him a gift for its fulfilment; at the same time that gift is looked on as imparted formally through the act of laying on of hands, authorizing him as an accredited teacher and minister, but used by God as the means of imparting to him a *charisma* for the ministry. The act of laying on of hands has been carried out by Timothy's teacher Paul, and by the presbytery acting together. It is possible, as Professor Daube suggests, that the laying on of hands of the presbytery (*epithesis ton cheiron tou presbyteriou*) is simply a Rabbinic term for "the ordination of elders" (*semikhath zeqenim, Bab. San.* 13 b). But it seems more likely that it means that the presbytery as a whole laid on hands, while Paul acted along with them and doubtless presided over them in the act of ordination. The fact that Timothy, who is put in charge of missionary churches by Paul and commanded to appoint elders in them, is not to lay hands suddenly on people, indicates that he would himself be the chief minister in ordaining presbyters in that area under his supervision, but that he should only do it after due and careful training. According to Rabbinic rules a man was not to be ordained to teach until he had reached the age of forty. It may be with that in mind that Paul exhorts Timothy not to let anyone despise his youth, for, young as he is, he is fully authorized by Paul and the presbytery to undertake his ministry.

This instance is of fundamental importance for a number of reasons:

(a) It provides us with a clear case of what even Professor Daube (who sees it, however, as parallel to Rabbinic ordination) calls "apostolic succession". Timothy is not appointed to be an apostle, but he has the full authorization of Paul the Apostle to do the office of a minister, and indeed of a bishop; and as such he is to fulfil the same office in ordaining others as Paul fulfilled in ordaining him.

(b) But this ordination is a corporate act of the presbytery. It was the presbytery that was the repository of authorization at the local level, although the presbytery had also to be acting within the sphere of the apostolic commission and mission, a link that was supplied by St. Paul. It is not suggested that it was the local presbytery that joined with Paul in ordaining Timothy. At any rate it is clear that the presbytery is the medium of ordination although Paul has a special part in it, and Timothy afterwards takes a similar place in the ordination of others. Presumably, however, he would not act apart from the presbytery, except perhaps in founding a new church and appointing and ordaining new presbyters, in which instance he would be the authorized person acting within the apostolic commission to undertake that; but once established the presbytery would act

as a body with Timothy. Here both "presbyterian" and "epis-
copalian" elements are clearly held together.

Now in interpreting what the New Testament has to say
about ordination and its adaptation of Old Testament rites, we
have to remember that nowhere does the New Testament take
over an Old Testament rite and develop it as such. What it
always does is to lay several images or rites together, elements of
which are then used in the freedom of the apostolic Church for
its own purposes in forming a new image or a new rite which
derives its significance not from the Old Testament ceremonies
or images as such but from Christ and from what the apostolic
Church makes of it. How then are we to interpret the New
Testament concept of ordination?

(1) The first thing to note is that by selecting this rite of
laying on of hands, which was essentially a *lay rite* both in the
Old Testament and in Judaism, the Christian Church made it
decisively clear that the Christian ministry was not to be interpreted in the sense of the priesthood of the Old Testament.
That had been fulfilled in Christ who alone is Priest. But because all that was fulfilled in Christ, permanent elements of
significance in it might well be transferred from Christ to the
interpretation of the Christian rite. That is what happened.

(2) The main element in the laying on of hands seems undoubtedly to be the commissioning of ministers of the Word to
proclaim the *kerygma* and teach the *didache* in obedience to the
apostolic witness to Christ and in following their example and
ordinances. Ordination is for those who labour in the Word
and carries with it acknowledged authorization to do so,
authorization that derives from the apostolic commission as an
attestation of the tradition of the apostolic teaching and preaching of the Gospel. Here we recall the old rites of consecrating
the king by filling his hands with "the testimony", and the consecrating of the prophet through whose Word it is God who
acts and rules.

(3) But this ordination has other elements associated with it;
the gift of the Spirit, the bestowal of a special *charisma* for the
ministry; and it is performed with prayer. It is difficult to resist
the conclusion that, while in the Old Testament three different
sets of expressions are used to describe three different forms of
laying on or lifting up of hands, the New Testament seems to

blend elements of all three together. That was certainly done
immediately after New Testament times. Thus in addition to
the strict concept of *samakh*, responsible commissioning with
authority to minister the Word, ordination also draws into its
orbit the concept of blessing the one ordained through prayer,
and calling upon him the gift of the Spirit, who brings a special
charisma to the one ordained for the fulfilment of his ministry.
But also the other idea found in the practice of *samakh* in the Old
Testament is not absent: that of offering or presenting the one
upon whom hands are laid before God, symbolized by the presentation of the seven before the apostles, as Joshua was presented before Eleazar by Moses when he ordained him, or the
Levites were presented before the Tabernacle and then offered
to God. That is a concept which Paul applies to his missionary
congregations; he offers them to God as an oblation. According
to Calvin this element is a powerful ingredient in ordination, for
the ordinand after the analogy of the Old Testament sacrifices
is through laying on of hands offered to God for His service and
so consecrated. This act of ordination takes place in the Name of
Christ the King and Head of the Church, so that all the ordinand does when ordained is to be done in the Name of Christ.
That Name is his sole authority; nothing is to be done apart
from it. But to ordain in the Name of Christ, and to act in the
Name of Christ, is to act within the Self-consecration of Christ
on our behalf, as the language of the Name of God declared by
Christ to the apostles in John 17 indicates.

(4) Ordination thus means ordination in the sphere where
we are all consecrated through participation in Christ's Self-
consecration on our behalf. We recall that the disciples were
specially related to the Self-consecration of Christ at the Last
Supper, for in His solemn prayer of consecration they were
associated by Christ with Himself as those who would take His
Word to others so that others would believe through their word
and be drawn into the unity of the one Church of Christ. We
cannot dissociate ordination in the Name of Christ from that
fact. Those ordained are to be regarded as drawn in a special
way within the sphere of Christ's Self-consecration so that it is
only as they share in His Self-consecration that they can minister
the Word to others in His Name. It is in this connexion then
that we have to see the relation of ordination to participation in

the Lord's Supper, and see the Lord's Supper as the New Testament counterpart to the meal of consecration in which Aaron and his sons participated at their consecration, "a meal of thanksgiving and praise". That expression is reflected in an important passage in Hebrews 13 which speaks of the ministry in several injunctions and adds: "Through him then let us offer up a sacrifice of praise to God continually, that is the fruit of the lips which make confession to his name continually." It was not unnatural therefore that in very early times, as in the *Apostolic Constitutions*, the rite of ordination to the ministry was looked upon as being brought to its completion when the one ordained first celebrated the Lord's Supper, for it was when the gifts of bread and wine were put into his hands that the Lord Himself fulfilled the act of consecrating His servant to His ministry, as He consecrated the apostle-disciples at the Last Supper. It is significant therefore that all the earliest consecrations and ordinations known to us took place in a Eucharistic context. This is a practice that should still be followed. The act of the presbytery in ordination should be followed by the celebration of Holy Communion in which the newly ordained person should dispense the Sacrament for the first time. The early Church of Scotland practice of "fasting" at ordination seems to have been derived from the old rite of the consecration of the priests with its seven days of separation.

The Doctrine of Ordination

In gathering up our discussion to present a doctrine of ordination we must consider it from three aspects:

(1) The source of ordination: its derivation from Christ through the ministry of the Church.

(2) The end of ordination: that to which a man is ordained determines the nature of ordination.

(3) What the act of ordination means and how it is carried out.

(1) *The source of ordination.* Who is it who ordains a man to the ministry? In answer to that question we have to give the unambiguous answer: Jesus Christ Himself. Ordination is His act. It is His authority that stands behind it, and therefore it can be done only in His Name. But Christ ordains within His Church

which He founded upon the apostles and it is through that Church that He acts. Here we are confronted with a fundamental duality, but it is also the fundamental duality of Revelation. Revelation is the act of Christ which is brought to bear upon us directly through His Spirit, but it is Revelation which He communicates to us through the Word historically mediated in the Holy Scriptures. The risen and ascended Lord has bestowed His Spirit upon the Church, but the Spirit utters to us what Christ has already said: He does not speak of Himself and does not teach us anything new, but takes what Christ has already revealed and leads us fully into its Truth. The Church is thus bound to the New Testament Scriptures, but in and through the New Testament Scriptures the risen and ascended Lord communicates Himself directly to His Church in the communion of the Spirit. So it is with ordination. It is the risen and ascended Lord who acts directly through His Spirit ordaining His servant to the ministry, but He does that in and through the Church which He has once and for all established in the apostles and bound to the Revelation which He has committed to the Church through the apostles.

The Church is bound to act in obedience to the apostolic teaching and commands, and through them it is bound to the historical Jesus Christ. When the Church from age to age ordains men to the ministry in the Name of Christ, it does that only within that obedience to the apostolic teaching and ordinances, and only within the sphere of the apostolic commission and mission given by Christ in founding the Church. That duality is apparent already in the New Testament Church. It is the risen and ascended Lord who bestows gifts upon the Church through the Spirit, but these gifts are bestowed for exercise within the one Church founded upon the apostles and within the sphere of their commission by Christ. The apostles appointed the rite of the laying on of hands to mark out and delimit the sphere of their commission, and to attest the propriety of a ministry within that sphere. That laying on of hands cannot be regarded as determining or delimiting the sphere of the operation of the Holy Spirit, for although Christ has bound the Church to its foundation in the apostles, He is Himself sovereignly free over the apostles as the risen and ascended Lord. The laying on of hands cannot be understood therefore as

securing or guaranteeing the presence or the operation of the
Holy Spirit, but as the apostolically given sign witnessing to the
presence of the Spirit, attesting the obedience of the Church to
its apostolic origins and binding its continuance, and the continuance of its ministry, within the sphere of the apostolic commission and authority. It is Christ, not the apostles, not the
Church, who bestows upon the ordained minister the Spirit and
the gifts of the Spirit for the exercise of his office; nevertheless it
is clear that the laying on of hands was given by the apostles
with the promise of Christ to impart spiritual gifts for the fulfilment of the ministry.

Ordinarily and normatively we are to understand the laying
on of hands as the apostolically appointed sign and instrument
used by the Spirit in bestowing the *charisma* for the ministry. Its
necessity is one of obedience to the apostolic ordinance, and it
attests that the ordination of the ministry derives from the
historical Jesus and His historically communicated authority to
the apostles. But the historical Jesus is risen and ascended, and
it is He who from generation to generation continues to bestow
His Spirit upon the Church and continues to bestow the grace-
gifts for the ministry of Word and Sacrament within the Church.
Therefore it is Christ the living Lord who is the actual Ordainer
in ordination, although He makes use of the ministers who have
been sent by Him already to carry out the ordinance within the
Church on earth. It is only in this togetherness of "the Risen
Lord" and "the historical Jesus" who is one Lord Jesus Christ,
the King and Head of the Church, that we must think of
ordination. The risen Lord sends us back to the historical Jesus
and sends us back always to the commission He gave to the
apostles, so that ordination is through the historical communication of the apostolic Word and the apostolic commission. The
historical Jesus still commissions His ministers through that external and historical succession, and therefore the historical
mediation or communication of ordination is of fundamental
importance as attesting the binding of the Church to the
historical Jesus and the historical Revelation.

The Church which separates itself from the historical Jesus
ceases thereby to be Christ's Church, for it cuts itself off from its
historical rooting and grounding in the historical Revelation
and Incarnation. But within that historical communication it is

the risen Lord Himself who ever comes to His Church acting obediently in His Name and Himself ordains. He Himself is really present where we meet in His name to obey His command, and He fulfils what He promises, and His presence in grace and in the power of His Spirit undergirds all our actions. We rely in all ordination therefore not upon the faithfulness of the Church, nor upon the unbroken nature of the historical succession, for these are all involved in the relativities and contingencies of this fallen world; but upon the faithfulness of Christ who remains with His Church that lives and acts in His Name. It is His covenant faithfulness undergirding our weakness and faltering faithfulness, and renewing our participation in Him, that is the ground of our reliance in every act of ordination.

It is this same fundamental duality in ordination that gives the concept of the so-called "validity of orders" its elusive ambiguity. Validity must refer absolutely to the fact that it is Christ the Lord who ordains, and ordains to ministry in the Church of God. He it is who honours that ministry as His own gift to the Church and makes it efficacious through His Spirit. But validity also refers to the responsible transmission of authorization from generation to generation, attesting the obedience of the Church in all its ordinations to the apostolic teaching and ordinances. Because this involves historical communication and responsible action it involves a duly intended and orderly act of ordination. It cannot be given in abstraction from the ordering of a Church's life, from its discipline and polity. Thus validity has also a juridical aspect, in which the term is relative to the legal structure of a Church in history. It refers to the responsible authorization of a Church in history, which orders its life and discipline in obedience to the apostolic Church and therefore is bound up with the canonical way of administering life and discipline in that Church.

In the Church of Scotland we ordain a man to the ministry of the Word and Sacraments in the Church of God, because we believe it is Christ Himself who ordains, but in ordination the Church (through its authorized ministers) commits to him due authorization to minister the Word and Sacraments within the discipline of the Church of Scotland within which he also promises at ordination to be subject to the Church. But the Church of Scotland does not thereby claim that, in that sense of

4—C.A.C.

authorization, it has authorized its ministers to administer the Word and Sacraments in every other Church. It does not necessarily acknowledge the authorization of those ordained in other Churches as giving them authority to administer the Word and Sacraments in the Church of Scotland, but it does not for that reason question the validity of their orders in the sense that their ordination is an act of Christ and is honoured by Him in making their ministry efficacious. The Church of Scotland does claim, however, that in obedience to the teaching and ordinance of the apostles "the laying on of hands of the presbytery" is the proper and responsible way of ordaining the ministry and of transmitting in the historical communication of the Church due authorization for the ministry of Word and Sacraments within the sphere of the apostolic commission and mission. While it acknowledges that authorization for the ministry of the Word and Sacraments is inescapably bound up with the discipline of the Church of Scotland and is therefore relative to its own structure and law, it claims that its careful and orderly transmission of ordination from generation to generation is in full conformity to the apostolic ordinance and teaching, and therefore reaches beyond what is merely relative to the particular legal institutions of the Church of Scotland itself to what is valid in the Church of God.

(2) *The end of ordination.* Ordination means ordination to the ministry of Word and Sacraments, that is to dispensing Word and Sacraments. Strictly, therefore, "ordination" should be used only for the order of those who dispense the Word and Sacraments. It is using "ordination" in a somewhat loose sense to speak of ordaining deacons or deaconesses or ordaining elders, for they are not ordained to dispense the Word and Sacraments but are set apart or consecrated to assist in that ministry, even although a rite of laying on of hands may be used. A rite of laying on of hands is used also in some baptismal rites or in confirmations, but it does not therefore mean that those who have hands laid on them are ordained—what determines ordination is the end to which ordination is directed and intended by the Church. This involves two important points.

(a) That which a man is ordained to minister, the Word and Sacraments, is more important than ordination. Ordination is in order to minister the Word and Sacraments, and therefore ordination is subordinate to the Word and Sacraments which it serves. In other words, the ministering of Word and Sacraments is subservient to the Word and Sacraments themselves. The ministry is but an earthen vessel, as St. Paul put it, but it contains the heavenly treasure, and must never be confounded with the heavenly treasure. Therefore in the ministering of the Word and Sacraments, the mysteries of God, the ministering itself must be dependent upon that which is ministered and can never exalt itself over it. Ordination does not give the minister authority over the Word and Sacrament, but sets him in a servant-relation to them. They are always transcendent to the ministry and their efficacy cannot be tied to the ministry or only be relative to the worth of the ministers. The very authority which a minister has for ministering Word and Sacraments lies in the Word and Sacraments and not in himself—that is another way of saying that the ministry is at every point dependent upon the apostolic Word and Ordinances, for it is through the apostles that we have committed to us the Word and Sacraments and it is only in obedience to the apostolic ordering of the ministry that we administer them.

(b) There can in the nature of the case be no higher ministry than that of the ministry of Word and Sacraments, for that would be to suppose that there was a higher authority than that of the Word and a higher sanction than that of the Seals of the Word directly instituted and given by Jesus Christ. If ordination is defined by its end in the ministry of Word and Sacrament, and Word and Sacrament are more important than the ministering of them, it follows that there is only one order of the ministry in the proper sense; that of the minister dispensing Word and Sacraments. The order of the presbyteral ministry is not only the highest order, but in the strict sense the only order of the ministry. Other so-called orders are either for the assistance of this order or for the convenience of maintaining unity and concord and discipline among those so ordained. The fact that there is only one order of the ministry in the strict sense is the meaning of the so-called parity of ministers in a Presbyterian Church, but this does not preclude distinctions in jurisdiction either in the Church Courts to which presbyters are subject or among presbyters themselves. Thus, as Calvin says, "The political distinction of ranks [i.e. distinctions in Church polity, not 'politics'] is not to be repudiated, for natural reason itself dictates this in order to take away confusion; but that which shall have this object in view, will be so arranged that it may neither obscure Christ's glory nor minister to ambition or tyranny, nor prevent all ministers from cultivating mutual fraternity with each other, with equal rights and liberties."[1]

There can therefore be no doctrinal grounds for any distinction between a presbyter and a bishop or a presbyter-bishop, nor any ground at all for a distinction in order, though there may well be ecclesiastical or historical grounds for making a distinction in function and therefore for adding some measure of jurisdiction to one presbyter to enable him responsibly to fulfil that extra function. But such a distinction in function could not make a bishop more of a minister or give him a higher ministry in relation to Word and Sacrament than that of any other presbyter. The doctrine of parity of ministers must not therefore be confused with differences in function or relative distinctions in jurisdiction. Thus in the Reformed Church we acknowledge that some presbyters are set apart and are acknowledged to have a special *charisma* for teaching doctrine and for keeping a "watching brief" over the purity of the Church's proclamation and doctrine in obedience to the teaching of the apostles. These are the "doctors" of the Church, and they are responsibly commissioned to exercise their functions with appropriate jurisdiction, not in their case in Church or pastoral government, and so they are not given ecclesiastical jurisdiction of any kind but in the teaching and training of the ministry and in doctrine. That does not in any way do away with "the parity of ministers" in the sense that the doctors have a higher ministry or a superior order to other presbyters. The same would apply to the "bishop-in-presbytery", although in that case where his special function would be concerned with pastoral discipline he would naturally be set apart for that in the appropriate way by the Presbytery, in "the laying on of hands by the Presbytery", so keeping him under its own authority but commissioning him to act responsibly for it in the ways the Church would lay down. Here the nature of "the laying on of hands" would be determined by the end intended and determined by the Church. In

[1] *Comm. on Num.* 3 : 5.

this instance it would not be determined simply by the Word and Sacraments, but by something else: a function to act as spiritual counsellor and guide to his fellow-ministers, and to act in a presidential capacity or even a representative capacity for the presbytery in its solemn acts and deliberations. But because the bishop-in-presbytery could be given no higher relation to the Word and Sacrament—that is in the nature of the case impossible—he could have no higher order than that of his fellow-presbyters.

(3) *What ordination is and how it is carried out.* Ordination is the solemn setting apart to the ministry of Word and Sacraments of a man who has been called to that ministry. It is an act in which the whole Church concurs, although the act of ordination itself is carried through by those who have already been ordained, for they only are the proper instruments for "regular" association of others with the commission they have received and which they in obedience to the apostolic ordinance devolve upon others. It is not that they thus transmit "grace," or the Holy Spirit, nor that they transmit divine authority; but in so doing they attest that it is Christ alone who acts, and they make evident that they are acting only in obedience to Christ's own commissioned apostles. But, as we have already noted, the act of ordination is also the lawful act in the discipline of the Church where responsibility in office is devolved in an orderly or canonical way upon others in succession to their fathers in the same office. It is an act that takes place in space and time: in the space or place of the Church where Christ has put His Name on earth, the visible Church, and in the time or historical continuity of the Church which Christ has sent out into history to proclaim the Gospel of His Kingdom until He comes again. Thus the physical, visible, and temporal action in ordination attests the binding of the Church to the physical, visible, and temporal incarnation and the Church once and for all founded by the incarnate Son on the apostles and prophets. Just as the Church's life and worship is neither timeless nor spaceless, but in the historical and risen Jesus Christ, so the act of ordination is not a spaceless and timeless act in which the visible and temporal element is of no importance.

On the other hand, the act of ordination is not a Sacrament in the proper sense—although Calvin himself was not averse to calling it a sacrament. It is certainly not a "Sacrament of the Gospel", that is a sign and seal of a saving ordinance through which salvation is bestowed in the unity of Word and appointed Sign; but because ordination is the appointed ordinance with its accompanying and appropriate sign for the ordering of the ministry of the Word and Sacraments, it necessarily partakes of the sacramental character of the Word and Sacraments and is rightly performed only within the Church as the Body of Christ, within the Covenant-signs-and-seals of the Church's incorporation into Christ. No unbaptized person can ordain or be ordained, for no uncovenanted person can be commissioned within the ministry of the New Covenant; and no one who is not himself a communicant member of the Church can ordain or be ordained, for no one who has not himself shared in the communion of the New Covenant and in the Self-consecration of Christ, sealed upon His own at the Holy Supper, can be a consecrated minister of the New Covenant. Just because ordination has this setting within the Church's incorporation into Christ in Word and Sacrament, it must take place in the context of Word and Sacrament as well as in the context of the Church's solemn judicial action in a Sacral Court.

This dual aspect of the rite of ordination reflects its dual character. It takes place in and through an act of the Presbytery met and constituted as a Sacral Court of the Church. Ordination is not properly and validly enacted by any association of presbyters, but by an association of presbyters duly convened within and according to the discipline and constitution of the Church by a resolution of the appropriate court as a whole; for it must be an act in which the whole Church concurs and which therefore has the acknowledged authority of the Church. That is the judicial aspect of ordination, which has its appropriate ceremonies such as the interrogation and response, the taking of vows and the signing of the formula in the Church's roll, and the solemn act of laying on of hands, which in part is an essential legal act attesting the lawful and responsible bestowal of a commission or the canonical conferring of authority to minister the Word and Sacraments within the bounds of the Church and its mission. This judicial part of ordination is not carried out in and by itself apart, but only within the whole spiritual action of ordination, though it is particularly in the laying on of hands that the overlap between the judicial and the spiritual aspects of ordination is most apparent.

Ordination is primarily a spiritual act within the Church in which Christ Himself is the Principal Agent, and in which the ordained ministers (those preaching presbyters to whom it belongs to act thus in Christ's Name) act as servants of Christ and only in obedience to His commands. The whole act of ordination is therefore dependent upon the Word of God as mediated through the apostolic tradition. If ordination is by Christ in accordance with His Word, then it is carried out only in "sacramental" dependence upon His Word—it is the Word which commissions to the ministry, and the Word which is the sole repository of divine authority in the Church and which bestows that authority as the Church acts in obedience to it. The Word is the sceptre through which Christ the risen and ascended Lord continues to govern and rule His Church and continues to call men into His ministry and to command them in His service. Ordination takes place therefore in accordance with the apostolic Warrant, in solemn declaration of the Word, and in the context of the Church meeting to wait upon that Word in its proclamation through the heralds sent by Christ to the Church. Only when the royal proclamation of the Word of the King has been made does the Church through its ministers act in obedience to it in the ceremony of ordination.

The other parts of this ceremony are prayer and the laying on of hands. The *Westminster Form of Church Government* puts the laying on of hands first, but the *Second Book of Discipline*, following the order of the *First Book of Discipline* and the teaching of Knox and Calvin, puts prayer first. That indicates that the primary element in ordination is the *epiclesis*, the response of the Church to God's Word made in the prayer calling for the bestowal of the Spirit upon him being set apart to the ministry. It is Christ Himself who ordains through the sending of His Spirit, and it is entirely the divine intention and act that determines the nature of the ordinance and its effect. The emphasis upon the act of prayer as an *epiclesis* also makes clear that the formal act of laying on of hands, necessary and important as it is juridically, is not to be regarded mainly as a legal act, but as the apostolically appointed sign attesting that it is Christ who ordains, that it is the Spirit who acts, and that the rite of ordination has its root and ground beyond in the Self-consecration of Christ in His own prayerful Self-oblation on our behalf. Within that act of prayer the laying on of hands has its essential and indispensable place. But when it is taken within that act of prayer we must say with Augustine: "*Quid aliud est manuum impositio quam oratio super hominem?*" The imposition of hands is primarily the lifting up of hands in prayer, so that actual tactual laying on of hands is really secondary. On the ground of biblical teaching, however, in which it is clear that the act of *samakh* was the main ceremonial act, we lay stress upon tactual imposition as well as the laying on or lifting up of hands in blessing; for in the biblical teaching tactual imposition itself is recognized as an act offering and presenting the one who is the object of laying on of hands to God in dedication and consecration for His service. It is because of this extremely close relation between laying on of hands in prayerful offering and the lifting up of hands in prayer in blessing that many of the earliest books of Church Order omit its actual mention, for the stress was laid upon the act of prayer and was considered to be implied in it. That was the attitude of John Knox in 1560, although in 1572 (if not actually earlier) the imposition of hands was restored in detailed action and has ever since been regarded as indispensable in the Church of Scotland.

Accompanying and preceding the act of ordination there are other rites which have their proper place and are designed to attest the fact that the person ordained is acknowledged as one who has himself received a divine call to the Holy Ministry, that his own private recognition of that call is confirmed by the Church acting through its duly constituted Courts, and confirmed by the congregation which has called him to be its minister in the Name of Christ. The act of ordination thus requires the *imprimatur* of the Church as a whole and the acclaim and acquiescence of the local congregation, who also take vows in support of the minister and in obedient acknowledgment of the fact that their minister has been *sent* to them by Christ Himself. The minister himself takes vows which bind him to the continuity of the Church's obedience to the apostles in doctrines and ordinances, and in which he solemnly promises to fulfil His ministry with devotion to Christ as His servant, and, without lording it over the flock, to seek their good in the Lord. At the same time he acknowledges that the government of the Church is agreeable to the Word of God, promises to be subject to its discipline, to take his due part in its affairs, and to seek the unity and peace of the Church. But in his undertaking these vows, as in the administration of ordination to him, the Church makes it clear that the minister acts not on his own charges or on his own resources, but only on the *command* and therefore only in reliance upon the *promise* of Jesus Christ who remains the same yesterday, to-day, and for ever, and who never fails to keep His Word.

2

THE GOSPEL AND THE KINGDOM

(a) *A Study in New Testament Communication*[1]

IT is often claimed that the problem of communicating the Gospel is the major practical problem facing the Church to-day, as it may also be the major theological problem. This concern is a very healthy sign, but it is becoming increasingly apparent that we are apt to be so concerned with devising new methods of evangelism as to forget the one factor of supreme importance: the burden of the Gospel itself, that is, to forget that the Gospel is not simply the message of divine love, but the actual way in which God communicates Himself to us in history. No technique that forgets that the Gospel has already been made supremely relevant to sinful humanity in the Incarnation and death of Jesus Christ will ever avail for the communication of the Gospel. This is therefore an attempt to probe into what the New Testament has to say to us about this, and into the way in which, as a matter of fact, the New Testament actually communicates the Gospel to us.

We may take as our starting point the Parables in the Synoptic Gospels with the parallels in the Fourth Gospel. According to Professor C. H. Dodd, "a parable is normally the dramatic presentation of a situation intended to suggest vividly some single idea".[2] Jesus used parables to "illustrate what Mark calls the mystery of the Kingdom of God"[3]—i.e. He presented His teaching in a concrete fashion and not in abstractions. However, because "there is no mere analogy but an inward affinity between the natural order and the spiritual order"[4] the Parables are so self-luminous that "the interpretation will show through".[5] Professor Dodd goes on to say: "The

---

[1] From the *Scottish Journal of Theology*, 1950, pp. 225–240.
[2] *The Parables of the Kingdom*, p. 165.
[3] P. 33, Mark 4: 11.
[4] P. 24.   [5] P. 20.

Kingdom of God is intrinsically like the process of nature and of the daily life of man . . . the sense of the divineness of the natural order is major premiss of all the Parables".[1]

In this view Dr. Dodd follows Jülicher in rejecting the idea that Parables are allegories where the elements are treated as mysterious cyphers or allegorical equivalents for eternal ideas, but he refuses to follow Jülicher in making "the process of interpretation end with the generalization". No doubt the Parable has the character of an argument but "the way to an interpretation lies through a judgment of the imagined situation, not through a decoding of various elements in the story".[2] "The Parables bear upon the actual and critical situation in which Jesus and His hearers stood: when we ask after the application we must look first not to the field of general principles but to the particular setting in which they are delivered. The task of the interpreter of the Parables is to find out, if he can, the setting of a Parable in the situation contemplated by the Gospel and hence the application which would suggest itself to one who stood in that situation."[3]

Unquestionably Professor Dodd has put us greatly in his debt for his exposition of the Parables, and for the astonishing light that his method of interpretation casts on them again and again. It is difficult to avoid the feeling, however, that his restricted definition of the Parable and the resulting method of interpretation are unduly narrow. A more balanced and, certainly to the preacher, a more satisfying account has been given by the Rev. R. S. Wallace in a previous number of this Journal.[4] In that article Dr. Wallace raised the question whether the relation upon which the Parable reposes is a natural or a sacramental relation. That is the point of crucial importance for a doctrine of communication. Is it really true, as Dr. Dodd maintains, that when we scrutinize the Parables and relate them to the original situation so far as we can reconstruct it, the conclusion regarding the original meaning and application follows or shines through?[5] That would mean that so far as we can reconstruct the original Jesus in His setting in history (*Sitz im Leben*), we can read off the divine Revelation because there is an inward affinity between the natural order and the spiritual order, and

[1] P. 22. [2] P. 23. [3] P. 26.
[4] 2, 1. pp. 13 ff. [5] C. H. Dodd, *op. cit.*, p. 31.

because of the divineness of the natural order. Surely that is not the message of the Synoptic Gospels, nor the teaching of the Parables. Undoubtedly the divine communication must involve analogy if it is to get across to men who can only think in terms of human and worldly analogies, but the whole significance of the Parable is that it is *analogy with a difference*, analogy which has at its heart an eschatological event which, until it actually overtakes us, nothing in the natural or historical order can begin to reveal. Even when it happens, absolutely necessary as the analogical elements are to convey the Revelation, they are unable of themselves to point to the truth. "Flesh and blood hath not revealed it unto thee, but my Father which is in heaven" (Matt. 16: 17). The extraordinary fact is that while Professor C. H. Dodd recognizes this teaching quite unambiguously,[1] he fails to carry it into the heart of his epistemology. In other words the eschatological relation upon which he has thrown such a flood of illumination is not truly realized in the depth of faith. That is the significance of the *mystery* of the Kingdom.[2]

The Synoptic passage which we must discuss here is Mark 4: 1 ff., especially 4: 11 ff. Professor Dodd's thesis is that the evangelist has misunderstood the Parables and the significance of the Parable itself, and the result is a series of interpretations attached to the Parables which he pronounces a confusion. This leads him to reject every New Testament interpretation of the Parables. In this instance Dr. Dodd's own method of interpretation does not allow him to make sense of the passage as it stands, and he is forced to mutilate and reconstruct it. In particular he lays the axe to the word *mysterion* as not being a genuine word of Jesus, in spite of the fact that an *agraphon* survives through Clement of Alexandria and the Clementine Homilies in which *mysterion* in a similar connexion is found on the lips of Jesus, apparently from a different source altogether, which makes the genuineness of *mysterion* in this passage all the more certain. However, it does not matter ultimately whether the word itself is scored out, for the thought is inextricably woven into all three Synoptic accounts as well as the Johannine, going back to Old Testament passages such as Deut. 29: 29; Ps. 78: 12; Is. 6: 9 ff.; 42: 18 ff.

[1] *Op. cit.*, p. 197.   [2] Cf. Wallace, *loc. cit.*, p. 14.

What did Jesus mean when He said, "How shall we liken the Kingdom of God?" or "the Kingdom of God is like" this or that? Surely that Kingdom or the Word of the Kingdom or the Mystery is difficult to express directly. It is like this and it is like that, and yet it is like this and like that. We cannot say, "Lo, here is the Kingdom of God" or "Lo, there is the Kingdom of God", for the Kingdom of God does not come like that. It does not come with observation. As the Fourth Gospel puts it, "Except a man be born again (from above) he cannot see the Kingdom of God."[1] "How shall I liken the Kingdom?" says Jesus. "I shall express it by a parable" (παραβολή).[2] The word of the Kingdom can be expressed only indirectly by a series of parallels on a different analogical level side by side with it. The Word of the Kingdom can be expressed to men of flesh and blood and concrete existence only by throwing a parallel in flesh and blood and in the language of humanity to the Word of the Kingdom. That means, as Jülicher and Dodd agree, that the parable is not an allegory, although to say that the parable yields *one idea* is to make it as much an allegory as if it yielded a series of ideas. Behind the parable, or rather beside it, there is the Kingdom which has broken into the midst, the *eschaton* which is here and now. Dr. Dodd agrees that it is this which gives the parables their peculiar significance. The *basileia* or *eschaton* is identified with the Word of the Kingdom. That comes out very clearly, as K. L. Schmidt points out, when we compare the Synoptic parallels. The parable therefore is the picturesque, dramatic and analogical speech thrown alongside the invisible Kingdom already in the midst, already "among you" (ἐντὸς ὑμῶν). "The Kingdom of God is come upon you" (Matt. 12: 28; Luke 11: 20: ἔφθασεν ἐφ᾽ ὑμᾶς ἡ βασιλεία). The parable is thus essentially two-sided. It has a visible side, the analogical; but that is thrown alongside the invisible Kingdom and is, so to speak, contrapuntal to it. The parable is essentially sacramental in form and that is always its intention on the lips of Jesus. Jesus Christ, in teaching and Person, is Himself the great Parable of the Kingdom of God.

If the Word of the Kingdom is identical with Christ

---

[1] Cf. 1 Cor. 2: 1 ff.

[2] The Greek word used by the evangelists is particularly significant. παραβολή indicates the act of throwing alongside (παρα-βάλλω).

Himself then it is clear why the Word cannot be expressed directly in speech. Christ Jesus cannot be put into words. In Him we
have the Word and the Act of the Kingdom, *logos* and *dynamis*,
in one: a Person in the midst. As Professor Dodd says, the parable describes an aspect of Christ's own ministry and the de-
veloping situation and the crisis which His coming has brought
upon history. But the design of the parable does not lie in itself
or in any symbolic meaning to be read off the face of it or even
in any single idea. It is designed to put a man into a situation
in which he is confronted with God and can hear for himself
the Word of the Kingdom which flesh and blood cannot reveal.
Consequently the relation between the Word of the Kingdom
and the parables is conceived in terms of *mysterion* or *krypton*.
It will help us to understand this if we remember that *mysterion*
is not used in any sense relating to the Greek mysteries. A
passage such as 1 Tim. 3: 16 is helpful, "Great is the mystery
of Godliness, God manifest in the flesh." That is the fundamental sense in which it is nearly always used in the New
Testament, in the Synoptics, in St. Paul's Epistles, and in the
Apocalypse as well.[1]

There is a very illuminating sentence from the Fourth
Gospel (8: 43) which throws a flood of light upon the situation
here. "Why do you not understand my speech (λαλιάν), because you cannot hear my word (λόγον)?" The Jews were
unable to make anything of the speech (λαλιά) of Jesus, i.e. the
parables (παραβολαί), because they could not hear or could not
bear to hear His Word (λόγος). If we ask the Fourth Gospel
what the relation is between the speech and the Word the
answer is given in the expression "abiding" (μένειν). It is
when a man abides in the Word or when the Word abides in a
man that the man understands the speech and knows the Truth
which will make him free. Thus the preaching of Jesus is
broadcast to all who hear it as speech but only he who has ears
to hear or who makes room for it (χωρεῖν), as the Synoptics say,
can hear the Word. In this way the Word is broadcast to all
and sundry through speech and parable, but only those who
are prepared to receive it in faith actually hear it as the Word
of the Kingdom. That comes out again and again in the Fourth
Gospel. The voice of God speaks; the unbelieving crowds say

---

[1] There is, of course, a counterfeit *mysterion* of evil.

that it thunders, but the believers say that it is the voice of an angel. "Lord, how is it that thou wilt manifest thyself unto us and *not unto the world*? Jesus answered and said unto him, If a man love me he will keep my word (λόγον) and my Father will love him and we *will come unto him and make our abode with him*" (John 14: 22, 23). That is the Johannine way of putting the Mystery of the Kingdom.

This helps us to understand the teaching in Mark and the Synoptic parallels. "To you is given to know the mystery of the Kingdom of God but to them who are without all things are spoken in Parables." Then Jesus declares that the clue to all the Parables is the same—the Word (λόγος). "Do ye not know this parable? How then shall ye know all parables? He who sows, sows the word (λόγον)."[1] And so Mark goes on to say (v. 33): "And with many such parables He spake (ἐλάλει) the word (τὸν λόγον), as they were able to hear" (καθὼς ἠδύναντο ἀκούειν: recall the οὐ δύνασθε of John 8: 43). "Without a parable He did not speak unto them (χωρὶς παραβολῆς οὐκ ἐλάλει αὐτοῖς)." There is little doubt therefore that the thought of the Synoptics is close to that of the Fourth Gospel.

We come now to what is usually reckoned exegetically most difficult, the scandal of a ἵνα (Mark 4: 11 f.), "Unto you it is given to know the mystery of the Kingdom of God but to those who are without, all things are done in parables, that seeing they may see (ἵνα βλέποντες βλέπωσι) and not understand (καὶ μὴ ἴδωσι): and hearing, they may hear; lest at any time they should be converted and their sins should be forgiven them." Several things must be said here.

(1) Its very harshness is the strongest argument for the authority of ἵνα.

(2) No doubt the Greek is harsher in sound than the Aramaic. It may be that the Aramaic was capable of ambiguous interpretation as Professor T. W. Manson avers.

(3) This ἵνα must be put side by side with ἐὰν μὴ ἵνα in v. 22, which indicates that the Parables, while they concealed

---

[1] K. L. Schmidt points out that in each Synoptic set of parallels Kingdom and Word of the Kingdom are equated with the key of knowledge (Luke 11: 52). The hearing of the Word is the key to knowledge, the key to the Parables of Jesus. Cf. G. Kittel, *Theologisches Woerterbuch zum N.T.*, 1, pp. 581 ff.

the mystery, only concealed it with the intention of revealing it (4: 21–23), while the expression in v. 33 καθὼς ἠδύναντο ἀκούειν also throws a flood of light upon the passage.

Why, then, does Jesus speak in parables?

(1) He speaks in parables in order to reveal that the Kingdom of God has come into the midst in His own Person and to direct men to believe in Him in such a way that there is evoked from them full decision. The parable is chosen by Christ as the means of confronting men with Himself, the Word, in such a way that men can choose Him in love and yet not be overwhelmed by His divine majesty. The Word comes through the parable in such a way that men have to choose God in order to know Him, to surrender to His will in order to understand. The Word is so nigh that it creates room for faith and decision. Jesus consistently avoids giving a compelling manifestation of Himself for that would leave no room for faith and decision and men would be fixed in their sin by the unveiled divine majesty instead of being wooed to belief and trust so that Christ can heal them. In the parable, so to speak, the Kingdom of God comes into the midst and throws a man into the crisis of decision, and yet by its veiled form the Word of the Kingdom holds man at arm's length away in order to give him room and time for personal decision.[1]

(2) We can say with Calvin that Jesus spoke in parables not simply for the purpose of instruction but to keep the attention of the hearers awake until a more convenient time. He kept the un-understanding and the unbelieving in a state of suspense till a fitter opportunity arrived. And so in the parable Jesus accommodated the Word to men's capacity who were yet rendered inexcusable by the amount of light they got from the surface of the parable but whose final verdict is suspended because as yet they were not sufficiently prepared to receive instruction. That is the force of the words "as they were able to hear" (καθὼς ἠδύναντο ἀκούειν, Mark 4: 33). Above all forms of speech the parable is calculated to have the greatest propensities for suggestion in which with the light and skilled thrust of a rapier Jesus gently touches men to the quick of their soul by the two-

---

[1] This necessary time-element is really eliminated by a realized eschatology which holds that "the time-scale is irrelevant to the ultimate significance of history" (C. H. Dodd, *op. cit.*, p. 71).

edged Word, summoning them to decision without crushing them to the ground by an open display of majesty and might. It is by means of the parable that Jesus pierces to the heart in such a way as not to crush the bruised reed or quench the smoking flax—καθὼς ἠδύναντο ἀκούειν. In Johannine thought, this means that Jesus did not want to judge the hearers on the spot in any final fashion. The *eschaton* had broken into the present but if men were confronted openly with the *eschaton* in the Word and presence of Jesus in their unbelief, they would be finally damned on the spot. But Jesus veiled the *eschaton* so that it encountered men obliquely. "I judge you not; but the word that I speak, that shall judge you at the last day" (John 12: 48). The Word of God is always creative. It always acts upon a man whether he will or no, but in the event of a man's "no", in the event of his unbelief, Jesus intends that the judgment shall fall with a delayed action still leaving room and time for decision and faith. The Word of the Kingdom creates ferment among men and sooner or later there must be an explosion. There may be conversion now, which is an eschatological event: "Repent, for the Kingdom of God is come upon you." It may be damnation in the *eschaton*: "Depart from me, for I never knew you."

(3) Jesus deliberately concealed the Word in the parable lest men against their will should be forced to acknowledge the Kingdom, and yet He allowed them enough light to convict them and to convince them. Jesus refused to reveal Himself to men in such a way as to command their assent and still leave them unbowed in the haughtiness of their pride. He revealed Himself in a way that often involved offence (σκάνδαλον) so as to cut across the grain of human pride and demand humility and rebirth.

We make a real mistake if we imagine that the Jews simply did not recognize Jesus as the Son of God. They did indeed, and yet they did not recognize Him. They were blind, but they were wilfully blind. They had such an obstinate disposition of soul that in the very act of perceiving the truth they insisted that it should not apply to them, for they could not bear the Gospel; they could not endure the Word of Christ because it cut clean across all their proud national aspirations, their rigid ideas and desires. Thus they rendered themselves morally and spiritually incapable even of understanding the speech (λαλιά)

of Jesus. In the language of St. Paul they deliberately held
down the truth in unrighteousness. When a man does that,
God delivers him over to a reprobate mind. That is God's
punishment for the perverter and evader of the truth; and so
Jesus said quite plainly, "For judgment am I come into this
world, that they which see not might see, and that they which
see might be made blind" (John 9: 39). That is the force, the
terrible force, of the ἵνα in Mark 4: 11. It is not, says Calvin,[1]
that the teaching of Christ by itself or by its own nature causes
blindness. "Where the Word of God blinds and hardens the
reprobate, as this takes place through their own depravity it
belongs truly and naturally to themselves, but is accidental as
respects the Word." The Word of God in its own nature is
always full of light, but its light is choked by the darkness of
man and it becomes a savour of death to death and a savour
of life to life (2 Cor. 2: 15, 16).

That is surely the meaning of this difficult passage. As we
have seen in the interpretation that follows, the Word of the
Gospel is broadcast to all and sundry. Only where it is received
in good soil does it bear fruit. That does not mean that the
Word presupposes an esoteric aristocracy and acts selectively
upon them. Professor C. H. Dodd points out that Jesus told
another series of parables to show how this selective activity (if
we may call it that) works. The appeal goes to all and sundry.
The saved are separated from the others by their free reaction
to the demands which the appeal of the Word involves.[2] This
selection is itself the divine judgment, though men pass it upon
themselves by their ultimate attitude to the appeal. That is
very apparent in the series of *pericopae* in Mark 10: 17–22 and
Luke 9: 57–62. The fact that in Mark 4: 11 we have a ἵνα and
not just a οἵ means that this is a divine judgment. That inevitably happens when the Kingdom of God comes into the
midst. It takes full charge of the situation and acts upon men
whether they will or no. God is always subject. He is the King.
This is the breaking of His sovereignty (βασιλεία) into the
midst of men's desires and decisions and choices, throwing them
all into critical ferment and giving them an essential form *vis-à-
vis* the Kingdom. Had Jesus spoken openly (ἐν παρρησίᾳ, John
16: 29) men would have been damned on the spot, but as He

[1] *Comm. ad loc.*   [2] *Op. cit.*, p. 189.

spoke in the veiled encounter of the parables men were judged in unbelief and yet given freedom still to believe. However, because in the breaking in of the Kingdom the emphasis is laid upon the action of God, the δύναμις of the λόγος, this experience is viewed as divine act.

So far we have been dealing with the relation of Word to speech, of mystery to parable, but here is another relation which is also central to the question of communication, the relation of Word (λόγος) to power (δύναμις). It will be sufficient to say here that in the Synoptics there is the closest relation between the Word and the Act in Jesus' preaching. Word and Act are inseparable and complementary. The Kingdom is essentially God's saving intervention among men, and that takes place in the preaching and the miracles of Jesus in inseparable unity. This identity of Word and divine Act is most obvious in Mark's Gospel (cf. 9: 1; cf. 1 Cor. 4: 20), but the notable passage is that of Matt. 12: 28 (with the Lukan parallel 11: 20). "If I by the Spirit (or finger) of God cast out devils then the Kingdom of God is come upon you"; and so Jesus went about *preaching* and *healing* (Matt. 4: 23) and sent the disciples out to *preach* and to *heal* (cf. Matt. 13: 15: καὶ ἰάσομαι αὐτούς). This "and to heal" (καὶ ἰᾶσθαι, Luke 9: 2; cf. Matt. 10: 7 ff.; Mark 3: 13 ff.) is of special importance as it throws considerable light upon Mark 4: 12 (and parallels), where Jesus says, "Lest they should be converted and I should heal them" or "Lest it should be forgiven them."[1] In the eyes of Jesus the Act of healing thus appears identical with the Word of forgiveness. The classic example of that identification is found in the case of the paralytic in Mark 2. There, however, for the purpose of faith there is a lapse of time inserted between forgiveness and healing—"That ye may know the Son of man hath power on earth to forgive sins." It is precisely that lapse of time or eschatological reserve between the Word of the Kingdom and the power (even the violence—βιάζεται) of the Kingdom that Jesus is concerned to preserve in the Parable where the *Word* is spoken in such a way that full Action is still suspended, even in the case of the believer who enters the Kingdom of God.

---

[1] This is a quotation from Is. 6: 9 ff.; the LXX has instead of "and it should be forgiven them" the words "and I should heal them", both of which come in the Synoptics.

Jesus is not one whose Action falls short of His Word. Therefore, though the Word of forgiveness is spoken in such a parable as that of the Prodigal, that same Word is acted out in Himself on the Cross. There the Word of pardon is enacted in flesh and blood and inserted as a reality into our history and life. There the Word of forgiveness becomes an actual fact, not just a mere idea, not just a word spoken into the air, but an accomplished fact. "It is finished."

We may now see further why the Word was indirectly communicated through the parable because the Act is also part of the Word. The Word of God is not mere speech ($\lambda a\lambda\iota\dot{a}$) but power of God ($\delta\dot{v}\nu a\mu\iota s$ $\tau o\hat{v}$ $\Theta\epsilon o\hat{v}$), Christ crucified, as St. Paul said. It is because the Word is also power that it cannot be conveyed in mere speech but has to be conveyed in saving acts, in miraculous signs ($\sigma\eta\mu\epsilon\hat{\iota}a$ or $\delta\nu\nu\dot{a}\mu\epsilon\iota s$) until the final great Act is completed. In the death of Jesus the Word and the Action are completely one. God is just and the justifier of the ungodly.

The next conception which demands our examination is that of *witness* ($\mu\dot{a}\rho\tau\upsilon s$). Fundamentally there are two kinds of witness in the New Testament. First there is witness in the sense of John the Baptist, the man sent from God to bear witness to the light of the world. He was not himself the light, but pointed away from himself to another. So much did he concentrate upon bearing witness to this other that he reduced himself, as it were, to a bony finger pointing and the voice of one crying "Behold, the Lamb of God." Here the light is not mediated through himself. He himself fades out of the picture. "I must decrease, He must increase." He is witness only in the sense that he is a voice. It is in that sense that the preacher of the Gospel is witness in the act of preaching. He does not call attention to himself, but points away to the Lamb of God, so that all the focus of attention is concentrated upon Him to whom witness is borne. It is such preaching that as a result there takes place an encounter, a conversation, and an abiding with Jesus Christ (cf. John 1 : 35 ff.).

Second, in the profoundest sense Christ is witness. He does not witness to a light that is other than Himself for He *is* the light of the world. Here, then, the witness and the light witnessed to are identical. Jesus Christ is in His own Person witness to Himself. That is why in the Fourth Gospel Jesus says: "I am the Truth." He is Truth in the form of personal being. He Himself is the Truth of God embodied forth in history, personally encountering man. Some of the most significant passages in the Fourth Gospel are concerned with this majestic *I am.* The most illuminating passage in this respect is that which describes Jesus before Pilate: "To this end was I born and for this cause came I into the world that I should bear witness unto the truth. Everyone that is of the truth heareth my voice. And Pilate saith unto him, What is truth?" Why did Jesus not answer Pilate?[1] Just because to ask Jesus Christ, who is Himself the Truth, a question about the Truth is to assume that He is not the Truth and that He only thinks *about* it or knows *about* it. Suppose we are talking to a man and then suddenly we say, "Do you exist?"; what can a man say if he is asked that question? He can only say something like this. "If you who stand here and talk to me cannot feel sure that I exist, what good can I do if I *tell* you that I do exist. If you do not believe that I exist you cannot believe what I say." That was the situation before Pilate. We can almost hear Jesus saying, "Pilate, if you do not hear my word you cannot understand my speech." But here we go a step deeper. "Pilate, if my person or my life does not open your eyes to what truth is, then it is utterly useless for me to *tell* you what the truth is." The word is identical with the Person of Jesus Christ. That thought comes out again in the trial with the majestic, kingly words of Jesus, ΕΓΩ ΕΙΜΙ, when the cry went up, "What need have we of further witness?" This man is witness Himself. He is a witness in which Word and Person are identical.

That event made a profound impression upon the early Church—indeed to such an extent that the fact that Jesus *witnessed a good confession* before Pontius Pilate became part of one of the earliest creeds of the Church.[2] The point is this: It is in His death that the Word and the Act of Christ, the Teaching and the Person of Christ become absolutely identical. It is there that He is supremely "the faithful and true witness" (Rev. 1:5; 3:14). It is there that the Captain of our salvation is made

---

[1] Cf. S. Kierkegaard, *Training in Christianity*, pp. 199 ff.
[2] Cf. O. Cullmann, *The Earliest Christian Confessions* (Eng. trans. by J. K. S. Reid), p. 25 f.

perfect through suffering. He is God's Truth done into flesh and blood. God's Truth in the midst of sin and guilt being true to itself. It is God's own witness in the flesh and blood of Jesus Christ, a witness consummated in His death. The New Testament calls that witness God's testimony (μαρτύριον): Christ crucified who is both Word (λόγος) and Power (δύναμις), that is, the Word made flesh, the witness who is Himself the Truth.

We must now ask in what sense we Christians are witnesses. How may we communicate the Truth by personal witness?

We are witnesses without doubt in the sense of John the Baptist when we preach, when we proclaim Jesus Christ in such a way that the person of the preacher fades out of the picture altogether and the Person of the living Christ is in the foreground encountering men face to face. But we must say more than that of Christian witness, for he that is least in the Kingdom of God is greater than John the Baptist. This Truth, to which we bear witness, is no longer a bare word but Truth in the form of personal being. The Christian has an intimate relation to the Truth such as John the Baptist did not have. Because Truth and personal being, Word and Deed are now one, the Christian does not know the Truth without being true, without in a profound sense becoming one with the Truth. That is why the New Testament uses such expressions as "doing the truth", "being true" and in particular ἀληθεύοντες ἐν ἀγάπῃ (Eph. 4:15), and so St. Paul could say, "It pleased God to reveal His Son in me." In a profound sense the Word becomes flesh in the Christian by his incorporation into Christ, i.e. not through any extension of the Incarnation but through an eschatological "repetition" of the Incarnation in faith. And that is why real faith is always a virgin birth in the soul, for Christ, as St. Paul says, becomes formed within the believer. John the Baptist could never have said, "It pleased God to reveal His Son in me"; but now that the Word has been made flesh and the Incarnation has been completed upon the Cross, the Truth is done into our flesh and blood. It is part of the *mysterion* that "he that is joined to the Lord is one Spirit". The word that St. Paul uses here is very enlightening. It is κολλᾶσθαι, the word that is used for the marriage union when a man shall cleave unto his wife and they shall be one flesh. Behind that lies an idea that comes out more clearly in the Johannine literature, expressed in the

Hebrew word *yada* which means both to *know* and to *love*. The knowledge of the Truth is an act of the most intimate union. And so the Christian is a witness to the Truth in a profound sense because he is in the Truth and the Truth is in him. He has a relation to the Truth which Paul calls "communion" (κοινωνία) and which John calls "abiding" (μένειν). Christ alone is absolutely identical with the Truth. No one can be a witness to the Truth in that unique sense except Jesus Christ. The Christian, however, can be a witness to the Truth in a parallel fashion in so far as he is in Christ and Christ is in him.

The early Church thought of this union with the Truth as begun in baptism where the believer is sealed with the Truth and joined to Christ in death and resurrection. What he is in baptism he becomes through suffering inasmuch as through the fellowship (κοινωνία) of Christ's suffering he becomes conformable to Christ. Just as Jesus Christ began His ministry as a witness at baptism, identifying Himself with men, and completed that in His terrible baptism of blood in which He was so straitened till it was accomplished, when He became God's Testimony, God's Word-deed, God's Witness in flesh and blood, so the Christian in the thought of the early Church follows his Lord beginning with baptism when he starts to be a witness (μάρτυς) but becomes a witness in deed and in life through suffering for Christ. Thus, it is in the Christian's suffering witness (μαρτυρία) or martyrdom that he becomes conformable to Christ, and there, as far as is possible for men, he, the martyr-witness, becomes in his death and resurrection at one with Christ the Truth, who in Himself has already wrought out that atonement. He is a complete witness in word and life and seals it with his blood.[1] This is not the same as truth mediated through personality in the modern sense. It is something vastly different. How different we shall see now as we discuss the New Testament thought of proclamation.

According to St. Paul (1 Cor. 2: 1) God's testimony, *martyrion*, takes place through proclamation (κήρυγμα). God's testimony, as we have seen, is defined concretely as Christ crucified, Power of God. *Kerygma* may be defined as the straightforward

---

[1] There is a similar thought in the Epistle to the Hebrews in the idea of the death of the Testator where the promise is sealed with blood and where the Christian bearing witness to Christ must resist evil unto blood.

proclamation of this *martyrion* in such a way that the original *martyrion* actually takes place in the experience of the hearer. That is to say, the original event becomes event all over again through the power of the Spirit so that in *kerygma* a man encounters the living Christ, Christ crucified but risen. No doubt the *kerygma* in itself is mere speech (λαλιά or simply λόγοι) but it is not in the enticing words of man's wisdom nor with the excellency of speech, nor indeed by human or logical demonstration that the *martyrion* takes place, but in the demonstration of the Spirit and of power (ἐν ἀποδείξει πνευμάτος καὶ δυνάμεως). In other words, God bears witness to Himself as men proclaim the crucified and risen Christ. Through the power of the Spirit God's Testimony is self-authenticating. Thus St. Paul goes on to say that *kerygma* is a revelation (ἀποκάλυψις, see also Rom. 16: 25) or a mystery (μυστήριον). In itself *kerygma* is simply speech (λαλιά) but it becomes the power of God (δύναμις τοῦ Θεοῦ)—that is the great mystery (μυστήριον): God manifest in the flesh. This is the treasure that we may possess in earthen vessels. The Christian is put in trust with the Word of the Gospel, the *mysterion*, and it is in that sense that it pleases God to reveal His Son in the Christian's witness, while the Christian's sufferings in witness are the signs and the marks of Christ upon him. We may put this in our own words by saying that *kerygma* is objective, sacramental preaching with an eschatological result such that the original event (Christ crucified) becomes event all over again in the hearer.[1]

In the parable, as we saw, the action of the Word was suspended until the Crucifixion. Now the Word and Act are one, as one they take the field in *kerygma*. Whenever Christ crucified is preached in the demonstration of the Spirit there is power (δύναμις). Whether a man believes or not, the creative Word continues activity. It cannot return void. It is the Word-Deed that always acts upon man, the unbeliever as well as the be-

---

[1] That is why we cannot reject outright the thought of *repetition* in the Roman Mass. In the teaching of the New Testament, however, this is not temporal repetition, but eschatological event. Thus there is also an element of truth in the Roman doctrine of the *opus operatum*, for the Word-deed of God, that becomes event and becomes flesh in the sacrament, is the creative Word, the creating Word, the active Word, the original Word-deed of God (cf. John 1: 1 ff.). It is that Word that is the *dynamis* in *kerygma*.

liever. Hence it becomes a savour of life unto life or of death unto death. Some eat and drink salvation; others out of the same cup and the same plate eat and drink damnation. The Word of God is never idle. It always accomplishes its action upon man in the *kerygma*.

No doubt that is a terrible thought for the preacher (κῆρυξ), to think that through his preaching some may be damned. That is what Paul called the "terror of the Lord". But the constraint of the love of God was so heavy upon him that he was unable to resist. He was impelled to go on preaching as an ambassador of the reconciling love of God in Jesus Christ.

It is at this point that we meet again with the difficult passage of Mark 4: 11. If we score out the ἵνα, then we deny the *kerygma* its gracious and yet dread urgency, an urgency that modern preaching has largely lost. In Jesus Christ God's Word and God's Action are absolutely identical. He is the *Eschatos* who confronts men in His own Person, in His teaching and in His work, with the final Word and Act of God, and demands absolute love and obedience. The situation has the urgency of finality, of salvation and judgment. It is that eschatological urgency that lies at the heart of *kerygma*. *Kerygma* is not the proclamation of ideas or a bare message, but such a proclamation of Christ, the Word-Act of the living God, that by the Holy Spirit it becomes itself the actualization of the Word-Act among men in salvation and judgment.

Kerygma has thus a dual significance corresponding to the eschatological tension at its heart. It is used by God to intervene Himself in the human situation as He who once and for all has wrought out His final Act in the death and resurrection of Jesus Christ, so that through the *kerygma* the hearer is brought face to face in the present with the *eschaton* and may pass from death to life here and now. That takes place in the Church of Jesus Christ where the age to come has already overtaken this age and overlaps it. In the mercy of God, however, Jesus Christ, the *Eschatos* by whom God will judge the quick and the dead, has withdrawn Himself visibly from history, *without being absent*, and has appointed a day when He will *appear* again in glory and power. Meantime the Word of the Gospel and the final Deed of God are partially held apart in eschatological reserve until the *Parousia* or the *Epiphaneia*. This is therefore the age of grace,

the age of *kerygma*, in which the Word of the Gospel is proclaimed to all, in which time and space are given for repentance
and decision. But this is the age too when by the Spirit of God
all who believe the *kerygma* of the Church may taste already the
powers of the age to come and with her enter into the Kingdom
of God. Because this Kingdom is neither an ideal nor a bare
message but actuality in the midst, the *kerygma* of the Church
is power of God, and through it the sovereignty of God (βασιλεία
τοῦ Θεοῦ) overtakes men and by the passion of Christ struggles
with them (Matt. 11: 12—βιάζεται). Those who lay violent
hands upon it (βιασταὶ ἁρπάζουσιν αὐτήν)[1] may press into it
(Luke 16:16—βιάζεται), but whether they will or no the grace
of God will abound and reign over all.

(b) *An Aspect of the Biblical Conception of Faith*[2]

Several scholars have recently called for a reconsideration of
faith as faithfulness answering to and dependent upon the Divine faithfulness. Certainly the New Testament conception of
faith (*pistis*) is much more than that, for in faith the intellectual
element of belief is powerfully represented, but even so this intellectual aspect of faith in the biblical context is grounded upon
the basic fact of the faithfulness of God and falls within the de-
termination of man's obedient and faithful response to the
covenant-mercies of God.

The Hebrew root that concerns us here is '*mn*, with the meaning of firm, steadfast, together with the terms '*aman* and
'*emunah*, with corresponding meanings, etc. As in the case of so
many Hebrew words, the fundamental significance of '*mn* seems
to be related closely to the intense family-consciousness of Israel.
Thus, as Arthur Weiser points out,[3] the *qal*, '*aman*, is applied to
a mother, or a nurse, or the guardian of a child, with reference
to the faithfulness and reliability of that relationship. Thus, too,

---

[1] Cf. Luke 24: 29: καὶ παρεβιάσαντο αὐτὸν λέγοντες, Μεῖνον μεθ'
ἡμῶν.
[2] Read before the Society for the Study of Theology, at Oxford, March,
1956; printed in *The Expository Times*, 1957, pp. 111–14.
[3] In the article on *pistis* in Kittel's *Theologisches Woerterbuch zum N.T.*, v.
183 f.

'*ōmēn*, *ōmeneth*, means a nurse, or a trustee, and '*omnah* means nursing or bringing up. And so '*ōmen* comes to refer to faithfulness in that light. Thus the vivid picture of the constancy and steadfastness of a parent to her child lurks behind the Old Testament conception of faithfulness.

This is the conception of steadfastness which in the Old Testament is applied to God in His covenant-faithfulness. For example, in Deut. 7: 9 it is used to speak of God's constancy in keeping covenant and *hesed* (RSV, "steadfast love") with His people, and in Is. 49: 7 it is applied to the faithfulness of God in His election of the Servant, to whom He will not only prove utterly faithful but for whom He will fulfil all His promises. Then this is described in v. 15 f. in the familiar words: "Can a woman forget her sucking child, that she should not have compassion on the son of her womb? yea, these may forget, yet will not I forget thee."

This conception of steadfastness or faithfulness is also applied in the Old Testament in a religious sense to people, such as the servant of God (Moses, Num. 12: 7), witnesses (Is. 8: 2; Jer. 42: 5), messengers (Prov. 25: 13), prophets (1 Sam. 3: 20), priests (1 Sam. 2: 35), and so on. But the conception of '*emunah* is applied above all to God.

To illustrate that, A. G. Hebert, in a recent article, cites Ps. 36: 5-7, and then comments as follows: "As the psalmist implies, the Hebrew word denoting steadfastness and firmness applies properly to God and not to man, who is repeatedly characterized as physically frail ('All flesh is as grass . . . the grass withereth, the flower fadeth: but the word of our God shall stand for ever'—Is. 40: 6-8) and as morally unstable (as in the first four verses of Ps. 36, where the ungodly man 'flatters himself in his own eyes' and his words are 'iniquity and deceit'). Hence the words 'faith' and 'to believe' (*he'emin*) do not properly describe a virtue or quality of man; they describe *man as taking refuge from his own frailty and instability in God who is firm and steadfast*. So in Is. 7: 9 the prophet says to the weak and timid King Ahaz, who is scared of the kings of Syria and northern Israel, 'If ye will not believe, ye shall not be established'—if you will not make-yourselves-firm (on God), you will not be made firm."[1]

---

[1] *Theology*, lviii, No. 424 (Oct., 1955), 374.

From this it is clear that we are faced with a problem when we have to translate the Hebrew into Greek, for the Greek *pistis* and *pisteuein* are not very happy equivalents for the words denoting faithfulness in Hebrew; *pistos*, however, is more applicable. Certainly the LXX is very uneasy about their use, and significant facts emerge which require far greater consideration than, I think, we have given to them. *Pistis*, for example, is never used in the LXX to signify "faith" or "belief", and *pistoi* is not used to describe the Old Testament "believers"—indeed it occurs but once in the canonical books in application to the members of the covenant-community, in Ps. 101: 6: "Mine eyes are upon the faithful (*pistous*) of the land", where clearly *pistoi* is properly rendered "faithful". The term *pisteuein* is used frequently in the LXX and used also in a strict religious sense, but this usage is dominated by the Old Testament conception of faithfulness.

The verb *'aman* has, it would appear, mainly a twofold usage. Primarily, it is used to mean "to make firm", "to establish", "to ground in the truth", and as such is sometimes translated in the LXX by *sterizein*. This meaning is apparent in many New Testament passages, of which we give two examples—

> 2 Thess. 3: 3: "Faithful (*pistos*) is the Lord who will strengthen (*sterixei*) you."
> Luke 22: 31 f.: "Satan has desired to have you, that he may sift you as wheat: But I have prayed for you that your faith (*pistis*) fail not: and when you are converted, strengthen (*sterison*) your brethren."

The other use of *'aman* which we may note refers to "believing in" or "relying on", where the LXX translates by *pisteuein* or a compound form of it. Here we may cite two typical instances.

> Gen. 15: 6: "Abraham believed (*episteusen*) God and it was counted unto him for righteousness (*dikaiosunen*)."
> 2 Chron. 20: 20: "Believe in (*empisteusate*) the Lord your God and ye shall be established (*empisteutheesthe*)."

In all these, and many similar instances in the Old Testament and the New Testament, the main emphasis is upon establishment or reliance upon God or upon the Truth in the Hebrew sense of the word for "truth".

That brings us to examine the concept of *'emeth*, the primary word in Hebrew for "truth". *'emeth* derives, of course, from the same root as *'emunah*, and indeed there does not seem to be a great deal of difference between *'emeth* and *'emunah*. There is a wide area, at any rate, in which they overlap in their meaning.

The usual translation of *'emeth* in the LXX is *aletheia*, but *aletheia* is not used to signify abstract or metaphysical truth, but what is grounded upon God's faithfulness, i.e. truth not as something static, but as active, efficacious reality, the reality of God in covenant-relationship. It is the steadfastness of God which is the ground of all truth. Primarily, truth is God's being true to Himself, His faithfulness or consistency. God's Truth means, therefore, that He keeps truth or faith with His people and requires them to keep truth or faith with Him. Thus the Hebrew *'emeth* is translated not only by *aletheia* but also by *pistis* and *dikaiosune*. There is no doubt that again and again where we have the words *pistis* and *dikaiosune* in the New Testament we must see behind them the Hebrew words, *'emeth* and *'emunah*, and where in the New Testament we have *aletheia* we must understand that not simply as a Greek word, but in the light of the biblical inclusion of *pistis* and *dikaiosune* in the concept of truth.

Because in the biblical context truth is grounded upon the divine faithfulness and the covenant-relation which it sets up, truth is also concerned with the event of the word through which relation between God and man, and man and man, takes place. It is in and through the word-event relationship that God's Truth is revealed and becomes efficacious reality among men. Here, of course, we have to do with the familiar Old Testament conception that when word and event coincide there is *'emeth* or truth. This is applied above all to God's Word, for when His deed corresponds to His Word, that is Truth. Truth is the faithfulness between God's actions and His Word. His Word accomplishing its purpose, actualizing itself, is the Truth with which men have to do, and it is with that Truth and Word of Truth that the prophets are burdened. The mighty Word of God enacts itself as Truth in the midst of God's people, for when through the prophets the Word of God reveals God and establishes His will, there is His Truth. Then God's Truth is fulfilled and actualized.

In the nature of the case this divine Word pressing to its Truth among men requires truth from the side of man in answer to it: man must walk before God in truth, and all his living, doing, speaking is to be a living of the truth, a doing of the truth, and a speaking of the truth. But when God's people prove unfaithful and untrue, His Truth becomes their judgment, and so *'emeth* is also used juridically or forensically. God keeps faith and keeps truth with sinners in judgment of sin, in vindication of the right, in justification. But out of this there arises the conception of God's Truth as a supreme eschatological and messianic conception, especially in Isaiah, Deutero-Isaiah, and in many Psalms. God is faithful who will bring His Word of Truth to pass in spite of all the unfaithfulness of His people, in spite of all the sin of man. When God's Word is finally established as Truth, when God has finally acted, the messianic Kingdom will be established. Truth will spring out of the earth, and a throne will be established in mercy and one shall sit on it in truth. It is this conception that forms such a powerful ingredient in the notion of the Servant in Deutero-Isaiah, for in and through the Servant the faithfulness of God both in judgment and in redemption presses toward its complete fulfilment in all the relations between God and His own.

When we turn over the pages to the New Testament and find this language being used and these conceptions being employed in the interpretation of Christ and the gospel, it becomes evident that Jesus Christ is understood as *the incarnate faithfulness of God*, the Word of God at last become event in our flesh in the fullest sense. "He is the Faithful and the True, the Amen." He is the Truth of God actualized in our midst—that is the Faithfulness of Christ Jesus (*pistis Christou Iesou*) of which St. Paul speaks so often.[1]

The New Testament conception of faith has a great wealth and variety which it is impossible to discuss here, where we are limiting ourselves to one main, fundamental aspect, but there are many passages where the usual translations are inadequate and where considerable light is brought to bear upon them from the Old Testament conceptions we have been discussing. Most of these passages have been adduced by Dr. Hebert in the valuable article referred to earlier. For our purpose here a

[1] See *The Church of Scotland Interim Report on Baptism* (1955), pp. 46–52.

selection will serve to indicate the line of interpretation that we must follow—

> 2 Thess. 2: 13: "God chose you from the beginning unto salvation in sanctification of the Spirit and faith of the truth" (*pistei aletheias*).

In Greek "faith of the truth" is an awkward expression, but it is clear from the Old Testament background that for St. Paul neither *pistis* nor *aletheia* will express fully what he is after, and so he puts both words together to convey what the Old Testament means by '*emeth* and/or '*emunah*.

> Rom. 3: 3: "Shall their faithlessness (*apistia*) make of none effect the faithfulness (*pistin*) of God?"

Difficult as the Greek is, the *pistis* of God, it expresses very excellent biblical teaching. The fundamental reality of our salvation is the divine faithfulness, and this in St. Paul's Epistles is equivalent to *dikaiosune*, righteousness, and in the Johannine writings, to *aletheia*, truth: all of these terms in the LXX may render the same Hebrew conception. Surely it is in this light that we are to translate

> Rom. 1: 17: "The righteousness of God is revealed from faith (*pisteos*) to faith (*pistin*)."

That is to say, the righteousness of God is revealed from God's *pistis* to man's *pistis*, but man's *pistis* is his implication in the divine *pistis*. God draws man within the sphere of His own faithfulness and righteousness and gives man to share in it, so that his faith is embraced by God's faithfulness. It is in precisely the same sense that St. Paul employs his favourite "*Pistos* is God who . . .", and then goes on to speak of man's salvation, or righteousness or faith in its utter reliance upon the divine faithfulness. That is the whole point of

> Rom. 3: 21–25: "God's *dikaiosune* is manifested through the *pistis* of Christ to all who believe (*tous pisteuontas*)."

Another set of significant passages we may take from the Epistle to the Galatians.

> Gal. 2: 16: "We . . . knowing that a man is not justified by the works of the law, but through the faithfulness of Jesus Christ (*dia*

pisteos Christou Iesou), even we believed (*episteusamen*) on Christ Jesus that we might be justified out of Christ's faithfulness (*ek pisteos Christou*), and not by the works of the law."

Gal. 2: 20: "I have been crucified with Christ; yet I live; and yet no longer I, but Christ liveth in me: and that life which I now live in the flesh I live in faith, the (*faithfulness*) which is of the Son of God (*en pistei te tou huiou tou theou*) who loved me and gave himself for me."

Gal. 3: 22: ". . . that the promise which derives from the faithfulness of Jesus Christ (*ek pisteos Iesou Christou*) might be given to them that believe (*tois pisteuousin*)."

In most of these passages the *pistis Iesou Christou* does not refer only either to the faithfulness of Christ or to the answering faithfulness of man, but is essentially a polarized expression denoting the faithfulness of Christ as its main ingredient but also involving or at least suggesting the answering faithfulness of man, and so his belief in Christ, but even within itself the faithfulness of Christ involves both the faithfulness of God and the faithfulness of the man Jesus. These typical passages from the Epistle to the Galatians give us the supreme difference between the Old Testament and the New Testament. Like the Old Testament, the New Testament also lays emphasis upon the faithfulness of God, and requires from man a corresponding faithfulness. But in the gospel the steadfast faithfulness of God has achieved its end in righteousness and truth in Jesus Christ, for in Him it has been actualized as Truth, and is fulfilled in our midst. Jesus Christ is not only the Truth of God but also Truth of God become man, the Truth of God become truth of man. As such Jesus is also the truth of man before God, for God, and toward God. Jesus Christ is thus not only the incarnation of the divine *pistis*, but He is the embodiment and actualization of man's *pistis* in covenant with God. He is not only the Righteousness of God, but the embodiment and actualization of our human righteousness before God. Thus St. Paul writes to the Philippians (3: 9): ". . . not having a righteousness of my own, based on law, but that which is through the faithfulness of Christ (*dia pisteos Christou*), the righteousness from God that depends on faith (*epi te pistei*)".

To expound this more fully we should have to go into the whole doctrine of the Atonement through the obedience of

Jesus Christ, and of our involvement in the whole movement of the Incarnation from the birth of Jesus to His ascension, and we cannot do that here. It may be sufficient to say that in the incarnate life of Jesus Christ, the Son of God become man among estranged men, we have the life of One who was God the Judge of man, and who was man judged by God; who was God bestowing Himself upon man in utter love, and who was man in obedient self-offering to God. In that life of union between God and man Christ manifested a twofold steadfastness or faithfulness: the steadfastness of God and the steadfastness of man in obedience to God; the steadfastness of God the Word revealing Himself to man, and the steadfastness of man believing and trusting in His Word and living faithfully upon it. Jesus Christ is God being true to Himself steadfastly and faithfully in the midst of our human estrangement, into which He entered in grace and steadfast love. Jesus Christ is man being perfectly true to God, steadfastly and faithfully obedient to God, the Amen of truth to God's truth. He is from the side of man, man's *pistis* answering to God's *pistis*, as well as from the side of God, God's *pistis* requiring man's *pistis*: as such He lived out the life of the Servant, fulfilling in Himself our salvation in righteousness and truth.

All that is remarkably summed up in 2 Cor. 1 : 18 f., according to which Jesus Christ is not only the faithful *Yes* of God to man, but is also the faithful *Amen* of man to God. He offers to God for us, and is toward God in His own person and life, our human response of obedience and faithfulness. Here there are two great aspects of the Christian gospel which need to receive from us much fuller consideration than they have found in modern theology.

(a) The whole of our salvation depends upon the faithfulness of God who does not grow weary of being faithful. It is God's faithfulness that undergirds our feeble and faltering faith and enfolds it in His own. In Christ Jesus we are in fact unable to disentangle our faith from the faithfulness of God, for it belongs to our faith to be implicated in the faithfulness of God incarnated among us in Jesus Christ.

(b) Jesus Christ is not only the Word of God become flesh, He is also Believer, but Believer for us, vicariously Believer, whose very humanity is the embodiment of our salvation. In

Him who is Man of our humanity, we are graciously given to share, and so to participate in the whole course of His reconciling obedience from His birth to His death. That He stood in our place and gave to God account for us, that He believed for us, was faithful for us, and remains faithful even when we fail Him again and again, is the very substance of our salvation and the anchor of our hope.

(c) *The Mystery of the Kingdom*[1]

It is sometimes said, without much theological inquiry, that the New Testament does not use the word *mystery* in any homogeneous sense, and that it cannot rightly be applied to the Sacraments of Baptism and the Lord's Supper. Certainly the New Testament does not apply the word *mystery* directly to the sacraments, but it does, I think, use it in a fundamentally homogeneous sense appropriate to the sacraments; for it is appropriate to the life of the Church in Jesus Christ.

It is the aim of this article to seek to give a positive account of *mystery* in the biblical doctrine of Christ and His Church by drawing out the theological significance of three important words: μυστήριον, πρόθεσις, and κοινωνία. In its fullest and deepest sense, μυστήριον refers to the union of God and man eternally purposed in God but now revealed and set forth in Jesus Christ as true God and true Man in one Person, a union which creates room for itself in the midst of our estranged humanity and through fellowship or communion gathers men into one Body with Jesus Christ. In these expressions *union* and *one Body* with Jesus Christ we have described the meaning of μυστήριον. In the expressions *eternally purposed* and *set forth* we have the significance of πρόθεσις. And in the expressions *creates room* for itself, *fellowship* or *communion*, and gathering into *one Body with* Jesus Christ, we have the significance of κοινωνία. All this has to be understood from beginning to end in terms of the Incarnation, of the union of God and man brought about in the Incarnation of the Word, the hypostatic union of God and Man in Jesus Christ. That hypostatic union is a union which recedes back into the mystery of the Holy Trinity, the con-

---

[1] French text published in *Verbum Caro*, 1956, pp. 3–11.

substantial communion of Father, Son, and Holy Spirit; but it is set forth in the incarnate life of Jesus Christ in terms of the reconciliation of man and God, for through His atonement and through His Spirit Jesus Christ who is God and Man in Himself creates out of the world a Church concorporate with Himself, or one Body with Him.

Primarily, then, μυστήριον refers to the union of God and Man in the one Person of Jesus Christ. In Him that union is thrust like an axis into the midst of our Humanity, making everything to revolve around it and have significance only in relation to it. That axis recedes into eternity in the eternal election or πρόθεσις of God, but it also manifests itself in history in the Church of Jesus Christ. Jesus Christ is Himself the manifestation, the setting forth (προτίθεσθαι, πρόθεσις) of the eternal purpose (πρόθεσις); and it is in communion with Him, through participation in the divine πρόθεσις, that the Church of Christ is called into being and maintained from age to age as the sphere through which Christ continues to manifest Himself, as the community (κοινωνία) in which He dwells by His Spirit, and which He who ascended to fill all things will bring to its fullness in His eternal purpose; for He, the First-born of all creation, will return again to consummate His eternal purpose in the new creation. Then the *mystery* consummated already in Christ will be revealed and manifested in the new heaven and the new earth.

We may put that the other way round. *Mystery* is the secret that lies behind God's creation. In the heart of that creation God created man, in the union of male and female as one flesh, to reflect the image of God within their relation of union between man and God. But that union between man and God was sundered, and the union within mankind making mankind one flesh, was sundered: the secret was lost to man, the mystery was wholly recondite. But the eternal purpose of God remained, and so at last in Jesus Christ, after long preparation in God's purpose with Israel, the mystery of God's will became incarnate; it embodied itself in the midst of our humanity, begetting in Jesus Christ the One in whom all mankind is gathered back into communion with God. By the atonement of Christ the God-Man, through at-one-ment and κοινωνία in Him, mankind is restored to the lost relation with God; restored in Christ to union with God. The Church is the sphere or κοινωνία in history, Christ's own Body, where that mystery of the Kingdom is proclaimed, revealed, and actualized, and there is created a new humanity through participation in Jesus Christ the First-born among many brethren, the First-born of all creation.

That in compendium is the significance of μυστήριον, πρόθεσις, and κοινωνία, but it needs to be controlled and modified by more detailed exposition of the theological significance of these terms.

(1) μυστήριον

Mysterion has a twofold sense in the New Testament—and an opposite sense, the counterfeit μυστήριον of evil which we will not consider. Primarily μυστήριον is the μυστήριον τοῦ Χριστοῦ as Paul calls it (Eph. 3: 4), but it is also the μυστήριον that has become actualized among the apostles and prophets and is to be described as the mystery of Christ and His Church (Eph. 5: 32). This mystery is *Revelation* that is identical with Christ Himself—and here one thinks of the Johannine record of the majestic word of Jesus: Ἐγώ εἰμι ἡ ὁδὸς καὶ ἡ ἀλήθεια καὶ ἡ ζωή (John 14: 6).

In 1 Tim. 3: 16 the mystery is spoken of as "the great mystery of godliness, God manifest in the flesh, justified in the Spirit . . .". That is the mystery of the Kingdom of which Jesus Himself speaks in the Synoptic Gospels (Mark 4: 11; Luke 8: 10; Matt. 13: 11): "To you is given to know the mystery (or mysteries) of the Kingdom of God." It is significant that both singular and plural are used by the evangelists, as if one wanted to emphasize the Person of Christ as the full content of the mystery, and another the knowledge of this mystery. Christ in the midst is the real focus of the parable—so that in Johannine language the mystery is the Ἐγώ εἰμι of Him who is one with the Father, God with us in Christ. In Synoptic language He is Emmanuel, but that Christ is the Son of the living God is not revealed by flesh and blood, but only by the Father. This mystery of the Person of Christ, however, has the same doubleness as the word to *reveal* in both Hebrew and Greek usage in the Bible, where *reveal* means not only an unveiling or uncovering of God but an uncovering of the ear, or an unveiling of the heart, of man. Thus the Revelation of this mystery refers not only to the secret of the Person of Christ as true God and true Man, but also to the revealing of it to men. It is highly significant, therefore, that this mystery, in the records of the Synoptic Gospels, gathers round it a conclave of twelve disciples to whom it is given to know the mystery as it is not given to those without. "To you it is given to know the mystery of the Kingdom; but to those that are without, all things are done in parables" (Mark 4: 11).

Several Old Testament passages are here in view and immediately leap into the mind of the reader, such as Deut. 29: 29; Ps. 78: 12; and especially Is. 8: 16 f. which speaks of the messianic testimony and instruction out of the Torah as sealed up among the disciples. "Behold I and the children whom the Lord hath given me are for signs and wonders in Israel." This is also recalled by an ἄγραφον or unwritten saying of Jesus recorded by Clement of Alexandria and the Clementine Homilies, in which Jesus speaks of His *mystery* which He has between Himself and the sons of His house (Clem. *Strom.* 5.10.69; *Clem Hom.* 19.20). Jesus and His disciples build together one Temple or Body in His mystery of the Kingdom.

No doubt there is also in view here the twofold fact of the Danielic vision that the Kingdom is given to the Son of Man and to the saints of the Most High (Dan. 7: 13 f., 27; cf. also 2: 44). The mystery of the Kingdom is thus not only the mystery of the union between God and man in Christ Himself, but the mystery of the One and the Many through atonement which Paul expounds in several of his Epistles. Christ who died One for all, forms all who believe in Him into one Body with Him, one New Man enshrining at its heart in Christ Himself the union of God and man. That is the mystery of Christ, God manifest in the flesh, and the mystery concerning Christ and His Church.

This same mystery is enshrined in the apostolic revelation and *kerygma*, for through His *Šālîaḥ*-Spirit Christ Himself dwells in the midst of the apostles, leading them into all truth and making them in a unique sense stewards of the mysteries of God and able ministers of His Spirit (1 Cor. 4: 1). It is on the foundation of this oneness between Christ and His apostles that the whole Church is built up and grows up into Christ the Head as one

Body with Him. This mystery which was concealed from the ages but is now made manifest in the *kerygma* of the apostles is spoken of in a doubleness corresponding not only to the significance of revelation but also to the significance of the οἰκονομία. This term οἰκονομία refers either to the dispensation of the mystery on the part of God, or it can refer to the *stewardship* of the mysteries on the part of the apostles which is given to them for the sake of the Church (see Eph. 1: 10, and 3: 2, 9; Col. 1: 25; 1 Cor. 9: 17; 1 Tim. 1: 4; 1 Cor. 4: 1 f.). That mystery is to be fulfilled in the οἰκοδομή and αὔξησις of the Church, and belongs in that fulfilment to the great gathering together into one of all things in Christ, things in heaven and earth, things visible and invisible, through the reconciliation of the Cross. In other words, the mystery concerning Christ and His Church reaches out in cosmic significance and redemption, and will be brought to its complete consummation to which we may well apply the language of the Apocalypse: ἐτελέσθη τὸ μυστήριον τοῦ Θεοῦ (Rev. 10: 7). That is the eternal purpose of God which He has purposed in Jesus Christ, and is now revealed and proclaimed in the Church.

(b) πρόθεσις

Like the word μυστήριον, πρόθεσις has essentially a twofold sense.

(1) It refers to the purpose of God and is used by Paul particularly of the eternal election which God has purposed in Himself and wrought out in Jesus Christ. It is the eternal purpose which in Rom. 8: 28 ff. Paul speaks of as ranging from predestination on the one hand to future glory on the other hand: it is at once pre-destination and post-destination, as it were, but the emphasis is clearly on the purpose of God in Christ as reaching out into the eternal and infinite mystery of God. That eternal πρόθεσις in the fullness of time is incarnated in Jesus Christ (Eph. 3: 11 f.), and it is defined in terms of Jesus Christ by whom all things were created and through whom all things are restored to the purpose of the divine Will. Thus πρόθεσις is pre-destination, the eternal election moving into time in Christ the Elect or the Beloved One, and reaching out to fulfilment and consummation in the Church as Christ's Body, the fullness of Him who fulfils all in all, as Paul puts it in Eph. 1: 22 f.

(2) πρόθεσις, however, has another meaning as *setting forth*—προ-θέσις, where it appears primarily to have had a liturgical significance. Thus in the famous passage in Rom. 3: 24 f. where Paul speaks of our justification freely by grace through the redemption that is in Christ Jesus, he adds, "whom God set forth (προέθετο) a propitiation (ἱλαστήριον) through faith in his blood, to declare his righteousness . . .". The language of Paul recalls the language of the Old Testament in Exod. 25: 17; 37: 6 and 1 Chron. 28: 11, and the thought that it is at the mercy seat where the blood of the covenant is set forth in atonement that God communes with His covenant people. He holds communion with them on the basis of the atonement wherein His covenant-purpose is ever renewed in the midst of Israel.

It is difficult also not to see associated in the mind of St. Paul, as in the Old Testament liturgy, the significance of the shewbread with that communion in covenant with God. By eating this bread the priests participated sacramentally in the Word of Life enshrined in the Holy of Holies: it was a kind of sacramental manna. In Hebrew this is spoken of as the bread of the face or the presence of God, and in Greek it is called the ἄρτος τῆς προθέσεως (cf. Heb. 9: 2). In Mark 2: 26 (Matt. 12: 4) we have a significant passage where Jesus asserts the authority of the Son of Man over the Old Testament regulations and in particular over the barriers the Jews had erected in worship in the House of God. Jesus deliberately broke down those barriers to inter-communion and gave as an example the act of Abiathar the high priest, who took of the sacred shew-bread of the priests and gave it to common men in their hunger. The thought here is that the Son of Man has authority to break down the φραγμός, the middle wall of partition as Paul calls it (Eph. 2: 14), dividing the Jews from the Gentiles, the inner from the outer court of the Temple. Jesus Himself spoke of this φραγμός as the fence or hedge which God had built round Israel His tender vine which He cultivated with such care (Matt. 21: 33, cf. Is. 5: 1 f.), but which had to be destroyed, while its inheritance was given to the nations of the earth (Mark 12: 1 ff.). The same word φραγμός is used in Jesus' parable of the wedding feast. God's servants are sent out to the highways and hedges or φραγμοί to compel people to come in and fill up God's house (Luke 14: 23). There they sit down to partake of the messianic meal, the heavenly manna and drink of the water of life. That is in parabolic form the counterpart to the apocalyptic description of the Great Marriage Supper of the Lamb, when the mystery will be completed and the Church will become one with the Word of God. But until then the Church is given the sacraments of Baptism and Holy Communion in which the Church as one Body with Christ continues to feed upon the Body and Blood of Christ. There in this sacramental fellowship, corresponding surely to the priestly meal at the Table of shew-bread before the face of God, the Church holds communion with God, feeding upon the heavenly manna on the very threshold of the Holy of Holies through the veil of which Christ has already entered, our High Priest.

Not all this, of course, is immediately related to the actual word πρόθεσις in its use in the New Testament; but it belongs to the whole context of the word in the κοινωνία of the Church. We may sum up the significance of πρόθεσις by saying: it refers both to the divine election or eternal purpose in Christ who is in Himself God and Man, and refers to the fact that the eternal purpose is set forth in the Incarnation (see also 2 Tim. 1 : 8 f.), and continues to be set forth in the midst of the Church in its κοινωνία. Through Word and Sacrament in the Church we are ever given to have fellowship in the mystery of Christ (as one reading of Eph. 3 : 9 puts it).

(3) κοινωνία

Like μυστήριον and πρόθεσις, κοινωνία has a twofold sense: a primary and a secondary sense. Primarily κοινωνία means participation through the Spirit in Jesus Christ, participation in the union of God and Man in Him—in the Johannine record that is profoundly given in John 17. Secondarily κοινωνία refers to the fellowship which is the Church, the communion which exists between members of the Body of Christ.

Primarily, then, κοινωνία means participation in the mystery of Christ. We have seen that μυστήριον is the union of God and Man in Christ, for in the eternal purpose that union was incarnated and bodied forth among men in the Word made flesh. That is the mystery of the Kingdom in its vertical dimension of πρόθεσις as it is inserted into human life and history, the axis of God's purpose of love. In Christ Himself that mystery is fully

realized and actualized. God and Man are uniquely and finally
One in Him, and in Him the Kingdom has fully and finally
come. Jesus Christ as true God and True Man is the mystery of
the Kingdom in His own Person. The whole work of atonement
and reconciliation is already wrought out in Him. It is a finished
work. κοινωνία means our participation in that completed union
between God and Man, participation in the finished work of
atonement and reconciliation. It is indeed only in that participation, in the κοινωνία of the mystery of Christ, that we *know*
the mystery of the Kingdom.

Secondarily, however, κοινωνία means fellowship in the
mystery as well as participation, but fellowship only on the
ground of participation. Through the eternal πρόθεσις actualized in the Incarnation of Christ the mystery of the Kingdom is
inserted, so to speak, into our fallen humanity, inserted into the
midst of our flesh, into the midst of our choices and decisions,
into the midst of our knowledge. The penetration of that
mystery of the Kingdom, of the mystery of the union of God and
Man, into our humanity means that it acts critically and
creatively in the midst of our life and society creating room for
itself, creating space for itself in the midst of our humanity.
That is, it creates the Church, the circle of fellowship in which
Christ Himself dwells. We have already seen that to belong to
the mystery of the Kingdom in its secondary sense as the
mystery given to the saints of the Most High, is realized first of
all in the apostolate: that is the nucleus of the κοινωνία, the
communio sanctorum. It is the κοινωνία of those who all together
have κοινωνία in the mystery of Christ.

These two senses of κοινωνία are inseparable and are mutual-
ly related. There is no participation vertically in the mystery
of Christ except by horizontal fellowship in the mystery, but
there is no horizontal fellowship except by joint participation
vertically through the Holy Spirit in the mystery of Christ who
is true God and true Man. Now it is supremely in the cross and
resurrection, by atonement and reconciliation, that the union
of God and Man is inserted with power into our humanity,
creating the Church as the Body of Christ, giving it to participate in His relation with the Father, but already that insertion
had begun in the birth of Jesus; it was continued throughout
His whole Incarnate life, and was enacted in the ministry of

Christ where already, therefore, the Church was founded as it was formed in the twelve disciples round the Person of our Lord, one Body with Him.

In the Incarnation the mystery of the union of God and Man, of the Oneness of God and Man in Christ, is inserted and enacted in our midst in a twofold way:

(*a*) It is inserted into the midst of our knowledge, and that takes place in the Teaching of Jesus and in the Revelation of the Father through the Son to the disciples, giving them communion or participation in God's knowledge of Himself. Thus Jesus says in Matt. 11: 25 f.: "I thank thee, O Father, Lord of Heaven and earth, because thou hast hid these things from the wise and prudent and hast revealed them unto babes. Even so, Father, for so it seemed good in thy sight. All things are delivered unto me of my Father: and no man knoweth the Son, but the Father; neither knoweth any man the Father, save the Son, and he to whomsoever the Son will reveal Him." Thus κοινωνία is participation in the relation of the Father and the Son, which takes place through the Holy Spirit—very clearly set out by the Fourth Gospel from ch. 14–ch. 17. It was the insertion of that mystery into the midst of Israel that created at once the band of disciple-learners and -receivers of Revelation, and yet called forth the reaction of resentment which culminated in the Cross. This is a κοινωνία which cuts across the face of man's knowledge of God and calls it radically into question: and men resent it. But in spite of all the contradiction of sin, the oneness of God and Man in mind is inserted into the knowledge of sinners, which is an essential part of Christ's reconciliation. The Teaching of Jesus was an essential part of the atonement, and the atonement could not have taken place apart from it.

(b) The oneness of God and Man in Christ is inserted into the midst of our being, into the midst of our sinful existence and history, into the midst of our guilt and death on the Cross. The inserting of the Oneness of God and Man into the deepest depths of man's existence in his awful estrangement from God, and the enactment of it in the midst of his sin and in spite of all that sin can do against it, is atonement. In a profound sense atonement is the insertion of the hypostatic union into the very being of our estranged and fallen humanity. That insertion of oneness by atonement results in κοινωνία, in the Church as the

communion in which we are made partakers of the divine
nature. The κοινωνία thus created by the atonement and resurrection of Christ is fully actualized by the outpouring of the
Holy Spirit, and is maintained by the power of the Spirit as the
Church continues in the fellowship of Word and Sacrament. We
cannot here pursue the doctrine of the Church, but it is important to see that the Church is founded first not simply by the
words of Jesus to Peter: "Upon this rock I will build my
church", but upon the oneness of God and Man which in the
birth of Jesus is inserted into our human existence, which
reaches throughout the course of His life and particularly of His
ministry, into the atonement and into the resurrection, and then
into the ascension. The Union of God and Man which is the
very life of the Son of Man is already of the essence of the atoning and reconciling work of Christ, and it is the same union
which, after resurrection and ascension, through the Spirit
gathers men into itself in and through the Church: that is in and
through κοινωνία the divine πρόθεσις enshrining the eternal
μυστήριον embodies itself horizontally in a community of those
who are at one with God through the reconciliation of Christ.

We may summarize this in more dogmatic language. The
mystery of Christ is the hypostatic union of true God and true
Man in One Person; and as that union is enacted in atonement
and in resurrection it issues in the community of the reconciled,
the community of the resurrection. The πρόθεσις refers to the
fact that what God is in Christ as God and Man in union, God
is antecedently and eternally in Himself, and so the πρόθεσις
speaks of the recession of the hypostatic union and its grounding
eternally in the communion between Father, Son, and Holy
Spirit. But πρόθεσις also is the setting forth of that union through
Christ, through the atonement in such a way that men are
given to participate in the communion of God the Father, the
Son, and the Holy Spirit. Thus πρόθεσις is, as it were, the pro-
jection (προ-θέσις) of that communion in and through Christ
into mankind, creating κοινωνία as its counterpart through the
communion of the Holy Spirit. Indeed it seems clear that these
three terms imply the doctrine of the Trinity; μυστήριον more
particularly the eternal Son, πρόθεσις the eternal Father, and
κοινωνία the eternal Spirit. This trinity of action is grounded
eternally in the Holy Trinity of Father, Son, and Holy Spirit.

Is not baptism in the name of the Father, Son, and Holy Spirit, the sacrament of the Trinity, and in that sense a mystery, because it points to the mystery of the Kingdom? And is not Holy Communion in which we feed upon Christ a communion in the mystery of Christ? For it is here at the Lord's Supper that the Church ever becomes what it is, the Body of Christ, and rejoices in the great mystery between Christ and His Church. If we are to use the term *mystery* of the sacraments, however, it is clear that this differs *toto caelo* from the way in which mystery was used in the mystery-rites of ancient Greece. But if in this sense we can recover the setting of the sacraments in the doctrine of the Church as the communion in the mystery of Christ, and in the whole context of the Trinitarian faith, should we not use the term *mystery* rather than the term *sacrament* which lays the stress not on what God has once and for all done for us, but on our responsibilities and our vows of response? The term *mystery* used in the biblical sense would help us also to recover the biblical idea that there are not two or many sacraments but two essential "moments" in the one whole relation of the Church to Christ, one "moment" speaking of the once and for all participation in what Christ has once and for all done, and the other "moment" speaking of our continual renewal in that perfected reality in Christ Jesus.

3

THE SACRAMENT OF BAPTISM

(a) *The Origins of Baptism*[1]

IT is by no means an easy matter to trace the precise origins of the rite of Christian Baptism both because there is a vast amount of material relevant to it and because the New Testament does not seem to offer any one clear line for consideration. It takes all this for granted and speaks of Baptism quite naturally, without any difficulty of communication and without any need for explanation. The derivation of the rite and the actions involved are everywhere presumed as familiar. That makes it all the more difficult for us, for we have to examine minutely the many allusions, hints, and images employed in the New Testament writings, and in particular the references, and citations (often very incomplete) from the Old Testament, in order to place ourselves as completely as possible in the position of the New Testament writers, and then from their *Sitz im Denken* as well as *Sitz im Leben* seek to unravel their presuppositions and interpret their meaning.

Perhaps one of the most difficult things for us to do to-day, after a century of exhaustive Old Testament investigation, is to get ourselves into the position from which the New Testament writers regarded and interpreted and handled the Old Testament. Take, for example, the very extraordinary passage in the sixteenth chapter of Ezekiel. The interpretations of this by Old Testament scholars appear to differ widely, but they differ radically from that found everywhere in the Rabbinic Judaism of the first three centuries A.D., e.g. in the older *Pesikta*. But how would the writers of the New Testament have interpreted it? One thing must be clear, that we cannot expect them to have understood it after the fashion of scientific Old Testament scholarship to-day. They did not have that sort of approach to the Old Testament and certainly did not have the equipment

[1] Lecture delivered to the University of Lund, October, 1956, reprinted from *S.J.T.*, vol. 11/2, 1958, pp. 158–171.

it requires. It is more likely that they would have looked at it as their Jewish contemporaries looked at it, as a parable of Yahweh's dealing with Israel after the fashion of Jewish adoption of a newly-born foundling child of heathen parents. In this way the parable was interpreted to speak of Israel as a child-proselyte from heathendom, baptized and cleansed and brought into the Covenant, and then when she grew of age assumed into the marriage-relationship. But alas! she proved unfaithful to her husband who had entered into covenant with her. Taken in that way, it is certainly a remarkable parable of Israel adopted to be the child of Yahweh, sealed with the seal of the Covenant, and then in renewal of the Covenant espoused as the Bride of Yahweh. This double sealing of the Covenant was Rabbinically discerned in the reference in Ezekiel 16 to the two "bloods", vv. 6, 9, 22, and was interpreted to refer parabolically to cir-cumcision and passover. This very language is still used to-day in the rite of circumcision.

Now that is quite definitely typical of Judaistic interpre-tation of the Old Testament during New Testament times, and we know that this passage and its interpretation played a fundamental part in the understanding of proselyte Baptism. Those incorporated by baptism into Israel were adopted into the Covenant in the same way that Israel itself was adopted by Yahweh. But can we say that the New Testament writers would have regarded Ezekiel 16 in this light? We have to allow for the fact that these interpretations, repeated *ad nauseam* in the Rabbinic literature, were embedded in the Jewish tradi-tion and conditioned the Christian reading and interpreting of the Old Testament, but on the other hand their interpre-tation of the Old Testament was decisively altered by the over-whelming and shattering fact of Christ, which drew to it all the lines of Old Testament teaching, fulfilling them and abrogating them in a sovereign manner.

That is what makes it so difficult to get into the *Sitz im Denken* of the New Testament writers to see precisely how they looked at particular passages in the Old Testament. They certainly looked at the Old Testament from a Christian perspective. That did not mean that their Jewish tradition of interpretation was altogether destroyed. On the contrary it was given reinter-pretation and made to point forward in a new way to Christ.

But just because all lines were now seen to point forward to Christ, the many lines made to converge on Him overlapped the nearer their point of convergence. That is particularly evident in the way the New Testament writers use images from the Old Testament. They lay them on top of one another and employ several together in their use of the Old Testament to express their understanding of the salvation fulfilled in Christ. That usage extends even to Old Testament words and phrases and part-sentences, which are brought together sometimes within a single verse in the New Testament. That process of conflating images and terms was already at work in Judaism, but now in the fulfilment of the ancient promises in Christ that is done in a new way, and with a sovereign freedom in handling Old Testament citations. The reality in Christ is not bound by the ancient shadow or image; that was only a signitive pointer to the reality and now that the reality has arrived it interprets itself, not by an arbitrary handling of the Old Testament, but by a significant and sovereign use of it, bending it in subservience to the New.

In all this there is a tendency to go back direct to the Old Testament, to read it with new eyes and the new insights imparted by the mighty events of the Gospel; but even so there could be no escaping from the oral Jewish tradition which for so long had shaped the reading and understanding of the Old Testament. Rather was this Jewish tradition itself taken under control and adapted in the reinterpretation of Israel in the Church. It is only when we get inside that complicated reorientation to the Old Testament and to Jewish interpretation of it that we can discern the significance of so many of the allusions and references of the New Testament to the Old and to Jewish tradition. It is in that light, for example, that Paul appears to make use of Ezekiel 16 in Ephesians 5: 25 ff., but if so, how radically different is his employment of Ezekiel 16 from that of Rabbinic Judaism when he uses it to speak of the Baptism of the Church as the Bride of Christ.

That is but one important allusion offered in the New Testament to the origin of the rite of Baptism, but how are we to thread our way through the maze of allusions and references in this connexion? I believe that we may profitably take our cue from the Judaistic conception of proselyte baptism. By that I do not mean at all that we are to see in proselyte baptism itself the source of the Christian rite, but that proselyte baptism helps us to see a line of interpretation embedded in the Jewish tradition which throws considerable light upon what the New Testament writers took for granted in regard to the origins of the Christian rite. The firm use of proselyte baptism appears in Judaism in the middle of the second century; allusions to it appear frequently in Justin Martyr's *Dialogue with Trypho*. There are references to it also in the *Mishnah* which allude to a time when the Temple was still standing. But perhaps our oldest evidence for it comes from the New Testament, particularly from the Epistles of St. Paul who appears to use the language of Proselyte Baptism in 1 Cor. 10: 1 ff.; 2 Cor. 5: 17; 6: 14 ff.; 7: 1; Rom. 6: 15 ff.; Eph. 2: 11 f., etc. Be that as it may, it is extremely difficult to conclude that the firm practice of proselyte baptism in second-century Judaism did not go back, like everything else, to authoritative sanctions in their tradition very much earlier, and that the written teaching of the second century did not have behind it a long oral tradition.

I do not say this in order to argue that Christian baptism depends on or derives from proselyte baptism, but simply in order to make it clear that it is a legitimate procedure to examine the hints that proselyte baptism gives us of formative lines of interpretation at work in Judaism long before the firm practice of proselyte baptism was established, or its rite and meaning fully set forth in the tractate *Gerim*.

Proselyte baptism involved three main elements: circumcision, the sprinkling of sin-offering water on the third and seventh days after circumcision, and immersion. This was the rite of incorporation into the Covenant-people and of taking on the yoke of the Torah. Behind the rite lay a powerful theology of participation in the Exodus redemption out of Egypt, the crossing of the Red Sea, and of sanctificatory cleansing in the establishment of the Covenant at Mt. Sinai. This is found with particular clarity in the *Pesikta*, and is still preserved in the *Passover Haggadah*. The "proselyte" to Judaism, the *ger*, meant more than a proselyte in our sense of the word. Even the Greek sought to render the fact that he is one who may "draw near" to worship God as one of His holy people engaging in the holy things of law and cult. But the Hebrew *ger* has also a fundamental significance, as Nahum Levison has recently pointed out,[1] close to the word *hibri* or Hebrew, the one from the other side, a foreigner. Thus what was prescribed for the *gerim* in their incorporation into the *hibri* throws a good deal of light upon the Hebrews as a Covenant-people. It is in this respect that Ezekiel 16 surely has part of its far-reaching significance. On the other hand, incorporation into the *hibri* must be one of the oldest and most telling ideas governing the conception of Baptism which it eventually demanded. By looking behind these rites incorporating proselytes into the Covenant-people we can find considerable help in understanding the teaching of the New Testament.

(1) *Circumcision*

In the account offered by the Old Testament itself, this rite was given to Abraham and his family as *hibri* in ratification of the Covenant and in seal of the divine promise attached to it, the promise of a country but also of a messianic future. The promise of the land was not fulfilled for four hundred years, for the Hebrews were themselves to be *gerim* in the land of Egypt (Gen. 15: 13). It was in connexion with the first Passover and the Exodus out of Egypt that the term *ger* seems to come into prominence in the Old Testament. There it is that we hear that the *ger* was to be circumcised (and all male members of his family), if he was to take part in the Passover. He was to come under the one Law of the one Covenant (Exod. 12: 43–49). That is further elucidated in Leviticus 19, where it was prescribed that Israelites should love the *gerim* as they loved themselves, for they also were *gerim* in Egypt—"I am Yahweh, your God", it is added, for the whole worship of Yahweh was at stake.

There are two main points I would like to stress here.

(a) The relation of circumcision to the messianic promise. Until the Hebrews entered the promised land they too were *gerim*. That is a conception that came to the fore in the later literature of the Old Testament, exilic and post-exilic, when the Jews came to think of themselves as sojourners and aliens resident in a foreign country. They were essentially pilgrims expecting the messianic country, the messianic Kingdom. They were God's *gerim*, a thought particularly clear in the Psalms

---

[1] *S.J.T.* 10/7, p. 45. On Proselyte Baptism, see *New Testament Studies*, vol. 1/2, 1954, pp. 150 ff.

where there is a return to the idea that they were children of Abraham waiting to take possession of the promised land. At the same time the status of the non-Israelite *gerim* came to be increasingly appreciated as in Isaiah 56: 3–5, which seems to have influenced the Zadokite community of Damascus and the allied Community at Qumran. Thus at the height of the Old Testament teaching we have the important idea that the circumcised children of Abraham are messianically to be regarded as *gerim* expecting a country, expecting the fulfilment of the ancient promises of the Covenant.

(b) The Covenant cut into the flesh. In circumcision the Covenant was cut into the flesh of Israel as a sign and seal of its promised fulfilment. The Covenant was such that it had to be actualized in the whole life of Israel, enacted in its flesh, done into its existence before God. From the Deuteronomic literature on this was given a deeper interpretation in terms of the circumcision of ears, lips, and heart—the whole "inner man", so to speak, had to be circumcised. That is to say, the Covenant will of God had to be inscribed by His finger or by His Spirit upon the tablets of the heart. That idea came to prominence especially in Ezekiel and Jeremiah, but it is clear that when that took place, the writing of God's Word and will in the heart through the operation of the Spirit, then the Old Covenant would take on a new form. It would be a New Covenant.

But how was this Covenant to be fulfilled in the flesh of Israel? How was it to be cut right into the existence of Israel and so fulfilled from within Israel, wholly and completely fulfilled? The answer given by the Old Testament is found in the Deutero-Isaianic doctrine of "the Servant of the Lord", as He who will fulfil and mediate the Covenant. (I am myself convinced that while the Servant represents Israel in its ordeal it has a further significance in which, without denial of the corporate character of the Servant, one Servant in the Midst of Israel is indicated, and that here it is ultimately the figure of Moses, "the servant of the Lord", that lies behind it.) The fulfilment of God's Word and Truth, His judgment and mercy, takes place in the life of the Servant, but in him it is vicariously fulfilled for all. In the later Isaianic prophecies we hear also of the Holy Spirit. The Servant is anointed with the Spirit and through Him the Spirit is bestowed. And in this connexion we may add the prophecies of Joel fulfilled on the day of Pentecost in the Baptism of the Spirit.

We are now in a position to gather up the results of this discussion and put it into New Testament language. Circumcision is fulfilled in the New Covenant, (a) in the blood of Christ, which is the blood of the New Covenant, that is in His total circumcision or crucifixion; and (b) in His gift of the Holy Spirit. With these two facts the Old Covenant no longer remains in force in the old form, and therefore the outward sign of it is abrogated or rather displaced by a sign appropriate to the fulfilled reality of the New Covenant in Christ. Here it is the Epistle of Galatians that is most instructive. If the Covenant still stands in its old form, then argues St. Paul, what Christ has done is of no avail. But actually the whole relation between man and God has entered upon a new age, in the New Covenant made by God in Christ. This is fulfilled once and for all in the breaking of the Body of Christ and in the shedding of His Blood, and in the outpouring of the Spirit upon all flesh, that is upon all who enter into the New Covenant in the Name of Christ. Baptism is therefore given to take the place of circumcision as the sign and seal of the New Covenant.

(2) *The Sprinkling of Sin-Offering Water, or the Water of Separation*

The significance of this has been much neglected, no doubt because of its obscurity to Western minds. However, the fact that in the majority of cases, where the Greek word *baptizein* is used religiously in pre-Christian Jewish literature, it refers to this solemn cleansing by sprinkling ought to be sufficient to indicate its importance in examining the background to the rite of Baptism. The commandments regarding this rite and the traditions connected with it make it clear that it was one of the most solemn and awful rites in the Old Testament except perhaps that of the high priest entering into the Holy of Holies once a year on the Day of Atonement at the very risk of his life. It is important to realize, as Levison has pointed out anew, that the language used of it in the Old Testament is incredibly strong, viz., *chatah*, meaning to *un-sin*. The language used in the *Mishnah* indicates that in some sense it was thought of as a baptism of death, a death to sin. The rite involved the total burning by fire without the camp of a red heifer as a sin offering, and the preservation of its ashes which were to be used along with the sprinkling of water for un-sinning and sanctification on occasions of grave defilement. Some scholars, not without justification, regard the rite as an Israelite substitution for the pagan rite of "passing through fire" children in sacrifice to Moloch. That may well lie behind the incident recorded in Numbers 31 where the purification of Israel and their Midianite prisoners was to be effected through the water of separation or impurity while the gold and silver, etc. captured were to be "passed through fire". What could not endure the fire was to be made to pass through water, that is, by means of this solemn sprinkling. Whatever the origin of the rite, cleansing by sin-offering water was a "vicarious rite" in place of a kind of baptism by fire.

Be that as it may, we find that the ordinance of separation and un-sinning in this awful way applied to the *gerim* as well as to the Israelite. It was this that added awful solemnity to the circumcision of the proselyte, and made his coming from circumcision to be like "a coming from the grave" as the *Mishnah* puts it.

To see the deep significance of this it is worth looking at the rites ordained for the cleansing and readmission of lepers to fellowship in Israel. Lepers were separated and banished from common life as utterly unclean and were regarded as having no civil rights. Healed lepers, however, had to be readmitted through a double rite, a ceremony of reconsecration through a sevenfold sprinkling of the water of un-sinning, remarkably parallel to that for the consecration to priesthood, enabling them to draw near to holy things, and a ceremony remarkably parallel to that of the Day of Atonement for the annual renewal of the Covenant between God and Israel. Only thus could a leper be reincorporated into the holy nation and priestly people of Israel. Something of that undoubtedly influenced Elisha in the commands he gave to Naaman, the Syrian leper, whose sevenfold baptism (the word *baptizein* is used in the LXX) corresponded to the sevenfold sprinkling of the leper.

It is in Psalm 51, however, that we see even more deeply into its spiritual significance. David after his fearful sin regards himself as cut off from God and deprived of His Spirit, and prays for cleansing as if he had become a leper or a heathen. "Purge (i.e. un-sin) me with hyssop and I shall be clean: wash me and

I shall be whiter than snow. Hide thy face from my sins, and blot out all mine iniquities. Create in me a clean heart, O God, and renew a right spirit within me. Cast me not away from thy presence; and take not thy holy Spirit from me. Restore unto me the joy of thy salvation and uphold me with a willing Spirit." It was only then that he could draw near with the customary sacrifices to be offered upon God's altar.

It is significant that at important points in the Old Testament writings this language was used with profound spiritual and even messianic significance. It was used by Ezekiel in his spiritual reinterpretation of circumcision, and above all in the important passage in 36: 25 where the messianic gift of a cleansing and quickening Spirit is spoken of as the sprinkling of "clean waters", resulting in a new heart and a new spirit. "And I will put my Spirit within you, and cause you to walk in my statutes, and ye shall keep my judgments and do them. And ye shall dwell in the land that I gave to your fathers: and ye shall be my people, and I will be your God." Israel regarded as still waiting to enter the promised land is promised a fulfilment of God's Covenant made with Abraham, but a Covenant fulfilled in a new way through the Spirit. This passage was cited times without number in the Mishnaic and Talmudic literature of Judaism, but nowhere perhaps more significantly than at the end of the *Yoma* where it is adduced to give interpretation to the baptismal ablution of the high priest on the Day of Atonement, and to interpret that baptism messianically as "the hope of Israel".

Thus circumcision came to be reinterpreted in terms of a messianic gift of the Spirit, but the association of the sprinkling of the water of separation added to that the idea of a baptism of the Spirit which was at once un-sinning and quickening. The association of this kind of baptism or sprinkling of the water of the Spirit with circumcision, and its messianic reinterpretation, can hardly be over-estimated so far as the origins of the New Testament rite are concerned. It is of course the Epistle to the Hebrews which particularly points to this line of tradition in the origin of the rite of Baptism. The Old Testament rites are regarded as fulfilled in Christ Himself, the Mediator of a New Covenant, who, like the red heifer, suffered in vicarious sacrifice without the camp. Thus in Christ we may "draw near with a true heart in fullness of faith, having our hearts sprinkled from an evil conscience, and our bodies washed with pure water". The reinterpretation of the Old Testament rites in Christ does not mean the abolition of the use of water, but the language of the old rites is used to interpret the relation of this baptismal rite to Christ's fulfilment of the Covenant and His opening up for us a new and living way into the holy presence of God.

(3) *Immersion in Water*

Where did this rite come from and what was its significance? We know that the Near East abounded in "baptist" movements at the turn of the era, and that even within Israel there were many sects practising baptismal ablutions, the best known of which were the Pharisees who had a rite of initiation into the sect by immersion of the whole family, including women and children, but who practised frequent and daily baptisms in which they carried late-Jewish purifications to absurd lengths. In Judaism, however, all these rites of baptismal ablution and purification seem to go back to the central rites associated with the Laver in the Tabernacle or the Sea in the Temple, at which washing in water was required by priests on entering or leaving the Holy Place, and also before solemn sacrifice. Washing of the victims was also required, a fact which may be reflected in the sacrifice by Elijah on Mount Carmel. The particularly solemn act of ablution was that of the high priest at consecration (the only instance of baptism of one at the hands of another, e.g. of Aaron at the hands of Moses, unless Solomon was given a similar cleansing at the Gihon at his consecration to be king) and again on the Day of Atonement. It would appear that the placing of the Laver in the Temple was originally designed, or at least later interpreted, to represent symbolically the crossing of the Red Sea together with the sanctification of Israel for the service of God within the Covenant, just as the placing of the Tables of the Law in the Ark within the Holy of Holies appears to represent symbolically and to recall liturgically the ascent of Moses to receive the Law in the thick darkness which shrouded the holy presence of God on Mt. Sinai. At any rate the Laver did represent a liturgical extension into the worship of Israel of its sanctification and cleansing as a people taken into holy Covenant with God. When this sanctification and cleansing was applied to the proselyte, Judaism certainly interpreted it in an elaborate doctrine of the crossing of the Red Sea and the sanctification of Israel before Mt. Sinai.

Thus the application to proselytes of an act of immersion at the end of their initiation meant their participation in the mighty acts of Israel's redemption out of Egypt at the Exodus, their entry into the holy and priestly people of the Covenant, and their readiness through sanctification to receive instruction from the Law of God and to come under its yoke. It meant that they shared in God's sanctification or hallowing of Himself in the midst of His people Israel, and separated themselves from the darkness and uncleanness of the heathen world to live within the light and purity of God's revelation and appointed way of life. In this way they took shelter in the Name of God and came under the wings of His Holy Spirit; born again out of heathendom, they were new creatures, no longer aliens and strangers but fellow-citizens of the commonwealth of Israel in the family of God.

When we turn from the Old Testament and its traditional interpretation to the New Testament we are confronted right away with the Baptism of John the Baptist, and the Baptism of Jesus by John. Did this rite appear in entire independence of what we have been considering in the context of Jewish thought and practice? That is most unlikely. Then how are we to regard the distinctive characteristics of John's Baptism and how are we to interpret them over against the tradition of prior and contemporary Judaism?

Here we are offered, it would appear, some real help from the so-called Dead Sea Scrolls, both in a general way and at two particular points which seem to me to be important.

Generally these Judaean documents, and in particular the Manual of Discipline, along with the Zadokite Fragments from Damascus, use not only the language but many of the ideas we have been discussing, such as spiritual circumcision, the sprinkling of sin-offering water for atonement messianically interpreted, and the application of priestly ablution from the Temple to all initiated members of the Covenant Community. In all this circumcision itself falls into the background. Indeed there is no mention of it in the two documents named except in a spiritual sense. What is important is its fulfilment in the anointing of the Spirit and in the illumination of the Thorah, which is accompanied by sprinkling and immersion. These rites are not regarded as efficacious in themselves but as symbolic of the divine cleansing and justification. Atonement is by the Holy Spirit of God, apparently replacing the blood of the Covenant and all animal sacrifices. And of course it is supremely noteworthy that on the ground of such purification in water and Spirit admission is given to the messianic meal of bread and wine.

The attempts that have been made to draw close parallels between these ideas and practices and those of John the Baptist to prove their direct and immediate influence upon him are not convincing, but it is significant that here we have some justification for the general line of interpretation of the origins of the rite of Baptism we have been pursuing. If the documents in question are to be dated just prior to the fall of Jerusalem or even sometime within the first century, they do indicate clearly that there was within Judaism a remarkable development in reinterpreting the Old Testament similar to that which appears to lie behind the pages of the New Testament in the Jewish tradition, a development which was radically and critically reinterpreted once again in the light of the mighty acts of God in Christ. The parallels between the conceptions embedded in the New Testament and those in these sectarian communities at Qumran and Damascus help us to understand the change that took place in Jewish Christianity as it emerged out of Judaism, although they do not supply us with actual source-material governing that change.

There are two particular points that demand closer consideration.

(a) Although the *gerim* are mentioned as a distinct group of novitiates in the Covenant Community by the Damascus document, and may well be implied in the Manual of Discipline, in both of them all members of the Covenant Community admitted by baptismal lustration and covenantal oath-taking tended to be regarded as proselytes to the Lord or converts to the New Covenant. The term used is *nilwim*, taken from Isaiah 56: 3, 6, to describe "messianic *gerim*", as it were. Here Israelites are somehow looked on as polluted and unclean like lepers, so that solemn purification is absolutely necessary.

Hence the solemn cleansing applied to lepers and to those polluted by death, and to the high priest on the Day of Atonement, is applied to them. In other words, it is no longer sufficient to be a circumcised Jew. All have to undergo repentance and purification, circumcised Jews and proselytes alike; they have to become converted as members of the messianic Community and as participators in the New Covenant. (It is also interesting to note that the Damascus Document refers to the idea, common also in Rabbinic literature, that Abraham was a proselyte even in the narrower sense of the word.)

(b) Along with this there is apparent a reaction against a crude and literalist practising of the Cult in favour of an attempt to translate the priestly Cult into the actual life and existence of the Covenant people. Thus the structural pattern of the Tabernacle or Temple seems to be transferred to "the Community of the New Covenant" or "the Covenant of friendship" (*berith ḥesed*), as Brownlee has translated it. Through their initiatory rites the people were shaped into a unity and were regarded as building together a sort of living Temple of people, a "House of Holiness" with its Holy of Holies, Holy Place, and its Outer Court for Israelites, and in the Zadokite Document from Damascus also a fourth peripheral group apparently corresponding to the outer Gentile precincts of the Temple. Moreover, priestly ablution and the priestly ephod were extended to all covenanted members of the Community, now regarded as a sort of corporate priesthood of "the anointed ones". In other words, here we have an attempt by rigorous discipline to carry out what I have called the requirement that the Covenant Will of God must be done into the very life and existence of Israel.

We are of course at once reminded of the teaching of the New Testament, notably of Paul and 1 Peter, of the Church as the Habitation of God, the Temple of the Spirit, as the Holy People or House of God built up of living stones, but here in the New Testament there is a radical difference: the living Temple is above all the Body of Jesus Christ, and His Body in two senses; in reference to Christ Himself and in reference to the Church of Christ which He adopts in His grace to be His Body. In other words, the difference between the conception of the Covenant

Community in the documents of Qumran and Damascus and the Christian conception is that the Church is the people of the New Covenant only because, and on the ground of the fact that, the Covenant has actually been fulfilled in Jesus Christ, who gathers up Israel in Himself and is the beginning of a New Israel embracing all who are gathered into the Name of Christ and are baptized with His Spirit. It is in and through Jesus Christ and by the power of His Spirit that the Covenant Will of God is at last enacted into the existence of God's people. Baptism is therefore into His Name, for He is the Mediator of the New Covenant, but "into His Name" includes also the Name of the Father and the Spirit, for the Covenant He mediates is that in which God wills to be our Father and determines us to be His children; and the nature of this Covenant is spiritual, inscribed in our hearts by the Spirit of God Himself.

(b) *Aspects of Baptism in the New Testament*[1]

All the four Gospels take time to speak about John the Baptist before they offer us any account of the ministry and teaching of Christ, and they are concerned to show the very close relation between the mission of John, preparatory though it was, and the mission of Christ the Son of God and Servant of the Lord. That connexion is nowhere more evident than in regard to Baptism which had been given such a central and significant role in the ministry and message of John, as Baptism into repentant preparation for the coming of the Christ. John came to be known as the Baptizer not only because Baptism occupied such a central place, but because He administered Baptism to others. Under him Baptism was no longer to be ministered by the subjects of Baptism to themselves, but was administered to them as passive receivers. As such, John's Baptism had a radical character appropriate to his radical message, cutting through all the claims and pretensions of the Jews to the very root of their existence as a people of God, in order to clear the way for the advent of the Messiah and to prepare for Him a people ready for an entirely new situation. Therefore John summoned the Jews to uproot themselves out of their nationalist existence

---

[1] Lecture delivered to the University of Lund, October, 1956, reprinted from *Theologische Zeitschrift*, 14.3, 1958, pp. 241–260.

and to become a people of God again, a pilgrim people expecting to enter into the messianic country. He stood on the banks of the historic Jordan and pointed the way through the water to the messianic Kingdom, insisting that it had already drawn near and was about to break in with eschatological swiftness and urgency.

Two facts stand out in the narratives. This Baptism and message proclaimed an uprooting and a radical judgment, but also a new era of the Spirit, and both were to be fulfilled by the Messiah. He would lay the axe to the root of Israel and cleanse the Temple (the threshing floor), but He would also baptize with the Spirit and a new sort of Abraham's children would be begotten.

Then into the midst of that situation stepped the Messiah Himself, Jesus, to fulfil all righteousness: to fulfil the divine judgment and to fulfil the Covenant-Will of God, to enact the mighty acts of God and so to bring redemption. It is made clear in various ways that Jesus steps in to do that as the Servant-Son, while His life and work as Servant-Son begins right away with this submission to the Baptism of John. Thus the Baptism of Jesus is regarded as one of the mighty acts of the Gospel, one of the saving acts inaugurating the Kingdom; for with it the heavens were opened and the power of the Spirit descended upon Christ the acknowledged Servant-Son, while the language of that acknowledgment from the Father to the Son indicates the nature and character of the relationship to God which this Baptism involved. The language of the Evangelical narratives appears to recall that of *The Testament of Levi* (18): "The heavens shall be opened and from the temple of glory shall come upon him sanctification, with the Father's voice as from Abraham to Isaac. And the glory of the Most High shall be uttered over him, and the Spirit of understanding and sanctification shall rest upon him." At any rate in His Baptism, Jesus was clearly consecrated and anointed as the Christ and sent out to fulfil His mission as the Son of God on earth. He was immediately thrust into the wilderness where He, who had just been baptized in solidarity with sinners with the Baptism into repentance, fasted forty days and nights, humbling and submitting Himself (Son of God though He was) as one of us to the Will of His Father. It was then that He was tempted and

entered upon His redemptive work, being obedient to the Will
of God where we were disobedient, and offering throughout the
whole course of His life an offering of obedience well pleasing to
the Father—all on our behalf, that in Him we might be brought
to the obedience of the faith and become children of the
heavenly Father.

When we examine the Gospel records, the Fourth and the
Synoptic Gospels alike, we discover that none of them gives an
account of John the Baptist, of his message or of his baptismal
rite, apart from the transformation of John's Baptism that took
place in Jesus' submission to it. They all interpret John's
Baptism from the perspective of Christ's Baptism by John, and
indeed of His death and resurrection and His gift of the Spirit.
This is much more in evidence in the Fourth Gospel than in the
others, but the principle is the same in all of them. So interpreted John's Baptism is the beginning of the Gospel, and they
actually use of it the distinctive word, *baptisma*, used only in
Christian literature, and not used of John's Baptism outside the
New Testament (e.g. by Josephus). *Baptisma* was clearly coined
to speak of Christian Baptism, but was therefore applied rightly
to John's Baptism; for his Baptism was not only into the name
of the Coming One, the Christ, but it was the Baptism of Jesus
by John which transformed John's rite of Baptism into Christian
Baptism.

There can surely be no doubt about the fact that John the
Baptist supplied the Church with its ritual act, the rite of
initiation by water into the messianic Age and Community,
into the New Covenant, while the origins of that rite lie
apparently along the line we have been tracing out; but the
doctrine of Baptism is determined not by any Old Testament
typology, nor by ideas derived from Judaism, but by the event of
Christ's Baptism and by all it involved for Him on our behalf.

To this assertion, however, a qualification requires to be
made. There are points in the rite of Christian baptism in which
it is modified or determined by the doctrine of the saving event
in Christ, and there are points in the doctrine where the exposition of it makes fundamental use of the pattern of the rite of
Baptism. Thus, for example, the Christian rite of Baptism derives from John the Baptist, but the form of that rite is determined by the event that took place in the Baptism of Jesus. He

went into the water to be baptized by John, but when He did
that the Spirit came down upon Him and, as Jesus claimed,
anointed Him. That gave Christian Baptism a double form; not
only Baptism in water from below, but Baptism in heavenly
water from above, that is, in the Spirit. The Semitic language
lying behind this—*mayim* = water, and *shamayim* = heaven, with
all the Old Testament teaching bound up with it, particularly
from Ezekiel—is reflected all through the literature of the early
Church, and not without reason. This twofold character of
Baptism was reinforced at Pentecost when the Spirit was
poured out in Baptism upon the Church, and immediately the
apostles summoned men and women, with their children, to be
baptized in water, calling upon God and entering into the fulfilment of His promise to pour out His Spirit upon mankind. A
typical text describing this double idea contained in Baptism
which reflects the twofold character in the actual rite is found
in Titus 3: 5. "According to His mercy he saved us, through
washing (or laver) of regeneration and renewing of the Holy
Spirit which He poured out upon us richly through Christ
Jesus our Saviour. . . ."

On the other hand, the doctrine of Baptism is expounded in
the New Testament after the pattern of the rite. In the ritual act
of Baptism there was a descent into the water and an ascent out
of it—language which really derives not from the Gnostic myths
but ultimately from the Old Testament cult, but possibly immediately from proselyte Baptism. In the New Testament this
language was applied to the doctrine of Christ, not only to
speak of His death and resurrection, but also to speak of His incarnation and ascension—the descent and ascent of the Son of
Man. There is every reason to declare that that was the primary
usage of this language, found according to the Fourth Gospel,
on the lips of Christ Himself in His discourse with Nicodemus.
In other words, "the baptismal language" of descent and
ascent applies fundamentally to the descent of the Son of God
into our mortal humanity and to His ascension to the right hand
of the Father. It is only by a false abstraction that this language
is applied to Baptism with reference only to the death and resurrection of Christ, and not also to His incarnation and ascension, all for us and our salvation. Certainly the early Church
regarded His Baptism in the Jordan not as His adoption to be

the Son of God, but as His manifestation and public consecration as God's Son pointing back to His birth from above of the Spirit, and regarded His ascent out of the Jordan and His receiving of the Spirit when the heavens were opened over Him, for our sakes, as having its fulfilled counterpart in His ascension to open the Kingdom of Heaven to all baptized into His Name and to pour out upon them the fullness of His Spirit. Thus Baptism, like the redemptive work of Christ, must be related to His Person, to the whole course of His obedient life, and to the whole act of His divine condescension to our lowly estate and exaltation of us in Himself to the Father. We cannot be true to the whole teaching of the New Testament unless we consider Baptism in that its essential context.

But now we must turn to look at the word which the New Testament uses to speak of this—*baptisma*. We have not paid sufficient attention to the fact that it is a new word that is used, and not the word *baptismos* (found in the New Testament only in Mark 7: 4, and Heb. 6: 2 to describe rites of ablution). *Baptisma* must surely be understood in close proximity to *kerygma* as referring to the mighty acts of God in Christ that are proclaimed in the Word and Sacrament—the content of *baptisma* is the same as the content of *kerygma*, but while it is the Self-proclamation of Christ that lies behind the *kerygma*, it is the Self-consecration of Christ that lies behind the *baptisma*, and as in the Church's *kerygma* it is Christ Himself who acts and is mighty to save, so in the Church's *baptisma* it is Christ Himself who acts confirming His Word and sealing His work of salvation. Even in the preparatory ministry of John the Baptist *keryssein* and *baptizein* were conjoined; so it is also in the ministry of the apostles—*baptisma* follows their *kerygma* and is given, not as the seal of faith, but as the seal of the Word of the Gospel, for faith cannot be the content of the *baptisma* any more than it can be the content of the *kerygma*, although both require faith.

This interpretation is reinforced by the fact that nowhere does the New Testament offer us a description of the rite of Baptism. It is not interested in the rite as such, but in the event behind the rite; nor is it interested in the human minister of the rite but in the One who fulfilled the Will of God and ordained the rite as the seal of His command and promise. It is not of course that the New Testament regards the rite itself with indifference, but that the rite is to be used like a window through which we look to something beyond it altogether. Just as we do not normally when looking out of the window look at the window-pane (except to note on occasion how far its imperfection distorts our vision); we look through the window-pane without noticing it. So it is with the New Testament *baptisma*. Just as *kerygma* does not call attention to the preacher or the preaching but only to Christ Himself, so *baptisma* by its very nature does not direct attention to itself as a rite (that would be as *baptismos*) or to him who administers it, but directs us at once beyond to Christ Himself and to what He has done on our behalf; that is, to the objective and fulfilled reality.

This being so, it might be best for us to speak precisely of *baptismatic* rather than *baptismal* relation to Christ. We do speak of "baptismal ingrafting into Christ", of "baptismal dying and rising with Him" and of "baptismal regeneration", and in so doing we use a "sacramental mode of speaking"; but the difficulty about this language is, that no matter how much the emphasis is laid upon Christ Himself, some foolish people will always take it to mean that it is the rite of baptism which ingrafts or regenerates us, or that it is actually in the experience of the rite that we die and rise again with Christ, which can only mean that they think of this ingrafting or regenerating or dying and rising as acts in addition to what has already taken place in Christ on our behalf and therefore already been fulfilled in us in Him. The New Testament nowhere teaches us that there is a saving act in addition to that which has once and for all taken place in Christ and for us in Him. There is only one Jesus Christ, the historical Jesus Christ who does not have to be made present but who is actually present with us to the end of the world; so there is only one mighty saving event (including all the mighty acts of God that took place in the incarnation, life, death, and resurrection of Jesus Christ) which is ever present with us, availing and effective and operative for us because we have already been involved in it, for it took place on our behalf in Christ. The event is inseparable from the Person of Christ. It is Christ in His life-act, Christ with His mighty acts wrought out for us, who is always present with us to the end of the world; so that when we in His Name proclaim the *kerygma* and administer the *baptisma* it is actually Christ Himself, really and fully present, who acts savingly in His Church, revealing Himself and baptizing with His Spirit. Only when we learn to get behind the false stress upon our own subjectivity in *kerygma* and *baptisma* can we fully appreciate the teaching of the New Testament, and at the same time fully understand the royal freedom for faith that both *kerygma* and *baptisma* involve.

But now we must speak more precisely of this baptismatic event. To do that we must return to consider the Baptism of Jesus Himself, and that means to return to the start of His ministry in His submission to John's Baptism. That great event pointed back to His own birth from above of the Spirit, an aspect particularly stressed in the first three chapters of the Fourth Gospel; but it also pointed forward to His death on the Cross, an aspect also stressed by the Fourth Gospel but particularly stressed by the Synoptic Gospels. It may be better to consider the latter first.

(1) *The Relation of the Baptism of Jesus to His Crucifixion*

As we have already seen, the Baptism in the Jordan is to be regarded as the consecration of Jesus to His mission as Suffering Servant. It was Baptism into His vicarious work. It was of course His consecration both as Victim and as Priest in one act —a theme of the Fourth Gospel which speaks of Jesus as the Lamb of God bearing the sins of the world, and also as the Son consecrated and sent by the Father and endowed with the Spirit without measure. But this mission of Christ is presented primarily in the Gospels in terms of His Servant-ministry. He was baptized into a life of vicarious passion, in which He went forth to bear our sins and sicknesses throughout the whole course of His public life right up to the Cross and there above all. As such, however, it was a Baptism in His obedience to the Father's Will, obedience as the Son of God within the conditions of our estranged and alienated humanity, and obedience unto the death of the Cross. It was thus into the Cross that He was baptized, so that His Baptism came to its fulfilment in His crucifixion. But between His Baptism in water in the Jordan and His Baptism in blood on the Cross His whole servant-existence and active obedience was His Baptism, for throughout the whole course of His obedience He was enacting the Will of God in our flesh, and doing that on our behalf. "I have a baptism with

which I am being baptized" (Mark 10: 38 f.), He said, with
reference to the work which He was accomplishing and with
which He was sorely pressed until it was finally accomplished.

It is sometimes said that by "the baptism with which He was
being baptized" Jesus was speaking only metaphorically or
figuratively of His death, and that His words contain no reference to Baptism as such at all. Those who say that make the
mistake of thinking that by *baptisma* the New Testament means
baptismos, and fail to see the dimension of objectivity in which
the New Testament always uses this term. But they make
another mistake—they give the word *baptisma* in this saying a
meaning which it nowhere possesses in all Greek literature. The
verb *baptizein* is used often in Greek, and several times in the
Septuagint, only metaphorically, to speak of drowning or dying,
but nowhere is the word *baptisma* so used. Thus, to give this use
of "baptism" by Jesus only a figurative meaning, they have the
impossible linguistic task of proving that in this instance only it
must be figuratively interpreted while in all other instances it is
used of Baptism. Of course Baptism contains a figurative element, but the association of *baptisma* with *baptizein* here is clearly
more than a Semitism; it is designed to drive home, with the use
of the specific and distinctive word coined by the Church for
Baptism, the fact that Christ deliberately linked His Baptism in
the Jordan with His death on the Cross, and with the whole
course of His ministry in obedience and passion on our behalf;
and thereby also to drive home the fact that our Baptism in the
Name of Christ is a covenanted consociation with Him in all He
did to fulfil righteousness from His Baptism in the Jordan to His
crucifixion on the Cross. In our Baptism we are drawn within
the range of His vicarious work in life and death, and are consecrated to God the Father in His Self-consecration on our
behalf.

We must say, then, that Christ's vicarious Baptism was His
whole living passion culminating in His death, His Baptism in
blood, once and for all accomplished on the Cross. That is the
objective event, the one baptismatic event in Christ, that lies
behind every administration of Baptism, the all-inclusive *hen
baptisma* that is the primary fact referred to every time the word
Baptism is used by the New Testament. But this objective event
has a subjective counterpart, in the Baptism of the Spirit at

8—C.A.C.

Pentecost. At the Jordan, Jesus wearing our humanity was baptized and anointed for us; at the Cross, suffering in our humanity, He was baptized for us in judgment and death; and in the resurrection He was clothed with power and raised for our justification. On the ground of His whole atoning act in life and death and resurrection He ascended to pour out His Spirit once and for all upon human flesh, upon the Church, giving it to share in His One Baptism.

We have not made sufficient of the essential relation between atonement and Pentecost, and of the fact that the Spirit was poured out only after Christ had been glorified. Melito of Sardis sought to expound this by relating the shedding of blood to the release of the life or spirit, thus laying stress upon the pouring out of Christ's Spirit as well as the pouring out of His blood as His atoning action. As we have already seen, the Jewish Community at Qumran related the atonement in the New Covenant to the work of the Spirit. Whether these particular ideas played a part in the minds of the New Testament writers or not, it is clear that as they thought of the Baptism in the Jordan as one of His mighty acts bringing in the Kingdom of Heaven, so they thought of His ascension and His pouring out of the Spirit in Baptism upon the Church as a mighty act of redemption and salvation. This was not a new act or something that had to be added to what Christ had already done, as if that were incomplete, but it was rather the full actualization of His redemption in the midst of His people on earth. In the language of Melito of Sardis, the Church was not only sealed with the blood of the Covenant but sealed with the Spirit. Indeed, both these are one and the same redemptive event.

Thus we have to say that the great baptismatic event includes the once and for all Baptism of Blood on the Cross and the once and for all Baptism of the Spirit upon the Church at Pentecost. There is *One Baptism*, and *One Body*, common to Christ and His Church, but each participates in it differently—Christ actively and vicariously as Redeemer, the Church passively and receptively as the redeemed Community. This baptismatic event is essentially corporate in Christ and in His Church—it is corporate because the Church was already included as "the many" in "the One" who suffered and died on their behalf. "Except a corn of wheat falls into the ground and dies, it abides alone", but in dying this One became many for He gave His life a ransom for many. That is why the New Testament can speak of the work of Christ as a work for the Church, although it was also for the world. "He loved the *church* and gave Himself up for it, that he might sanctify it, having cleansed it by the washing of water with the word, that he might present it to himself, a glorious church, not having spot or wrinkle; but that it should be holy and without blemish" (Eph. 5: 25 f.). It is only within that One Baptism of Christ for the Church and of the Church in Himself that the administration of Baptism to individuals has its proper place. In other words, it is only through and within the Church created by the corporate Baptism of the Spirit at Pentecost, and drawn and established within the fulfilment of the Covenant-will of God in the obedient life and death of Christ, that when from generation to generation the Church in obedience to Christ's command baptizes in water, others are added to the Church that they may share in what has already taken place for them and live in the power of the Name of Christ, as members of the Body of Christ who was crucified for them and raised again in justification for them. Thus the Baptism of the individual, child or adult, is not a new Baptism, but an initiation into and a sharing in the One Baptism common to Christ and His Church, wrought out in Christ alone but bestowed upon the Church as it is yoked together with Him through the Baptism of the Spirit.

(2) *The relation of the Baptism of Jesus to the Incarnation*

Here we come to a much neglected line of teaching in the New Testament. Some people appear to have difficulty in accepting Matt. 28:19 as the authentic utterance of Christ: "Go ye into all the world and disciple all nations, baptizing them in the name of the Father and of the Son and of the Holy Spirit, teaching them to observe all things whatsoever I have commanded you: and lo I am with you always even unto the end of the world." The textual authorities for this verse are overwhelmingly strong, so that doubt about it can be only on purely *a priori* grounds, in a refusal to believe that the name of the Father, Son, and Holy Spirit could be brought together like that on the lips of Jesus. But hesitation in that way must arise from a myopic reading of the Gospels, the Synoptics and the

Fourth Gospel, for all through them we have to do with the relation of the Son to the Father and with the presence and power of the Spirit. That is nowhere more clear than at the Baptism of Jesus in the Jordan where we have the voice of the *Father* in address to the *Son*, along with the manifestation of the *Spirit*. Perhaps it is only when we fail to give the Baptism of Jesus by John its full and proper place in Christian Baptism, and so make a false abstraction of Baptism from the whole course of Christ's ministry from the Jordan to the Resurrection, that we have difficulty in thinking of Matt. 28: 19 as our Lord's own direct command. Although it has always been to that verse that the Church has looked for its dominical warrant for Baptism, Baptism is grounded upon the whole life of Christ going back to His Baptism, and even to His birth of the Spirit.

But here we must pause to think of the significance of Baptism into the Name of the Holy Trinity. It means that we are not baptized in the Name of Christ alone, but equally into the Name of the Father and of the Spirit. Therefore Baptism cannot be interpreted exclusively as Baptism into the death of Christ, for neither was the Father crucified for us, nor did the Spirit become incarnate on our behalf. Baptism in the threefold Name is a rite essentially appropriate to the trinitarian character of the baptismatic event, which includes throughout it the relation of the Son to the Father through the Spirit. Baptism is thus concerned with the act of the Father in sending His Son, with His eternal love which He has poured out upon us in the incarnation of His Son that through Him we might be adopted into sonship and assumed into fellowship with the Father. But Baptism is also concerned with the work of the Spirit through whom Jesus was born of the Virgin Mary, by whom He was anointed as the Christ at His Baptism, through whom He cast out demons and brought the Kingdom to bear redemptively upon the needs of men, through whom again He offered Himself without spot to the Father, and according to whom He was raised from the dead by the Father. It was this same Spirit whom Christ after His ascension as the Son to the right hand of the Father poured out upon His Church, renewing them in the power of the resurrection, giving them to share in all that He had done for them, and enabling them to cry, in echo of His own prayer, Abba Father. Baptism in the Name of God the

Creator and the Father is the seal of His Covenant promise to be our Father, and Baptism in the Name of the Spirit is the actualization of that promise, the sealing of us as belonging to the Father, the creative renewing of us as His children in God's image. In inseparable relation with Baptism in the Name of the Father and the Spirit, Baptism in the Name of Christ has direct reference to His birth on earth as the Son of the Father, to the whole course of His obedience, as well as to His death and resurrection, and it also has reference to the ascension of the Son to the Father where He stands in for us as our Surety and Advocate and where He confesses us as His brothers and presents us to the Father as His sons.

What I wish to stress here is the much neglected fact that Baptism has essential reference to the whole incarnational event: to the coming of the Son of God into our mortal humanity, to His whole life of obedient self-oblation well-pleasing to the Father, and to His ascension in which wearing our humanity He brought back with Him many sons to glory. As we have already noted, the language of descent and ascent, used to speak of the death and resurrection of Christ, is also used to speak of His descent into our mortal humanity and His ascent in our resurrected humanity to the right hand of God. Thus behind baptism into Christ there lies the whole incarnation and ascension of the Son of God, spoken of as the descent and ascent of the Son of Man. Ultimately the Sacrament of Baptism is grounded in the incarnation in which the eternal Son immersed Himself in our mortal human life and assumed us into oneness with Himself that He might heal us and through the whole course of His obedience reconcile us to the Father in an abiding union and communion with Him.

The significance of this will be apparent if we say that while Baptism is usually spoken of only as the Sacrament of our incorporation into Christ, it is ultimately grounded upon the fact that in Jesus the Son of God incorporated Himself into our humanity. It is indeed only because of the union with us effected in His incarnation that we can be given to share in all that He has done in our humanity on our behalf, and so have part in His vicarious death and resurrection. If Baptism as a Sacrament of the death and resurrection of Christ is detached or abstracted from this primary fact of His incorporation into us in the Incarnation, then baptism too easily becomes the sacramental mystery of a timeless dying and rising known also to the Semitic and Hellenistic religious mysteries. It was precisely this that the early Church resisted, and they did so by grounding Baptism upon the whole of the New Testament witness to Christ the incarnate Son, and not simply upon Rom. 6. That is to say, alongside the important fact that Baptism is the Sacrament of the death and resurrection of Christ they laid the important fact that Baptism is the Sacrament of the Incarnation, the Sacrament of the Nativity, as it was sometimes called.

In Baptism we are adopted to be sons of God the Father; we are born again of water and of the Spirit—but this is grounded in the Birth of Jesus of the Holy Spirit from above, for it was in and with His birth as well as in and with His resurrection that the regeneration (*palingenesia*) of our humanity was brought about. In the language used earlier there are not two acts of regeneration, incorporation, etc. but only one, that which has already been wrought out in Jesus Christ and in which we are given to share through the Spirit, so that it is in Christ that we are born again through sharing in His birth, and it is in Him that we are converted through sharing in His obedient life, and in Him that we are resurrected through sharing in His resurrection. He was not born on earth for His own sake, but for our sake. His birth for our sake was part of His reconciling and redeeming work, and Baptism is grounded primarily upon that basic event, His incorporation into our humanity, and therefore upon His obedience unto the death of the Cross in expiation of our sin and guilt, and in His resurrection out of our mortality as the New Man.

This is a favourite theme in the Johannine literature in the New Testament. It is apparent in John 1 : 12 f.: "To as many as received him to them gave he the right to become children of God, to them that believe into His name; who were born not of blood, nor of the will of the flesh, nor of the will of a husband, but of the will of God." All the patristic citations of this verse in the second and early part of the third centuries (Irenaeus, Tertullian, Hippolytus, etc.) cite it in the singular with direct reference to the virgin birth of Christ; but whether that is the original text (as seems most likely) or not, it contains a clear indirect reference to the fact that we are born again in Christ's miraculous birth. That is the point also of Jesus' conversation with Nicodemus, that our birth of water and of the Spirit is not a carnal but a spiritual event, from above, and behind it lies the primary reality of Christ's birth, for it is He who is the One born from above, who descended from heaven. Thus what is true of Christ in the reality of His virgin birth is true of us also who believe in Him and are baptized into His Name in virtue of the right (*exousia*) which He gives us. Again this is the teaching of the Johannine writer in his first Epistle, e.g. in 1 John 5: 18: "Whosoever has been born of God (*gegennemenos*) does not sin, but he who was born of God (*gennetheis*) keeps him." Christ's birth described in the aorist tense was a specific event, but the Christian's birth described in the perfect tense is rather the result that accrues from that rather than an event in itself; it is the effect or fruit of that unique event, and is not something in addition to it, but a sharing in it.

There is a very definite parallel to this in the teaching of St. Paul about our participation through Baptism in the New Man, the New Adam, the Man from Heaven, the First-Born of all creation, and so of our adoption in Christ through the Spirit who makes us to call upon the name of the Father like Christ Himself. We are adopted to co-sonship with Christ and share in His birth and resurrection. That aspect of Pauline teaching, which is particularly strong in the Epistle to the Galatians, has to be considered together with the two passages which speak of Baptism as our sharing in the death and resurrection of Christ found in Rom. 6 and Col. 2.

All this does not mean that we are to neglect the very important aspect of Baptism as the Sacrament of Christ's death and resurrection, but that we must balance that by regarding it also as a Sacrament of His miraculous birth of the Spirit, and therefore as a Sacrament of our regeneration in Him through sharing in His new Humanity. What binds these two aspects together is the simple but often neglected fact that our incorporation into Christ is grounded entirely and primarily upon His incorporation into us. It is, moreover, just because He incorporated Himself into our estranged humanity under the divine judgment, and through that incorporation fulfilled that judgment both in His holy life in condemning sin in our flesh and by submitting and offering our humanity in Himself to the final judgment of God, that Baptism also has an aspect as baptism into judgment and into repentance, into the sphere where the Spirit convicts of sin, righteousness, and judgment.

It is from this point of view that we can see in a deeper way the integral relation of John's Baptism and message with that of Christ, and understand why Christ began His ministry by proclaiming the same message as John and, it would also appear, by continuing (through His disciples) for a while at least to administer Baptism and make disciples like John. It is significant that even John the Baptist could speak of God as being able to raise up a new generation through this Baptism into judgment and repentance, just as He could raise up children to Abraham out of the stones lying in the river Jordan. In other words, what we find in the teaching of the New Testament is that the conceptions of birth and death and resurrection are all brought together. It is through Baptism that we are given to share in the death of Christ, but in that way, argued St. Paul, we are made to grow together with Him, in order that we may be resurrected unto newness of life. It is through the Cross, through atonement and reconciliation, that we are given to share in the new life of Man which began with the birth of Jesus and was completely manifested in His resurrection. Just as the atoning work of Christ reached back from His Cross to His birth, or rather reached forward from His very birth to His Cross, so our sacramental participation in the whole baptismatic event involves a sharing in the Birth of Christ and in His death and resurrection, as it reaches out also to the final Parousia when our life now hid with Christ in God will be fully unveiled. Apart from our sharing in His death and resurrection we can have no share in the new life and the new humanity begotten in Jesus Christ when He was born of the Virgin Mary, or be assumed into a life of fellowship with the Father through the obedience of the incarnate Son.

We must now address ourselves briefly to the question of our relation as individuals to the corporate baptismatic event that has taken place in Christ and is common to Christ and His Church. This is perhaps best approached from the fact that Baptism is the Sacrament of "the One and the Many", but we may expound that by using the language of the Covenant. When God made His Covenant of grace with Abraham it was

none other than the Covenant of grace which He established
with creation of the world, and which took on a redemptive
purpose with the rebellion and fall of man. But with Abraham
that Covenant assumed a particular form within history and
with one race elected from among all the races of mankind in
order that God might prepare a way within humanity for the
fulfilment of His Covenant Will for all men. "I will be your
God, and you shall be my people." "I will be a God to you and
to your seed after you." With such words the Covenant was
established in which God willed to be the Father of His people
and willed that they should be His children, and He gave them
as a seal of this Covenant and its promise of blessing, the sign of
circumcision, which we have already considered.

This Covenant was re-enacted with Israel as a people after its
redemption out of Egypt as God's first-born son, but now the
Covenant took on more specific shape. "I am holy, be ye also
holy." As Head of the Covenant God required a corresponding
holiness from His covenant-partner, for He willed that His
people should live in fellowship with Him and share in His own
Holiness. But God knew that His people were unable to fulfil
the Covenant, and so in His Fatherly mercy He provided a way
within the Covenant of obedient response to Himself and a way
of sacrificial worship as a witness to His readiness to cleanse and
forgive His people within the Covenant. The bounds of the
Covenant had already been marked out by the rite of circumcision, which also indicated that the holy Will of God had to be
fulfilled in the flesh of His people and that His promises availed
for their seed from generation to generation. But then within
these bounds God provided in the Law a revelation of His Will,
commandments to show the way of obedient conformity to
Him, and along with these God provided in the Cult solemn
symbolic indications of the way in which He Himself was ready
to provide fulfilment of His Covenant both from His own side
and from the side of Israel in all its weakness and frailty. The
whole Covenant thus rested upon the divine faithfulness, and
pointed ahead to a future in which this divine provision would
be translated from the realm of symbolic ritual into the actual
existence of His people. The worst thing that could be done with
such a Covenant would be to turn the symbolic ritual into an
end in itself, as a means of acting upon God and bending His

will to serve the ends of men. That is precisely what Israel tried to do again and again, so that God sent the prophets to protest against their use of the Cult and to demand obedience rather than sacrifice. But with the prophets He also began to reveal more and more His purpose for messianic fulfilment of His Covenant in a Servant who would not only fulfil the Covenant vicariously but be the Mediator of a New Covenant, in which the Will of God would be written upon the hearts of His people by His Spirit.

That fulfilment we have in Jesus the chosen Servant-Son, who fulfilled the Covenant both from the side of God and from the side of man, and so mediated a New Covenant which set the relations of men with God on a wholly new basis. This is the new form of the Covenant which is freely proclaimed to all men in the Gospel. It was as a sign and seal to this New Covenant that Baptism was given, not a sign and seal like circumcision of a Covenant yet to be fulfilled in the future but a sign and seal of a Covenant already fulfilled once and for all in Jesus Christ. Hence the seal of this Covenant took on a form appropriate to the nature of that which it sealed, namely, an accomplished fact, a finished work, a completed act of pure grace. Here too the essential pattern of the Covenant remains the same. God wills to be the Father of all men, and enacts a New Covenant in which they are to be His children; but here in sheer grace, and in merciful knowledge of our frailty and unfaithfulness, He has provided us with a covenanted way of response in the obedient life and sacrifice of Jesus Christ, His righteous Servant, His be-loved Son. In Jesus Christ God has not only done a work of grace for us and upon us in which He has done away with our guilt and sin and set us free, but He has also provided us in the obedient humanity of Jesus Christ with a perfected communion between man and God in which the Covenant-union is fully and finally actualized. It is in that obedient Humanity, and in that perfect communion between the Son and the Father lived and worked out to the uttermost within our human existence, that we are mercifully given to share. That is to say, in Jesus Christ the Covenant faithfulness of God has been met and answered by a Covenant faithfulness within our humanity, so that that divine-human faithfulness forms the very content and substance of the fulfilled Covenant which is the New Covenant. Thus the

Covenant relationship is now filled with the relationship or communion between the Son and the Father, and it is in that communion that we are given to share by the Spirit. We really can be given to share in it, for the Covenant Communion was wrought out and perfected in union with our humanity in Jesus Christ.

With that change in the form and content of the Covenant the sacramental seal becomes the seal of union with Christ and of communion with the Father through union with Christ. The form that this Covenant-Communion takes is the Church, the Body of Christ, and the sacrament of initiation into that communion and of participation in the relation of the Son to the Father is holy Baptism. In the nature of the case, Baptism is the sacrament of what has already been fulfilled for us and on our behalf in Christ; more specifically it is the Sacrament of the obedience of Christ offered in our stead in which He throughout His life and in His death stood in our place and gave to God an account for us, submitting to the Father's judgment upon our sin and guilt; and therefore it is also the Sacrament of the Father's satisfaction in the life and work of His Beloved Son whom He sent to carry through this redemptive work on our behalf. More briefly, Baptism is the Sacrament of the fact that in Jesus Christ God has bound Himself to us and bound us to Himself, before ever we have bound ourselves to Him.

"Before ever we have bound ourselves to Him"—that has to be emphasized. Baptism is not the Sacrament of a Covenant voluntarily made between two partners, and which is only made when both partners freely and willingly enter into contract. In that event Baptism would be partially the Sacrament of God's act, and partially the Sacrament of the individual's act—and so it has been, and still is, frequently expounded. But in the biblical teaching God's Covenant is quite a different thing from a contract, for it is wholly and graciously made by God, and depends therefore entirely upon the divine faithfulness. But in the biblical Covenant there are not only two factors, God and man, but a third, the Mediator of the Covenant, who is not a third in one sense, for He is Himself God on the one hand, and Man on the other hand. It is this divine-human faithfulness and divine-human fulfilment which is proclaimed to man in the

Gospel as the good news of salvation: namely, that God the Son become man has offered to the Father a human response and a human obedience and a human fulfilment of His Covenant Will, doing in our stead and in our place and on our behalf what we are unable to do, and doing it freely that we may freely share in it. Our part in the fulfilment has already been completed, and so Jesus Christ invites us in the Gospel to bring all our burdens to Him and to be yoked together with Him, for He has already made Himself responsible for us. When therefore Jesus had fulfilled all righteousness, as He was baptized to do, He gave His Church the ordinance of Baptism to be administered as the Sacrament of His fulfilled work and as the sign and seal of His promise extended to all men in the proclamation of the Gospel. Baptism is above all the Sacrament of that vicarious obedience of the Son to the Father which we are given to share through the Spirit; but as such it is a sharing in a finished work to which we cannot add one iota of our own, it is a participation in a righteousness not our own, in a justification which is a reality independent of our faith. Therefore we can only come to Baptism to receive and to rely upon the Mediator.

Just because in Baptism we are drawn into the covenanted communion and covenanted way of response, we are drawn into the sphere of obedience to the Father; just because we are given to share in the obedience of Jesus to the Father, we are covenanted to a life of obedience in His Name. Baptism requires faith and obedience, just because it is the Sacrament of our sharing in Christ's obedience and faith. Hence the Sacrament of Baptism tells us in unmistakable terms that it is not upon our own faith or our own faithfulness that we rely, but upon Christ alone and upon His faithfulness. Baptism is primarily and fundamentally, then, the Sacrament of Christ's obedience on our behalf, and of His faithfulness, and therefore it is the Sacrament which covenants us to a life of faith and obedience to the Father in Him. He who is baptized by that sign and seal relies not upon himself but flees from his own weakness and faithlessness to the everlasting faithfulness of God; but he also attests before men that he renounces reliance upon himself and his own works of obedience or faithfulness to God's Will. That is the faith and faithfulness in which we are baptized, the faith and faithfulness in which we baptize our children, for the promise is not only to us but to them also in the faithfulness of Christ who commands us to present them to Him.

It is when we keep this biblical perspective and refuse to let go as the very essence of the Gospel the fact that God has bound Himself to us and bound us to Himself before ever we bind ourselves to Him, that we have no difficulty about infant-baptism, for infant-baptism is then seen to be the clearest form of the proclamation of the Gospel and of a Gospel which covenants us to a life of obedience to the Father. But whether baptism is administered to children or adults it is administered with the same doctrine and with the same form, for it is only as little children that we enter into this inheritance of the Kingdom freely bestowed upon us in the New Covenant; and we enter into it relying not upon ourselves in any way but solely upon Him who has already laid hold of us by His grace, and who wills to have fellowship with us on that basis that we may be free to love and trust Him all our days.

(c) *The Meaning of Baptism*[1]

What is the meaning of Baptism? That faces us right away with serious questions of New Testament interpretation which it would not be right to set aside. It was Friedrich Schleiermacher, more than a hundred years ago, who posed for us the two main problems which are still being debated. (1) Interpreters of the New Testament have to face the fact that while the language of the New Testament comes from the Greek world, the thought of the New Testament emerges out of the world of Hebrew Religion. Thus even though the words remain the same the inner meanings are different, so that something more than a grammatico-historical interpretation is necessary. The solution which Schleiermacher offered lay in psychological analysis. (2) In regard to the actual content of the New Testament Schleiermacher drew a radical distinction between what he called the "sensuous" and the "spiritual" elements in it, and advocated the reinterpretation of the "sensuous" into the "spiritual" by means of the religious consciousness.

---

[1] Broadcast address on the Third Programme of the B.B.C., May, 1956; reprinted from *The Canadian Journal of Theology*, 1956, pp. 129–34.

To both these problems Schleiermacher offered a fundamentally subjectivist solution which came to exercise a dominant influence in the nineteenth and twentieth centuries, still apparent in the views of Rudolf Bultmann. Certainly the idiom has changed, but the issues remain the same, while the solution offered is still rather subjectivist. Instead of psychological analysis, we have existential analysis; instead of the distinction between the "sensuous" and the "spiritual", we have a distinction between the "mythological" and the "scientific"; and instead of the religious consciousness we have self-understanding. Yes, the idiom has changed, but it is doubtful whether Bultmann has taken us much beyond Schleiermacher.

But what of the other side of the picture? Against this whole movement of idealistic and existentialist reinterpretation of the Christian message there has been growing up a massive revolt. In its secular form this revolt is most apparent in Marxist thought and its movement down to earth and work-a-day humanity. In its Christian form this revolt is seen most clearly in the recovered emphasis upon the Incarnation and the reconciliation of man in his flesh and blood reality to the living God. It is with the latter that we are concerned here: with the return to a Christian realism, and a theological objectivity.

All this requires of us an interpretation of the New Testament at a deeper level. Schleiermacher's hermeneutical analysis went to the heart of the matter, but his solution does not meet the demands of scientific objectivity. We cannot by-pass the real problems by psychology. We have to take the speech of the New Testament with all its Hellenistic affiliations and by arduous historico-critical study of its usage in the actual life and worship of Israel and the Church build up a correct understanding of the distinctive meaning of the New Testament concepts. This impels us to think out the whole relation of the Church to Israel, of the New Testament to the Old Testament, and of theology to worship.

At the same time Schleiermacher's radical dichotomy between a realm of sensuous events and a realm of spiritual ideas must be rejected on the ground that it mutilates the actual evidence and denies the very essence of the Gospel of the Incarnation. It disrupts the whole significance of reconciliation which involves not only the reconciliation of man with God but the binding together into a new unity of the two aspects which Schleiermacher wanted to divide asunder. Much the same argument must be advanced against Bultmann's programme of demythologization.

This means that it is the doctrine of Jesus Christ who is God and Man in one person, and who wrought out in Himself the reconciliation of man to God, which comes again to assume the central role in theological interpretation which it has always had in the heart of the Gospel.

What then are some of the theological issues raised about Baptism?

The New Testament writers employ an unusual word for Baptism and attach to it a distinctive meaning. This is the term *baptisma*, which is to be interpreted in much the same way as another important New Testament term, *kerygma*. *Kerygma* refers to the proclamation of the Gospel, and yet not so much to the proclamation itself as to what is proclaimed, namely, Jesus Christ; not so much to the act of proclaiming as to the saving work of Christ. When the Gospel is proclaimed it is Christ Himself the crucified and risen Lord who is present and active for our salvation. Similarly in regard to Baptism, the New Testament is not interested so much in the outward rite as in what stands behind the rite; not so much in the subjective experience of the baptized as in the death and resurrection of Christ; and therefore it is not interested in the human minister but in the One into whose name we are baptized.

This is not to say that the outward rites are dispensable; on the contrary, they are quite indispensable; but the main focus of attention is directed on to the objective reality in the person of Christ and His finished work on our behalf. This indicates that Baptism is to be interpreted not in relation to what we do but in relation to what God in Christ has done and will do for us; its meaning does not lie in the rite itself and its performance, or in the attitude of the baptized and his confession of faith, important though they are. It lies beyond—in Christ. It was not Baptism that was crucified for us, nor was it faith that was crucified for us, but Jesus Christ. It is therefore only with the greatest reserve that we can speak, as the New Testament does occasionally, of faith or of Baptism as saving us. Certainly we are summoned to believe if we are to be saved; and we are commanded to be baptized; but Baptism tells us that though faith is required of us it is not by our believing that we are saved but by Christ Himself.

But this raises another issue. We are not baptized into the name of Christ only, but also into the name of the Father and of the Holy Spirit. This is very important, for it indicates that the meaning of Baptism cannot be determined exclusively with reference to Christ. Baptism is concerned with the eternal love of the Father and with His gracious decision to reconcile us in His Son, and to adopt us as His children; and it is equally concerned with the sanctifying and renewing work of the Creator Spirit. Thus Baptism in the name of the Father speaks of the prevenient love of God, and tells us that long before we learned to love and believe in Him He loved us and chose us to be His own; and Baptism in the name of the Holy Spirit speaks of the supernatural presence and work of God, telling us that our coming to love Him and our learning to believe in Him are the creative work of the Holy Spirit within us. It is only within that context of Baptism in the name of the Father and of the Holy Spirit that we can speak rightly of Baptism in the name of Christ.

On the other hand, because the eternal love of God was incarnated in Jesus Christ, and because the Father sends us His Holy Spirit in the name of Christ, it remains true that the significance of Baptism is essentially Christocentric. Two primary aspects of Baptism have to be mentioned in this connexion.

(1) Baptism is into the name of the whole Christ; not just into the name of the dying and rising Christ, but the Christ who was born of the Virgin Mary, who was baptized at the Jordan, in fact the whole historical Jesus. Baptism into Christ includes therefore a sharing in His birth and His human life, as well as in His death and resurrection. When were you born again? In your conversion? In your Baptism? The profoundest answer you can give to that question is, when Jesus Christ was born from above by the Holy Spirit. The birth of Jesus was the birth of the new man, and it is in Him and through sharing in His birth that we are born again. Modern theology has tended to neglect the reconciling and renewing significance of the birth of Jesus—but that is, I believe, an important element that needs to be restored to the doctrine of Baptism. If the miraculous

birth of the infant Jesus is the sign of the wonderful way in which the Love of God begins with our humanity, bringing forth out of it a new life born of the Spirit, learning obedience and growing in wisdom and grace, then is it not in sacramental likeness to the birth and growing life of Jesus, as well as His death and resurrection, that infant-baptism is to be understood as the sign of the way God deals with us? On the ground of what He has already done for us in Christ He quickens us by His Spirit and gives us to learn obedience, growing in wisdom and grace, until we grow up into the full stature of the manhood of Christ.

(2) When Jesus was baptized at the Jordan, identifying Himself with the sinners He had come to save, God the Father openly acknowledged Him as His beloved Son and the Holy Spirit manifested His descent upon Him. That not only pointed back to Jesus' birth of the Spirit as the One who had come to save men from their sins, but it pointed forward to the death of Jesus on the Cross when He was to fulfil the whole work of atonement. That is the objective reality of our Baptism which witnesses to it and shows it forth. When we are baptized in the name of Christ, we are baptized into a work that has already been completed on our behalf in the whole course of Christ's obedience, from His birth to His resurrection. Baptism is not the Sacrament of what we do but of what Christ has already done and which we could not do for ourselves. Baptism is the divinely given ordinance which directs us and our children not to something which only becomes real when we believe, but into the saving act of God's love which He has already fulfilled for us in Jesus Christ, and into which we enter as the great inheritance offered to us in the Gospel.

We must now turn to the place of faith in regard to Baptism. The fundamental significance of faith lies in the fact that in it man takes refuge from his own frailty and instability in the steadfast love and unswerving faithfulness of God. Only when we think of Baptism truly as the attestation not of our faith but of God's faithfulness, as the sign and seal not of something that begins with our human decisions but with the prior decision of Christ, can we give faith its full place. It is not enough to say that the primary emphasis is upon the initiative and the work of God, and that the subsidiary emphasis is upon the response of faith. Even if my salvation depends on God for ninety-nine per cent of its efficacy and only one per cent on me, my salvation is nevertheless as uncertain as my own frailty and weakness. The strength of the chain is to be measured by the weakest link. No, we are to think of this in another way. We are entirely dependent upon the divine decision, but that is a decision which overlaps and undergirds my decision and gives it ground and room and freedom for full personal activity. When I take my little daughter out for a walk, holding her by the hand, and she stumbles, she does not rely so much on her little grasp of my hand as on my strong grasp of her hand. It is when her little grasp is wholly enfolded in my own that it is secure and reliable.

Let me illustrate that from the Gospel account of the conversion of Zacchaeus. Some people interpret this by saying that Jesus saw that Zacchaeus had it in him to be a disciple, and that behind his wicked greed there was embedded an essential goodness, and so Jesus waited long enough in Jericho to draw it out of him and to effect his change of heart. There is no evidence in the record to substantiate that. What we are told is that this wicked extortioner wanted to see Jesus without being seen by Him; short in stature, he hid in a tree where he could observe Jesus as he liked without being noticed. But Jesus broke into the fortress of this man's security and announced His decision that He intended to lodge in Zacchaeus' house, and He told him to make haste and come down. Then the astounding thing happened. This man who did not have it in him to change his heart, who was not free to rid himself of his own selfish will, found himself free to make a decision for Christ, because Christ had already made a decision on his behalf.

That is the very heart of the Christian Gospel: that the Son of God has come into our world where men are enchained in their self-will and crushed down with the responsibility for their sins, in order to take that burden wholly upon Himself and to give an account of it to God. "Come unto me all you that labour and are heavy laden and I will give you rest", Jesus says. That is the Gospel which cannot be truly preached in such a way that the awful responsibility for our sins and for our salvation is taken off the shoulders of Christ the Lamb of God and laid back again on the head of the poor sinner. It is because Christ has already shouldered the burden of our sin and in our stead has given an account of it to God, that He makes it possible for us freely to believe in Him, to love God and our neighbour.

There is one more question we must discuss: Baptism as the sign and seal of regeneration. The whole point of this aspect of Baptism is missed if two primary facts are forgotten. (1) The concept of regeneration applies first of all to Christ Himself, to His birth of the Spirit and to His resurrection from the dead. Christ is the One in whom the regeneration of our humanity has already taken place. (2) The concept of regeneration is also applied by the New Testament to Christ's second Advent in power when He will come to judge the quick and the dead and renew His creation. Baptism as the Sacrament of regeneration is the ordinance of promise given by Christ to His Church in its life between His two Advents, between what has already taken place in the Incarnation and what will take place in the resurrection. It is not of course the rite of Baptism which regenerates, but in Baptism our regeneration in Christ is declared, and shown forth, and promised: it is *sacramentally* enacted as an image and likeness of the birth and resurrection of Christ. But our regeneration is more than a symbolic likeness of the birth and resurrection of Christ. It is their effect upon us, and yet not effect in the sense of a different and subsequent event. Our regeneration has already taken place and is fully enclosed in the birth and resurrection of Christ, and proceeds from them more by way of manifestation of what has already happened than as new effect resulting from them. It belongs to the peculiar nature of Baptism that it promises us a redemption which has already been accomplished in Christ; and therefore in Baptism the end is already given to us in the beginning. Baptism is not simply the starting of a process which we have to carry on and to which we have to make our own additions if we are to be saved. It is the initiation into a wholly new life which has been freely bestowed upon us in Christ, and which awaits His coming again for its full revelation and consummation. That is why the promise of Baptism and its fulfilment cannot be tied down to the enactment of a ceremony or be exhausted in this life. It is a promise that is valid for the whole of our life and reaches out beyond into the resurrection and the new creation.

When we look into the waters of Baptism we see our faces

reflected in it, not very clearly, but very brokenly. In the Sacrament of Baptism we see the image of our regeneration only, as it were, "in a glass darkly", in an enigma. It is essentially a sacramental mystery which under the veil of water directs us back to the work of our renewal which has once and for all taken place in Christ, and directs us forward to the day when we shall see Jesus face to face and become like Him.[1]

[1] See further *The Biblical Doctrine of Baptism*, St. Andrew Press, Edinburgh, 1958.

THE SACRAMENT OF THE LORD'S SUPPER

(a) *Toward a Doctrine of the Lord's Supper*[1]

THERE can be little doubt about the fact that the doctrine of the Lord's Supper as at present formulated in all the Churches of the Reformation is conditioned by reaction against the Roman aberrations and innovations which began particularly with the ninth century, but reached their culmination in the Tridentine decisions. The Churches of the Reformation sought to go behind these aberrations and in various ways to recover the teaching of the New Testament and the early Church, but they themselves were not able to escape making other innovations, if only by way of protection against the deformed conceptions from which they sought to be delivered in reform of the Mass. These Churches have developed their own characteristic traditions both in emphasis and practice, and these also need to be put to the rigorous test of the Word of God in the light of our understanding of Holy Scripture and of the teaching and practice of the early Church. This is not to say that there are to be no developments at all in the celebration of the Lord's Supper, but that such developments are only legitimate if they are in agreement with the teaching of the Holy Scripture and if they serve an important purpose in the celebration of the Supper in the differing circumstances of Churches in different ages and peoples and contexts. At the same time it ought to be manifest that simplicity should be an essential feature of the rite, in accordance with its inherent nature and pattern as manifested in the pages of the New Testament, so that elaborations should be very fully and critically examined. That is not the subject of this essay, however, but rather an examination of some of the main features in the doctrine of the Lord's Supper which require from us to-day careful thinking, if we are to go

1 Prepared for the Creed Association of the Church of Scotland.

forward to a formulation of the doctrine in such a way that it embraces the fullness of what the Church throughout history has learned of the apostolically ordered ordinance and of the apostolic instruction upon it.

(1) *Preliminary Considerations on the Origins of the Supper*

Is the Lord's Supper to be regarded as a reinterpretation of the Passover Meal or a Covenant Meal or simply a *kiddush*; and is it to be regarded as the memorial continuation of "the Last Supper" or as an extension into the Church's history of the Messianic Meal, of which there are traces in the Gospel records? These questions raise many difficult critical and linguistic problems which we cannot go into here, although they must not be avoided in a complete and thorough examination. Some of these questions in detail at least are probably insoluble, but when all is said and done, there are certain results that stand out and (in spite of their ragged edges) demand fairly full acknowledgment.

The origins of the Lord's Supper evidently lie in the Passover Meal, to which there had already been assimilated the Covenant Meal with its cup of wine. The original Passover according to the records in Exodus is rather different, for example, from the Passover celebration that we find to-day in the Jewish *Passover Haggadah*. The latter has of course developments in detail that may or may not be legitimate extensions of the original rite, but the essential pattern found in the *Passover Haggadah* is clearly one in which the original elements of "the Passover of Egypt" (as it was called in Judaism) have been enlarged and somewhat transformed by assimilation to the Covenant Meal of the Israelites at Mount Sinai, which took account of the mighty events of Israel's redemption that transpired after the celebration of the first Passover. There was added to the Passover Meal the consumption of wine, for it was a joyful and thankful feast before the presence of God, and this was called "the Passover of the Generations". It would appear that the *kiddush* with its rite of sanctification using a cup of wine and water, observed at the beginning of the festivals, also reflects a similar tradition, so that its influence upon the Last Supper must also be taken into account. Likewise we must take into account the *chaburah* meal with its rite of thanksgiving or blessing along with the breaking of the bread at the start of the meal and along with the cup of wine at the end.

Whether or not the Last Supper was enacted through the transformation of a *chaburah* meal or not, it is difficult to exclude the influence of this upon what took place even in the Passover of the Generations. Again, we cannot leave out of account, especially in view of the early chapters of the Acts of the Apostles, the rite of *'erub*, in which the use of a common dish or of a whole loaf was employed in an act of associating together or common participation with a view to reaching a common mind at a festival or in the convocation of a court. Whether or not this was actually in the mind of Jesus as He inaugurated the New Covenant in the breaking of the bread and the distribution of the cup, we do not know, but there is every reason to believe it came to play a part in the apostolic perpetuation of the Supper.

No doubt when these various Jewish rites are set over against one another in pride of place as antecedents of the Lord's Supper, the discussion is endless, but in some way or other they all appear to have had their influence. At any rate it is clear that the act of Jesus involved the use of bread and wine with the significance of the Passover and with the deliberate intention of founding the New Covenant in His Body and Blood.

There are other elements we have to take into account which we find in the Gospel records, in the various parables of Jesus about the Wedding Feast or Royal Supper, in His own acts in feeding the multitudes, the four and five thousand, and the occasions when He deliberately ate and drank with publicans and sinners, the excommunicated and lost sheep of the house of Israel, and justified it on the ground of the great Messianic Meal of the future when they would come from the East and West and sit down together with Abraham, Isaac, and Jacob in the Kingdom of God. These distinctly Messianic acts of Jesus at meals, especially in the light of His teaching about the divine constraint put upon the outcasts to come in and fill the house and partake of the Great Supper, are very important—neglect of them in considering the institution of the Lord's Supper belongs to the general failure to give the whole historical life and ministry of Christ its proper place in His saving work.

In addition to all that has so far been adduced, there is still the supreme fact of the appearances of the risen Jesus to His disciples, notably those in the same Upper Room where the Supper was held a few nights previously. According to Luke it was at their Easter Evening meal that Jesus first returned to His disciples as a body. The incident of His being made known in the breaking of bread to the two disciples at Emmaus is likewise significant, as well as the Johannine account of the meal with the risen Jesus at the lake-side. It can be argued, of course, that these are but incidents which have no explicit reference to the solemn participation in the Lord's Supper, but even then it must be granted that after the resurrection the disciples could not participate in the Supper as if Jesus had not risen and as if He were not present with them in it. The resurrection inevitably modified the character of the meal, as it was intended to do, so that the Lord's Supper as celebrated in the Church was not just the prolongation of the Last Supper (when did this expression *Last Supper* first arise?) but was a "sacramental" continuation of the acts of Christ in the miraculous feeding of the multitudes (as with manna) and entailed the "sacramental" extension into the Church of the resurrection meals of the risen Lord with His disciples. The relation of the Lord's Supper as celebrated in the Church to the Last Supper as celebrated on the night in which He was betrayed is, therefore, not unlike the relation between "the Passover of Egypt" and "the Passover of the Generations". Thus, in distinction from the Last Supper, the Lord's Supper enshrines both the historical Supper before the crucifixion of Jesus and a celebration of the resurrection. The Lord's Supper is a historical action in remembrance of Christ, after the fashion of the Last Supper, and a Messianic Meal with the risen Lord, joined together in one. That conjunction also affects the meaning of *anamnesis* in the Supper.

That was the Eucharistic meal of the early Church, held especially on the Lord's Day, the Day of the Resurrection, and significantly, in the context of a love-feast with its mutual sharing of God's gifts. To get the full tradition regarding this Meal we have to take the Synoptic accounts of the Last Supper with the Johannine accounts of Jesus' discourses and His high-priestly intercession at the Supper, together with the Johannine and Synoptic accounts of the events of Easter Evening when Jesus came into the midst of His disciples as they ate bread together, showed them His wounds, gave them His peace, breathed on them His Spirit and recommissioned them as His covenanted apostles. "As the Father hath sent me, so send I you." Then we have to conflate that with the Pauline account of the formed tradition as he received it and delivered it to the Corinthians, and consider the whole in the light of the actual practice of the Church as reflected in the Acts of the Apostles, the teaching of the Epistle to the Hebrews, and the illuminating allusions in the Apocalypse.

(2) *The Reformation of the Roman Mass*

The Reformers reacted very strongly to the Pelagian conceptions of atonement, and the Pelagian notions of the priesthood of the Church, which they found to be embedded in the Mass. These took the form of a repeated sacrificial immolation of Christ even in a propitiatory sense, which gave the Church control over men's salvation, and the form of a sacerdotal control over the Body of Christ which through the words of consecration fetched it down from heaven and brought it to rest upon the altar. These are crude ideas. They were not held in that crude form by the best of the Roman theologians even during the period of the Reformation, but they were not repudiated. The view they represent was given dogmatic definition in the decisions of Trent in a way that has for ever involved the Roman Church in excommunion from the rest of Christendom. For the Romans a priest was a *pontifex*, one who builds a bridge and so mediates between God and man; the priest fulfilled that mediation by re-enacting the sacrifice of Christ. But for the Reformers the Incarnation had radically altered the whole conception of priesthood, for only He makes a bridge between God and man who is Himself that bridge. The unity of act and person in the One Mediator, and the vicarious fulfilment in the Humanity of Christ of our response to God in obedience and sacrifice once and for all, made any view such as the Roman quite impossible. It was in radical conflict with the apostolic tradition. For the Calvinists, it was the teaching of the Epistle to the Hebrews (which brought together in such a fundamental way the priesthood of the incarnate Son who opened up in Himself a new and living way to God, and the once and for all perfection of His priestly work) that shattered the Roman error and directed the obedient Church away from those deviations back to the apostolic teaching and ordinance. Behind this lay also the change in the conceptions of God, the recovery of a full

Christology both in the doctrine of Christ itself and in its application to correlative aspects of the faith, and a recovery of the doctrine of justification through the grace of Christ alone, or more concretely, as John Knox always preferred to put it, through the Blood of Christ alone.

In their reconstruction of the rite itself the Reformers revolted against the idea of the Mass as a timeless rite, and returned to the conception of the historical Supper. True to their whole doctrine of God and their faithfulness to the Christology of the early Church they insisted in grounding the Supper again in the action of the historical Christ, upon His inauguration of the New Covenant with the disciples on the night in which He was betrayed, and upon the once and for all act on the Cross that cannot be repeated. What was partly at stake here was the assimilation of the Eucharist to the pagan conception of the mystery of the dying and rising god and to the process of deification and transmogrification that involved. That reduced the Sacrament to a *mythos*, the counterpart in time, dramatically ritualized, of a timeless reality. Against all that the Reformers sought to get back to the historical perspective of the biblical revelation, to the historical Jesus, and the historical character of the Supper in the tradition of the apostolic Church.

The Supper thus restored to its native historical character was not separated, however, from the presence of the living Christ, the Lamb who was slain but is alive again, ascended to the right hand of God and reigning as Priest and King over His Church. Hence the element of eschatology has such a full and powerful place in the Reformed understanding of the Supper, the very element which (doubtless in sheer reaction) the new Roman liturgies that appeared after the Council of Trent did their best to eliminate. Nowhere is this eschatological element more in evidence than in Calvin's stress upon the ascension of the risen Christ, and therefore upon the *sursum corda* in the celebration of the Eucharist itself. The Lord's Supper is a communion with the risen and ascended Christ through the Spirit which He pours upon His Church, and in it He who was crucified comes to show us His wounds in His hands, feet, and side, to give us peace and forgiveness through His passion and to quicken us again by the breath of His Spirit that we may go from the Supper to fulfil our calling in obedience to His sending, meditating upon the future life, working for the extension of Christ's Kingdom, and waiting for the day when He will return to take up His power and reign.

In this Supper the Church is given to taste and experience already the powers of the age to come; it is essentially a prelude to the new creation. The Sacrament of the Lord's Supper takes place therefore in "two times", and "two kingdoms" or "two ages", as Luther and Calvin both put it, or, as we would put it to-day, in the overlap of the two ages, the present age and the new age that has overtaken us in Jesus Christ and is already actual in our midst through His Spirit. It is above all in the Lord's Supper that the new age which overlaps the old, and is therefore veiled by it, is sacramentally unveiled in anticipation of the great unveiling of the Kingdom of Christ at the final Parousia. This means that we have to distinguish in a doctrine of "the real presence" between the Eucharistic Parousia of Christ and His final Parousia in judgment and new creation. Jesus Christ is really present under the veil of the bread and wine, but in such a way that He holds back the full power and majesty of His presence to give us time on earth and in history to fulfil His Will before He comes again. Therefore, as Calvin reminds us, we pray at every celebration of the Holy Supper, "Thy Kingdom come; thy will be done on earth, as it is in heaven."

The union between these two aspects in the Reformed doctrine of the Lord's Supper is in sharp contrast to the views of the Supper which (a) look upon it merely as a memorial of the historical Last Supper; and (b) which transmute it into a timeless rite of mystical repetition. The one involves an un-Christological separation between the sign and thing signified, and treats the sign as the sign of what happened historically in the past alone; and the other involves an un-Christological confusion between the sign and the thing signified through a doctrine of transubstantiation. Calvin held very strongly that because in the Eucharistic Communion we partake of Christ our relation with Him reflects and images His own nature. In participating in Him we become conformed to Him so that we participate also in our own way in the union of the divine and human natures in Christ. Thus the mode of sacramental relation reflects the mode of hypostatic union in Christ. But transubstantiation destroys that whole analogical relation of participation and conformity to Christ, and so disrupts the basic Christological nature of the Sacrament. It destroys it in its character as a communion in the mystery of Christ. Precisely by refusing to preserve the distinct propriety of the two sides involved in the sacramental relation, it makes it impossible for it to image or reflect the image of Christ in whom divine and human natures, while remaining distinct, are joined in such a way that neither is converted or changed into the other. But Calvin opposed equally those who held that the two sides in the sacramental relation are disparate and separable, that the Supper is only a historical act in memory of the historical death of Christ carried out in obedience to Christ's command. That view, often but quite falsely attributed to Zwingli, was held by the humanists in the Reformation era both within and without the Roman Church, and notably by the Anabaptist groups, as it is widely held to this day in many Protestant Churches. Here the emphasis upon the simplicity and historical character of the Supper has been given a humanist twist which depreciates the supernatural presence of Christ and diminishes severely the Christocentric nature and pattern of the ordinance.

(3) *The Formulation of the Doctrine of the Supper*

When he wanted to give a brief exposition of the Lord's Supper Calvin frequently spoke of it under three heads, which may serve a useful purpose here: *signification, substance* or *matter, effect* or *action*.

(a) *Signification.* The terms signification and representation have each a double reference in Calvin's thought. Here we are concerned with something which is not usually admitted and then it is simply an ambiguity. Signification may be the equivalent to "meaning", but it may also refer to the "thing meant". It is doubtful whether Calvin ever employs signification with regard to the Sacraments except in conjunction with its concrete sense as the "thing signified". The same applies to his use of represent, which means more than represent or symbolize, namely, *re-present*; it represents only in the concrete act of re-presenting. This means that it is not really possible to discuss signification in abstraction from the matter or the substance of the Sacrament.

The Lord's Supper as celebrated in the Church is a sign with a meaning; it is signitive, pointing beyond itself to what Christ has done and does for us, and so it figures our union with Christ in His death and resurrection and ascension, and relates us to His future advent. A true sign, however, has in it something of that which it signifies; it is analogous to the thing signified, and corresponds appropriately to its nature. In the ordinance of Christ, through His command and promise, the outward sign and the inward reality belong together as form and content of the sacramental communion; although the form is not the content, and the participation in the outward sign as such is not the communion, nevertheless it is the form in which the content is communicated to us, so that apart from the specific form commanded and to which the promise has been attached we cannot conceive or receive the reality. Wherever the outward sign or form is neglected or repudiated the inner content inevitably goes with it.

Two things must be noted here. (1) In this sacramental signification we must think of the relation of the sign to what it signifies as involving neither a relation of identity nor a relation of difference, but of analogy involving something of identity and something of difference. (2) But this relation of sign to the matter signified depends entirely upon the nature of the matter, so that the analogical relation is determined by the nature of Christ Himself, who is the substance or the matter signified. The analogical relation by itself tells us nothing, for that is just the bare form of the sacramental relation; but the content of it is Christological, that is union with Christ, and, as we have seen, such a union that it reflects in itself the nature of Christ.

Now it belongs to the nature of Christ that He is *mystery*; that is the incomprehensible union of God and man in one Person. It is Christ alone in the strict sense who must be spoken of as *mysterion*, but the Church is given to have communion in the mystery of Christ, and it is the Sacraments which are the appropriate signs of that mystery in the life of the Church. Thus in a secondary sense we may speak of the Sacrament as *mysterion*, inasmuch as it is a sign of Christ who is Himself the thing or matter signified. Now traditional theology especially since Augustine had been accustomed to speak of this in terms of *res* and *signum*, but Calvin like others of the Reformers, notably Bucer, Martyr, and John à Lasco, felt that the term *res* was not as appropriate as the term *mysterium* to denote the reality signified, namely Christ Himself as God and Man in one Person, the Mediator. The use of the terms *res* and *signum* tended toward a static and metaphysical interpretation of the sacramental relation, but the use of the biblical terms *mystery* and *seal* had the advantage of preserving both the Christological mystery behind it all, and the dynamic character of the union and communion involved in participation in Christ. Moreover, the term mystery made it clear that the sacramental relation which reposes upon the relation of God and man in Christ can no more be explained positively and put into precise rational terms than the hypostatic union which is stated by the Church only in negatives.

Calvin was therefore rightly adamant at every point in guarding the mystery of the sacramental relation, and it was at this point as well that his stress upon the ascension and so upon the *sursum corda* played such an important part. In our participation in the mystery of Christ we must raise up our minds and hearts above and beyond our senses and our abilities to provide in rational categories an explanation of the act of communion in the Body and Blood of Christ; for this is by its very nature a union wrought by the Spirit and therefore far transcends the capacities of our minds to grasp. The only way we can approach understanding of this is to conceive of it after the pattern of Christ Himself, and therefore, in accordance with the wonderful union of divine and human natures in Christ so clearly expressed in the Chalcedonian Christology.

(b) *Matter* or *substance*. The matter or substance is not any mystical event but Jesus Christ Himself, the *totus Christus*. As He is not only the agent or instrument of our salvation but its very substance, so the matter of the Sacrament is to be found in the substance of Christ Himself. (It should be noted of course that by "substance" Calvin has reverted to patristic rather than scholastic usage, just as his use of "matter" is obviously different from that of Mediaeval Romanism.) At this point it was characteristic that he should lay the emphasis upon the *Humanity* of Christ. "The thing requisite must be not only to be partakers of His Spirit, but also to participate in His humanity in which He rendered all obedience to God His Father, in order to satisfy our debts, although properly speaking one cannot be without the other; for when He gives Himself to us, it is in order that we may possess Him entirely." There are clearly two points here: our sharing in the obedience of Christ, that is, the whole historical self-offering of Christ in obedience to the Father's Will; and our participation in and union with Christ's human nature. It is only through union with Christ's human nature that we can really and fully share in His obedience, so that justification in Christ reposes upon union with Him.

On this matter Calvin used powerful language that has often been criticized by those who fail to understand the fundamental significance of what he has to say. "We acknowledge without equivocation that the flesh of Christ gives life, not only because we once obtained salvation by it, but because now, while we are made one with Christ by a sacred union, the same flesh breathes life into us, or, to express it more briefly, because ingrafted into the Body of Christ by the secret agency of His Spirit we have life in common with Him. For from the hidden fountain of the God-head life was miraculously poured into the Body of Christ that it might flow from thence into us." That citation is taken from the *Mutual Consent of the Swiss Churches*, and is not simply a private opinion of Calvin, but part of the basic Reformed agreement on the Sacrament.

The danger in using such language, of course, is that it might suggest a fusion or commingling between us and Christ in the sacramental union or in faith-union. That was precisely the kind of confusion that Calvin opposed in Osiander and Servetus, for it was a form of monophysite heresy transferred to the Sacraments. For all his strong language about union with Christ and participating in His "vivifying flesh" Calvin took care to guard it from metaphysical explanations of the mode of Christ's presence with us and union with us—for such explanations, he held, could only be shameless intrusions into the essential mystery of Christ which is more to be adored than expressed. But Calvin had two fundamental interests here which must not be neglected. What he wished to stress was that the Lord's Supper is the ordinance whereby Christ gives us to communicate in His sanctified and sanctifying life, that in and through Him we may share in all the benefits of the Covenant fulfilled in the flesh of

Christ; and that through sharing in Christ's humanity we may be brought within a covenanted union with God to be thought of as enduring event or permanent reality. Christ's own human nature is risen and exalted to the right hand of the Father, and it is in that incorruptible human nature that we are given to participate so that we have perpetual reconciliation and communion with God.

That is why Calvin interpreted the discourse of Jesus in John 6 not as referring specifically to the act of Eucharistic participation but as referring to our permanent and abiding union with Christ and our continual feeding upon Him. Because in Christ human nature is everlastingly united to His divine Person we are assured of everlasting life and salvation through our sharing in His human nature, so that through Christ we share in the very life of God. "Christ Himself is in us through His flesh, and we are in Him, while that which we are in Him is in God. While He is in the Father by the nature of His Deity, we are in Him by His corporeal nativity, and He on the other hand is in us by the mystery of the Sacraments. Thus perfect union was taught by the Mediator: while we were remaining in Him, He remained in the Father, and remaining in the Father, remained in us, thus advancing us to unity with the Father, since while He is naturally in the Father, in respect of His nativity we are naturally in Him, and He remains naturally in us."

(c) *Action* or *effect*. If Christ is Himself the matter of the Sacrament, "the effect flows from this that by the sacrifice of His death our sins are expiated, by His blood we are washed, and by His resurrection we are raised to the hope of life in heaven". That is to say, the action in the Sacrament is none other than that which Christ has already accomplished on our behalf once and for all. We are not concerned here with a new or a different effect, but with the one saving action of Christ effectively extended to us and continuously operative for our salvation. It cannot be emphasized enough that here we have to think of the whole action of Christ for us, in His Incarnation, obedient life, His Self-sacrifice for us on the Cross, His Self-offering to the Father in His ascension on our behalf and His eternal advocacy of us or intercession on our behalf. Union with this Christ cannot therefore be construed in terms of metaphysical or static relationship but in terms of dynamic movement. As Calvin puts it in the *Institutes*:—"This is the wondrous exchange made by His boundless goodness. Having become one with us as the Son of Man, He has made us with Himself sons of God. By His own descent to the earth He has prepared our ascent to heaven. Having received our mortality, He has bestowed on us His immortality. Having taken our weakness upon Himself, He has made us strong in His strength. Having submitted to our poverty, He has transferred to us His riches. Having taken upon Himself the burden of our unrighteousness with which we were oppressed, He has clothed us with His righteousness."

This in turn transforms the whole conception of the analogical relation in the sacramental participation. Not only is it one which has Christological content, but it is an *active analogy*, the kind by which we are conducted upward to spiritual things, and are more and more raised up to share in the life of God. This is an elevation or exaltation into fellowship with the divine life through the amazing condescension of the Son who has been pleased to unite Himself with us in our poverty and unrighteousness, that through redemption, justification, sanctification, eternal life and all the other benefits that reside in Christ we may be endowed with divine riches, even with the life and love that overflow in Christ from God Himself.

This stress upon the action of God in the Sacrament is reflected in the actual rite itself when the emphasis is laid upon the verbs "broken for you", "shed for you", which are figured and attested by the outward action of the minister. What Christ has commanded to be figured and attested in this active way, He undoubtedly performs, giving His broken Body and shed Blood for our nourishment, and effectively applying His death and resurrection for our salvation. The Sacraments are in no sense deceiving, lying symbols; what He has promised in His ordinances He perfectly and completely fulfils.

How are we to think of this action as taking place in the sacramental relation, and how is it different from the direct action of Christ when He was here on earth or when He will come again in glory? Just as there is a sacramental mode of relation, so there is a sacramental mode of action or operation. In Christ's direct action His Word and His Act are absolutely identical and coincident, but in the sacramental mode of operation they are held partially apart in order to make room for personal relations in decision and faith and repentance, and so for the growth of personal communion in union and love. We may illustrate that from the Gospels. In the healing of the paralytic let down through the roof Jesus deliberately held apart His *Word* of forgiveness and His *Act* of healing—"in order that ye may know that the Son of man hath power on earth to forgive sins", that is, in order to make room for knowledge and faith. Similarly in a number of parables He spoke of the Householder or King going into a far country and spending time—*chronizein*—there and returning to reckon up with His servants—parables which not only have reference to Israel, but apply also to the time between the ascension and the final advent.

The very institution of the Lord's Supper was designed for the same reason, as a sacramental measure for operation between the ascension of Christ and His coming again; an institution that very clearly reveals that our Lord contemplated a long period of waiting before He returned, a long period in which the Church would have time to grow and develop in union and communion with Him. Thus in the sacramental mode of operation He not only declares His Word and truly performs what He declares, but performs it in such a way that its final fulfilment is yet to take place in the consummation of the Kingdom. That is why we have two Sacraments; one which seals His once-and-for-all work of salvation, and one which continually seals our renewal in that finished work and gives us to participate in its effective operation until He comes again in power and glory. There is then in the Lord's Supper both a sacramental fulfilment and an eschatological suspension, and these belong together inseparably, and therefore it is most important to hold Baptism and the Lord's Supper closely together; if they are allowed to fall apart, the essential relation between the finished work and the future consummation tends to be radically misunderstood, as when the whole sacramental relation and operation is divided up into seven stages of increase in "grace".

So far we have discussed mainly the action of Christ in the Lord's Supper; but what about its effect in our reception of it? The all-inclusive effect is our abiding union with Christ and through union our participation in all the benefits of Christ, which we have already considered. But here we may add that

this union and communion with Christ and sharing in His benefits has two "moments". The first "moment" is that of receiving His gift of Himself in all that He has done on our behalf,
and that receiving is effectuated through our communion in His
Body and Blood, through which we are renewed in our membership in His Covenant and our incorporation in His Body.
But this union with Christ through receiving Him in communion involves a union with Him in the whole of His obedient
Self-oblation to the Father; that is to say, it engages us to
participate in the prayer of His obedient life on earth (and so
we pray in the Lord's Supper "Our Father which art in heaven,
hallowed be thy Name, . . ."), but it also engages us anew in
the eternal Covenant in which Christ stands in for us as our
Advocate before God, our High Priest who ever lives to make
intercession for us (and so through the Spirit we echo in the
Eucharist our Lord's high-priestly prayer which we are given to
overhear in John 17). Not only in word does Christ put His own
prayer into our mouth, but in the communion of the Lord's
Supper He takes us with Him into the hallowed place where we
are asked to watch and pray with Him in His passion of intercession as He alone bears and bears away the sin of the world,
and bends our will back into union with the divine: "Not my
will but Thine be done".

All this is reflected in the signification and figuration of the
sacramental rite. As the Son of God descended and taking upon
Himself our humanity offered Himself in vicarious sacrifice on
the Cross, thus giving His life for us and bestowing Himself in
utter love upon us, so the Lord's Supper represents His Self-
giving for us and His Self-impartation to us. As He rose again
from the dead triumphant and ascended as our Mediator and
Intercessor and Advocate, the Lord's Supper represents His
advocacy and prayer for us. Thus the Sacrament is an action in
which we receive Christ and feed upon His Body and Blood by
faith, giving thanks for what He has done in the whole course of
His obedience, but it is also an action in which we set forth the
bread and wine and plead the merits of Christ, taking shelter in
His sole and sufficient Mediation and advocacy on our behalf,
and lift up our hearts in praise and thanksgiving for His
triumphant resurrection and for His ascension, in which we
cling to the royal intercessions of the ascended Lord who is set

down on the throne of God Almighty. He has ascended to present Himself before His Father, and to present us in Himself as His brothers and as those whom He has redeemed with His Blood and given to share in His own filial relation to the Father. It is in His Name that we draw near, and worship and pray in the Lord's Supper. The Supper, therefore, has to do both with the death and with the resurrection of Christ; it is both a memorial in thanksgiving of His sacrifice once and for all accomplished, and a eucharistic memorial before God in which we lift up our hearts in responsive obedience to His ascension and are made to sit with Christ in heavenly places. It is our entering within the veil through Christ, who ever lives to make intercession for us and our consecration before the face of the Father.

(4) *The Lord's Supper as Eucharist*

The Lord's Supper is essentially a prayer and hymn of thanksgiving, dramatic prayer acted out in the broken bread and poured-out wine which Christ Himself puts into our hands through His ordinance, and bids us do in remembrance of Him. The use of the words "blessing" (*eulogia*) and "thanksgiving" (*eucharistia*) from New Testament times indicates that this is a primary aspect of the Lord's Supper deriving from our Lord's own words in blessing and giving thanks at His institution. In the old custom of the Church of Scotland the "Communion season" lasted several days, and the "Communion" itself lasted throughout the whole of the Lord's Day, although it came to be broken up into "Communion" at the morning service and the "Thanksgiving" at the evening service. That has tended to have the unfortunate result of separating the eucharistic aspect of the Supper from the communion. Therefore this aspect requires further and deeper consideration by us to-day, lest it be allowed to slip away from us, especially in reaction to modern misunderstandings of "the eucharistic sacrifice".

Calvin and Knox both drew a very clear distinction between the "propitiatory sacrifice" and the "eucharistic sacrifice". Christ alone has offered to God a propitiatory sacrifice in the sacrifice of Himself in obedient life and obedient death once and for all, and we can only offer to God praise and thanksgiving for what He has done and finished for ever on our behalf and in our stead and for our sakes. Because Christ is our High Priest who has taken our place and offered once and for all an all-sufficient sacrifice on our behalf, it is only "by the right hand of Christ" that we can offer anything to God at all, as John Knox put it. Or, to put it otherwise, Christ's high-priestly prayer recorded in John 17 is perpetual in its virtue and ever obtains mercy for us in the presence of His Father; it is that intercession of Christ that stands behind our prayer when we approach God in the Name of Christ and plead His passion on our behalf, and offer ourselves to Him as sinners whom Christ has redeemed by His Blood, adopted as His own and covered by His righteous Name. It is therefore under the cover and shelter of Christ's sacrifice that we draw near to God in the Holy Supper, bringing nothing in our hands but clinging only to Christ's Cross, in order to pray and to offer intercessions in the Name of Christ the Mediator.

But sincerely to pray to God means that we present our bodies to Him as a living sacrifice, holy and acceptable unto God as our reasonable service; and sincerely to intercede for others for Christ's sake means that we pour ourselves out in the service of others for whom Christ died. Thus "under the sacrifice we call eucharistic are included all the offices of charity by which while we embrace our brethren, we honour the Lord Himself in His members; in fine; all our prayers, praises, and thanksgivings, and every act of worship which we perform to God. All these depend on the greater sacrifice with which we dedicate ourselves, soul and body, to be a holy temple to the Lord. For it is not enough that our external acts be framed to obedience, but we must dedicate and consecrate first ourselves and secondly all that we have so that all which is in us may be subservient to His glory, and be stirred up to magnify it." In those words of Calvin we see that eucharistic sacrifice ultimately means directing ourselves and all that we have and do in the Name of Christ *to the Glory of God*, which is accompanied by the fruit of our lips in praise and thanksgiving to His Name. "This kind of sacrifice", Calvin continues in his *Institutes*, "is indispensable to the Lord's Supper in which, while we show forth His death and give Him thanks, we offer nothing but the sacrifice of praise. From this office of sacrificing, all Christians are called 'a royal priesthood', because by Christ we offer that sacrifice of praise of which the

Apostle speaks, 'the fruit of our lips, giving thanks to His name' (1 Peter 2: 9; Heb. 13: 15). We do not appear with our gifts in the presence of God without an Intercessor. Christ is our Mediator, by whose intervention we offer ourselves and our all to the Father. He is our High Priest who, having entered into the upper sanctuary, opens up an access for us, He the altar on which we lay our gifts, that whatever we do attempt, we may attempt in Him; He it is, I say, who hath 'made us kings and priests unto God and His Father'."

In order to get Calvin's teaching about this fully before us, it may be helpful to look at his comments on Num. 19, which describes the solemn rite of the sacrifice of the red heifer without the camp and the application of that sacrifice through the sprinkling of its ashes mixed with water upon those needing cleansing. Calvin looked at the passage in the light of Heb. 13 and it led him to speak of our offering of Christ to the Father. "In order that we may be partakers of cleansing, it is necessary that each of us should offer Christ to the Father. For although He only, and that but once, has offered Himself, still a daily offering of Him, which is effected by faith and prayers is enjoined upon us, not such as the Papists have invented, by whom in their impiety and perverseness, the Lord's Supper has been mistakenly turned into a sacrifice because they imagined that Christ must be daily slain, in order that His death might profit us. The offering, however, of faith and prayers, of which I speak, is very different, and by it alone we apply to ourselves the virtue and fruit of Christ's death." Then with reference to the fact that in the Old Testament rite "the people offered vicariously by the hand of the priest", Calvin added: "In this way also at present, although we set Christ before God's face in order to propitiate Him still it is necessary that Christ Himself should interpose and exercise the office of a Priest."

Calvin thus objected to the conception in which Romans thought of the Eucharist as a propitiatory sacrifice, as in the Creed of Pius IV: "I profess that in the Mass there is offered to God a true, proper, and propitiatory sacrifice for the living and the dead." But once that is resolutely set aside, Calvin can even speak about offering Christ to the Father and setting Him before the Father's Face—that is precisely what is done in faith and prayer at the Lord's Supper, but surely not in order to propitiate God(!) as Calvin put it, but in taking shelter under Christ's advocacy and in thankful pleading of His passion in the knowledge that once and for all we have been reconciled to God in Christ, and now for ever have a place in Christ's Self-consecration on our behalf and Self-presentation before the Face of the Father in Heaven. It is in communion with that risen and triumphant and ascended Lord and by His right hand alone that we offer our worship at the Lord's Supper to the Glory of God's Holy Name.

(5) *The Corporate Nature of the Lord's Supper*

This is an aspect of the Eucharist that has always been strongly emphasized in the teaching and practice of the Reformed Church. It is the Sacrament of the communion in the Body of Christ and is therefore rightly celebrated with the whole Body of the Church in heaven and earth. That is given its active signification in the assembling of the whole congregation to Holy Communion, in which Communion is held conjointly with the Lord and therefore with one another in Him. It is in no sense a private rite of a few, it is the Sacrament of the New Covenant in which Christ gave Himself a ransom for many, and all are to eat the bread and all to drink the wine; for there is one loaf and one cup, as there is One Lord in whom the many are reconciled to God and formed into One New Man.

It belongs to the essence of the Sacrament that each is a deacon to the other at the Holy Table, and serves him in love as Christ washed the disciples' feet at the Last Supper, giving us an example of what we should do to one another both in giving to one another and in receiving from one another humble, even menial, service in the name of the Crucified. This corporate Sacrament enshrines not only the mutual relations in love of the members of Christ's Body but a two-way relationship between the spiritual and the physical, the invisible and the visible. The communion in Christ is physically acted out in the dividing and eating of the bread, in the distributing and drinking of the wine, and the participants go from it to live and act it out in their daily life and work and in all their personal relations within the Household of faith, but also to shew forth the death of Christ to all men until He comes again. The Sacrament cannot be restricted to a cultic act, for by its very nature it presses out to fulfilment in the whole life and mission of the Church in all its spiritual and bodily existence and action.

Three things here demand further consideration.

(a) In the corporate act in which all join and in which there is a conjunction between the visible and invisible, the physical and the spiritual action involved, there arises the problem of the *manducatio impiorum*, as it has been called, of those who eat and drink unworthily to their own judgment. This requires that the Table be "fenced", for it is a Holy Table, and holy things are to be given only to the holy. Each Church therefore administers the Supper within its discipline, although in so doing it must acknowledge at every point that it is the Lord's Supper and not the prerogative or the possession of the Church. But what of those who come unworthily to participate; do they too eat the Body and drink the Blood of Christ? We must surely answer this question by recalling that the action in the Supper is not another action than that which Christ has already accomplished on our behalf, and which is proclaimed in the Gospel. But even in the proclamation of the Gospel some who refuse the light are blinded by it, and others who receive the light are illuminated by it, so that the Gospel is, as St. Paul put it, a savour of death unto death to some and of life unto life to others. We may take another illustration, from the Johannine account of the prayer of Christ answered by the voice of the Father from heaven which some heard only as thunder whereas others heard it as the voice of an angel; or the Lucan and Pauline account of the encounter of Saul of Tarsus with Jesus on the Damascus road, when Paul alone discerned the Voice of Jesus while others who saw the light heard no voice. Surely it is in that way that we are to think of those who come to the Table unworthily without faith. It is the same Christ giving Himself in His Body and Blood who is extended to all; but while some receive in faith so that Christ dwells in their hearts, others are blinded and judged by the very gift of grace extended to them, by the Body and Blood of Christ, for it is only by the Body and Blood of Christ that they can be judged; Christ does not therefore dwell in their hearts, for they do not feed on Him by faith.

(b) The Church that partakes of the Body and Blood of Christ at His Table is committed to engage in His mission of reconciliation, to proclaim the Gospel to all nations and to live it out as a fellowship of reconciliation bringing healing to a divided world. The Church must see to it therefore that its daily life and work are in agreement with its communion in the Body and Blood of Christ, and that the ordering of its whole life is in worthy correspondence with the Gospel. It is pledged to that in the most solemn and awful way by the Body and Blood of Christ, and cannot resile from that without seriously damaging its own life and quenching the Holy Spirit in its midst. No doubt it is because of failure at this point that the Churches in our day are so weak and sickly, repeating the lapses of the Corinthian Church which drew upon them the rebuke of St. Paul.

(c) This brings us also to face the vexed question of intercommunion. We cannot forget that so long as the Church is divided within itself it betrays the Gospel of reconciliation, and cripples the effectiveness of its mission in the proclamation of reconciliation to the world. But how is the Church to keep holy discipline over the celebration of the Supper, to acknowledge that it is the Lord's and not its own Supper, and to find a way in which common participation between the Churches can be achieved again with sincerity? We cannot forget the parable of Jesus about the man who went to lay his gift on the altar and remembered he had a quarrel with another; he was commanded to go and *first* be reconciled with his brother and then to come and lay his gift on the altar. That applies to intercommunion, for how can we sit down at the Holy Table together and pretend that we are one there when we refuse to seek or work out a way of reconciliation in which our outer life in the ordering of our mission and ministry is in agreement with the Gospel proclaimed at the Supper? But how can we go to the Lord's Table at all if that is so? for the parable tells us that we cannot go at all until we are first reconciled with our brother.

Where is the Church that dares to take this parable seriously? Surely the very discipline that Churches profess to exercise means that they wish to celebrate the Supper only in truth and sincerity; if so, none of these Churches should go to the Table without resolving to seek a way out of our divisions and without seeking to do all it can to work out, along with others, an ordering of the ministry and mission of the Church which is in worthy agreement with the Gospel enshrined and enacted in the Holy Communion. The Unity of the Church is a gift of Christ freely bestowed at Holy Communion. Woe to the Church that receives this gift in the broken Body and shed Blood of Christ and then hides it or refuses it because it loves its own man-made traditions and prejudices more than that which has been bought with the Blood of the Saviour. Behind all the problems of intercommunion there lies deep failure to grasp the true nature of this sacrament of reconciliation, refusal to believe sufficiently that it is an efficacious Sacrament, effective as well as signitive of unity, but also a failure to enter very far into the Garden of Gethsemane and to enter into the passion of the Lord. That applies as much to those who claim to have "open communion" but refuse to respect or listen to the sincere conscience of others, as it does to those who have erected again "the middle wall of partition" (the *phragmos*) which Jesus deliberately broke down in parable and in act, and at last in His crucifixion on the Cross.

(b) *Eschatology and the Eucharist*[1]

It is a significant fact that in the last thirty or forty years the difference between the Roman Catholic Church and the Evangelical Church in their teaching on the Eucharist has been narrowed down considerably. That is most evident in the abandonment by many leading Roman Catholic theologians of the Tridentine explanation of the sacrifice of the Mass in literal terms, and in their return to a deeper understanding of the sacramental and eschatological significance of the Eucharist. The outstanding event in this movement was the publication of *Mysterium Fidei* by Maurice de la Taille after the First World War, and since then other notable works have appeared moving more or less within the same orbit of thought.[2] To the Reformed theologian much of this discussion is still hampered by unreal scholastic distinctions and a too literal approach to the eucharistic sacrifice, but he cannot but be impressed with two major elements in it: (a) the distinct sensitiveness of Roman theologians to the Protestant criticism of the pre- and post-Reformation

---

[1] Prepared for the World Conference on Faith and Order at Lund, and published in *Intercommunion* (edit. by D. M. Baillie and John Marsh, S.C.M. Press), 1952, pp. 303–50.

[2] Cf. the works of Baumstark, Cabrol, Guardini, Héris, Masure, Casel, Vonier, Bardy, Warnach, Söhngen, Schmaus, Jungmann, etc.

doctrine of the Mass, and the concern of all to maintain the unique character of the sacrifice on the Cross as an unrepeatable event; and (b) the fresh understanding of biblical teaching and consequently a rediscovery of the eschatological nature of the sacraments of Baptism and Eucharist. In spite of this *rapprochement*, however, we cannot blind ourselves to the fact that the difference between the Roman Catholic Church and the Evangelical Church is very deep,[1] and much deeper than anything which divides the branches of the Evangelical Church.

In the branches of the Evangelical Church, that is in the Churches of the Reformation, differences have also been narrowed down considerably. To a certain extent the modern liturgical movement has tended to harden those differences through its search for a definitive shape of the liturgy, but on the whole it has served rather to bring the Churches together by taking their differences to a deeper level and testing them by the prophetic and apostolic foundation of the Church. Here it has become apparent that difference in practice has carried divergence in belief farther than it actually is. That is a heartening discovery; for it indicates that in the Evangelical Church, where we do not have to do with irreformable pronouncements of faith, a fresh understanding of the apostolic message may so undermine our differences and correct our several traditions that intercommunion will become a compelling necessity for all who confess "one Lord, one faith, one baptism, one God and Father of all". This essay is an attempt from within the Reformed Church to engage in discussion at this stage, and if possible to penetrate below the existing principles governing intercommunion to theological foundations in the hope of laying bare the significance of the Eucharist as the divinely given Sacrament of unity, indeed the medicine for our divisions.

I

The Sacraments and Eschatology

We may begin with the word *sacrament*, and note that the New Testament does not speak of sacraments, but rather of Baptism

---

[1] This difference is made very clear by the new Roman dogma. Instead of the Evangelical *solus Christus* at the right hand of the Father, the Roman Church substitutes *Christus et Maria*.

and the Lord's Supper. If we are to penetrate to the biblical foundations, therefore, we must avoid thinking about Baptism and the Eucharist as if they had to fulfil some man-made definition of a sacrament from Augustine, for example, or Aquinas or Calvin, helpful as they may be. When we set aside for the moment the centuries of theological discussion and turn to the pages of the New Testament Scriptures, we become aware of the fact that again and again the language it uses about Baptism is interchangeable with that it uses about the Eucharist.[1] Indeed, Baptism and Eucharist are just as parallel, and just as one, as *in Christ* and *Christ in us*. If anything, the emphasis is laid upon Baptism, as in the confession of unity cited above, "One Lord, one faith, one baptism", where the Eucharist is not mentioned, while whole Epistles such as that to the *Romans* do not mention it either. That would not be understandable were it not for the evident fact that the New Testament regards Baptism and Eucharist as two aspects of the same event, and that it is Baptism rather than the Eucharist which is all-inclusive. Both have to do with incorporation into Christ, but whereas Baptism is all-inclusive and final, the Eucharist is the continual renewal of that incorporation in time. The Eucharist cannot be understood except within the significance of Baptism, although the once-and-for-all significance of Baptism bears upon history only through the Eucharist. We may say, therefore, that strictly speaking there is only one sacrament, and that Baptism and Eucharist belong to this indivisible whole.[2] It is the sacrament of the *Word made flesh*, of the *Christ-event*, which includes the life, teaching, death, and resurrection of Jesus Christ. It is the same Word which sacramentally becomes flesh in both Baptism and the Eucharist, and it is in that action of the Word becoming flesh that they have their underlying and indivisible unity. In the action of the Church the relation between Baptism and Eucharist is through the *kerygma*: it is a *kerygmatic relation*.

---

[1] Cf. especially Mk. 10: 38 f.; 1 Cor. 10: 1 f.; 12: 12, 13.

[2] This is borne out very clearly by the art of the Roman Catacombs—cf. Vladimir Weidlé *The Baptism of Art*. The unity of Baptism and Eucharist has been remarkably conserved by the Orthodox Church. It became also a point of cardinal importance in the Reformation writings of Calvin and Peter Martyr, following Augustine.

In the elucidation of this we may recall the meaning of the Christ-event as the Word made flesh. It is the Christian message that in the Incarnation of the Son of God the eternal Word has entered into history, and partakes of the relativity of history, without ceasing to be God, and without at the same time destroying the continuity of ongoing history. In the historical Jesus the eternal Word is made flesh so that He is seen and heard in the flesh in history, and yet because He does not cease to be the eternal Word He cannot be seen or heard except in His eternal recession in God. That is why the Synoptic Gospels speak of the Word as *mysterion*. Jesus can be known historically as part of human flesh, but the real significance of the historical Jesus is not apparent except to faith. The Word has become flesh, and cannot be known by men of flesh and blood except in the flesh; but it is the Father in heaven alone who reveals Him, and not flesh and blood.

That, however, is only part of the significance of the Christ-event. The Word is not only eternal Truth but the act of the Eternal in time. That is why in the Gospels there is the closest relation between the Word and the act in Jesus' preaching. Word and act are inseparable and complementary. The Word of the Kingdom is God's saving intervention among men, and that takes place in the preaching and miracles of Jesus in inseparable unity. We may put the matter thus. Jesus is not one whose action falls short of His Word. Therefore, though the Word of forgiveness is spoken in a parable, that same Word is acted out in Himself on the Cross. There the Word of pardon is enacted in flesh and blood and inserted as a reality into our history and life. It becomes an actual fact, not just a mere idea or a word spoken into the air. That was why on the lips of Jesus the Word was indirectly communicated through the parable because the act is also part of the Word. The Word of God is not mere speech but power of God, Christ crucified, as St. Paul said. It is because the Word is also power or act that it cannot be conveyed in mere speech but has to be conveyed in saving acts, in miraculous signs. The parables were designed not to convey a symbolic meaning which can be read off their face but to confront men with Christ Himself as the Word of God, and the miracles were designed not just to prove the divinity of Christ but to confront men with the mighty power of God already at work among them in Jesus Christ. Both parables and miracles, however, pointed beyond themselves to the crucifixion and resurrection, where in the fullest sense the divine Word and act were one in the person of Jesus Christ.

That happened once and for all, and is absolutely decisive for all men and all time. It was not a once-and-for-all event merely in the sense in which every other historical event happens but once and is unrepeatable, but once and for all in the sense of eternal finality. As such, however, it is not merely a piece of past history, but is an enduring event with critical and decisive significance for all time.[1] Everything else will pass away, but this will not pass away. How does this unique and enduring event bear upon men in time now that Jesus Christ has withdrawn Himself from visible participation in history? It is here that the New Testament speaks about *kerygma*, and also about Baptism and the Lord's Supper.

Kerygma means both the thing preached and the preaching of it in one. It is the proclamation of the Christ-event, but such proclamation that by the Holy Spirit it becomes the actualization of that event among men. It is such proclamation that in and through it the living Christ continues to do and to teach what He had already begun before and after the crucifixion. *Kerygma* is the Word of the Kingdom that cannot be conveyed in mere speech, but is used by God to intervene Himself in the human situation as He who once and for all has wrought out His final act in the death and resurrection of Jesus Christ, so that through *kerygma* the Church is continually being called out of history to become the very Body of Christ, and by the communion of His Holy Spirit is given to taste the powers of the age to come and to stand already on the side of the resurrection. Accordingly, even after the Lord Jesus was received up into heaven and sat on the right hand of God, the disciples "went forth and preached everywhere, the Lord working with them, and confirming the Word with signs following". That is the twofold event of *kerygma*.

This means that *kerygma* is in the fullest sense the sacramental action of the Church through which the mystery of the Kingdom concerning Christ and His Church, hid from the founda-

[1] Cf. E. Brunner, "The Christian Understanding of Time", *Scottish Journal of Theology*, 1951, Vol. 41, pp. 1 ff., and his *Eternal Hope*, ch. 5.

tion of the world, is now being revealed in history. Just as in the Incarnation the Word was made flesh, so in *kerygma* the same Word continues to be "made flesh" in the life of the Church. Thus we read in the Acts of the Apostles of the Word as increasing and multiplying. By that is not meant that Christ the Word grows or increases, but that His living Word acting in and through human witness works creatively among men, building upon earth the Church which is concorporate with the all-inclusive Body of Christ. It is within this sacramental and kerygmatic activity of Church and Spirit that Baptism and the Lord's Supper are given their place in the New Testament. As such they may be regarded as bearing a relation to the *kerygma* of the Church similar to that which the signs and miracles bore to the *kerygma* of Jesus. Jesus took care in His preaching never to give a compelling manifestation of Himself, lest by an open display of His majesty and might He might crush men to the ground, leaving no room for faith or repentance or decision. In Him the *eschaton* had broken into the present, but if men had been confronted openly with the *eschaton* in the Word and Presence of Jesus they would have been faced with the final judgment. Jesus deliberately held the Word and its action apart in order to leave room for repentance and faith, but at the same time He followed up the Word with a sign which gave ample evidence of His saving power. The classic example of that is to be found in the Markan account of the healing of the paralytic, where for the purpose of leaving room for faith ("that ye may know that the Son of Man hath power on earth to forgive sins"), an interval of time was inserted between the Word of forgiveness and the act of healing. It was precisely that lapse of time or eschatological reserve between the Word of the Kingdom and its power that Jesus was concerned to preserve in His *kerygma*.

A similar relation between Word and act is to be found after the death and resurrection of Jesus, for though it is as one that they take the field in the *kerygma* of the Church, Jesus has withdrawn Himself from visible participation in history, reserving that for the *parousia* or the *eschaton*. Here, however, both the unity between the Word and action and their eschatological tension are intensified. The Church is redeemed not in Word only but also in power, and yet it waits for the redemption of the body. The new age has already overtaken it and through the Spirit it stands on the resurrection side of the Cross, and yet it still waits for the day when the form and fashion of this world will be torn aside and the new creation will be revealed. The Church lives between those two moments, between the Cross and the *parousia*, between the Word of forgiveness and the final act of healing, between Pentecost and the resurrection of the body. In the mercy of God the Word of the Gospel and the final deed of God are partially held apart in eschatological reserve until the *parousia*. This is the age of grace, the age of *kerygma*, in which the Gospel is proclaimed to all, in which time and space are given for repentance and decision. But this is the age, too, when by the Holy Spirit, who inhabits the Church and energizes its kerygmatic ministry, all who believe in Jesus Christ may taste the powers of the age to come through sacramental incorporation into the new creation.

It was said above that the relation between the sacraments and the *kerygma* of the Church is similar to that between the signs and the *kerygma* of Jesus—but there is this supreme difference, that now the death and resurrection of Jesus Christ have taken place and the great act for the redemption of the world has been completed. It is true indeed that the unveiling of the full reality of that act is still to take place, but it is equally true that with the death and resurrection of Jesus Christ the Kingdom of God and with it the new creation have already interpenetrated the age in which we live, so that this is already the fullness of time. The two sacraments of the Word made flesh, Baptism and Eucharist, are essentially *signs* belonging to this fullness of time, and as such are charged with the power of the resurrection. They enshrine in time the great *mystery* concerning Christ in His Church.

We must be clear, however, about the meaning of these two words, *sign* and *mystery*. The sign is to be understood in terms of the miraculous activity of Christ, as *kerygma* is to be understood in terms of Christ the living Word. These may be distinguished from each other in thought, but are actually inseparable. As the virgin birth and the resurrection are miraculous and active signs of the Word made flesh, so Baptism and Eucharist are miraculous and active signs of the Word made flesh in the Church as the Body of Christ. The great difficulty about the word *sign* in traditional theology is the unfortunate fact that *signum* corresponds to *res* and involves a quite unhebraic and unbiblical denotation as static matter or significant thing.[1] Even the expression *effective sign* used by the Reformers is inadequate.[2] Sign is essentially event, the worldly form which the Christ-event assumes in action, the point at which Revelation embodies itself actively in history. Sign is not, however, a complete or final embodiment, as if Revelation completely passes into or is absorbed in history, but such an embodiment in conditions of time as to point beyond itself to an infinite fullness. Before the Cross the miraculous signs were actual anticipations of the saving act of God in the death and resurrection of Jesus; afterwards they are the miraculous signs charged with the incarnate presence of the crucified and risen Lord which point beyond to a fullness which, as signs, in the conditions of our fallen world, they cannot altogether contain. In other words, the whole significance of the sign is bound up with the fact that the ascension comes in between the resurrection of Jesus Christ and His second advent. *Parousia* means both a presence and a coming. The sacramental signs are charged with the real presence, but it is a presence which is also yet to come, a presence whose full reality is yet to be unveiled and consummated.

That takes us to the significance of the word *mystery*. Here it is the Greek idea which has confused understanding. Like *sign*, *mystery* is essentially event, but event as that which is not yet fully disclosed in conditions of the fallen world. It is the event of Revelation in time in so far as it recedes into the eternal, in so far as the sign bears witness to the fullness beyond. In the New Testament, mystery is spoken of in relation to the *kerygma*, and not directly in relation to Baptism and the Lord's Supper, but its bearing upon the sacraments was inevitable. In its fundamental sense mystery refers to God manifest in the flesh, but as the great sign of that event is the Church of Jesus Christ, the relation of Christ to His Church is also spoken of as mystery. It is in that sense that the word may legitimately be applied to the sacraments. We may put it this way. Through its ministry of *kerygma* the Church is regarded in the New Testament as the great sacramental sign, for it is the visible counterpart of the

---

[1] Cf. E. Gaugler, *Das Abendmahl im Neuen Testament*, pp. 7 ff.; K. Barth, *Die christliche Lehre nach dem Heidelberger Katechismus*, pp. 88 f.

[2] This did enable Calvin, however, to teach a doctrine of *dynamic presence* in the sacraments.

resurrection-body of Christ. As such the Church can neither be fused with Christ nor separated from Him. As the God-Man Christ was Himself the embodiment in the world of the mystery of the Kingdom, but as the Church is the embodiment of the Spirit of Christ (for "he that is joined to the Lord is one Spirit"), it is also in its way the embodiment of the same mystery. The sacraments of Baptism and Eucharist are therefore the miraculous and active signs through which that mystery is embodied in the Church on earth, but, be it noted, embodied in such a way that, while they anticipate, they point to an eschatological fullness beyond. The sacraments are given to us because of the ascension and cannot be made to impugn it as if they contained a presence fully identical with that of the *parousia*. Had Christ not withdrawn Himself visibly from the world there would doubtless have been no need for sacraments, not in our sense at any rate. When Christ comes again and the Marriage Supper of the Lamb is consummated, the sacraments will give way to literal reality. Until that day comes the sacraments have to do with the breaking of the Christ-event into time here and now, and with our participation in the new creation.

To understand that more clearly we must recall the nature of the Christ-event, which, while it is once and for all in a final sense, is also an abiding or enduring event that can never pass away. The union of God and Man in the Incarnation also involves the union of eternity with time, and though that union is inserted into our history with its limitations and relativities it is a union that is carried through the contradiction of sin and death itself into the resurrection. There we have revealed the new creation in the risen Body of Jesus Christ. But just as the original creation involved the creation of time, so this new creation involves new time, time that is no longer at variance with the eternal through sin, but time that is cleansed and restored to union with the eternal. The Christ-event is absolutely unique and decisive in that through it redemption has been wrought once and for all, nevertheless it is an event that involves this new time, and as such it transcends the limitations and relativities of history as we know it from day to day, and endures for ever. It endures and abides for ever as new time just because it is indissolubly united to the eternal. That is the significance of the session at the right hand of God the Father, but it is also the significance of the continuity of the new creation in the Church, the Body of Christ.

We may say that as God and man are united in the God-Man in such a way that the two natures may not be identified with or separated from each other (we recall here the Chalcedonian formula), so the sacraments involve on another plane, in conditions of this fallen world, a like union between divine action and human action, but here let it be noted that the "divine" action is the action of *Totus Christus*, of the God-Man, and not of God *simpliciter* apart from the incarnation. There is then in the sacraments a union between the divine action and human action, between the *actio* of Christ Jesus and the *re-actio* of the Church, and *actio* and *re-actio* can neither be identified with, nor separated from, each other. Just as God and Man in Christ Jesus are united in the *communio consubstantialis* of the Holy Spirit, so here in the sacraments the divine action and the human re-action are united in *communio substantialis* through the same Holy Spirit.

This means that the sacraments do not have to do simply with a union between the present and the future, but with a union between the Church in history and the new creation as an abiding union here and now even in the heart of the world's estrangement. It is because that union is only partially revealed in the sacraments that we must talk about it in terms of mystery, and it is because that union will be fully revealed in the future that we must speak about it in terms of eschatology. The sacraments tell us, however, that the reality of the new creation is temporal fact here and now, even though its reality, veiled since the ascension of the Lord, is yet to be unveiled at the *parousia*. The New Testament emphasis upon the future is not so much the future of the reality but the future of its full manifestation, so that the eschatological tension involved in the sacraments is the tension between the time of a present but hidden reality and the time of the same reality revealed in the *parousia*.

It is because the eschatological relation involves both the relation between the present and the future and the relation between the new creation and the old, here and now, that the one sacramental relation between the Church and Jesus Christ has two particular "moments": Baptism and the Lord's Supper. Just as the Christ-event had its two supreme "moments" in the virgin birth and in the death and resurrection of Jesus Christ, although neither "moment" can be understood except as it involves the other, so here in the sacramental union where the Christ-event breaks into the historical life of the Church incorporating it into Christ as His Body, there are two corresponding "moments", Baptism and the Lord's Supper, each of which involves the other in a single whole. The doubleness of the eschatological tension is enshrined in both of them, but the emphasis upon the once-and-for-all incorporation into Christ or union with the new creation falls most heavily upon the sacrament of Baptism, while in the sacrament of the Eucharist we have emphasized most the breaking in of the new creation as the enduring event in, and in spite of, the conditions of this sinful and historical world. If at Baptism we think of our having died and risen with Christ so that we are born anew in Him, so that old things are passed away and all things are become new, at Holy Communion we think of that not only as a *datum* once and for all, but also as a *dandum* which must be given anew, day by day, in the conditions of our fallen world. Every time we communicate is eschatological time until we drink it anew in the Kingdom of God. It is just because, in the sign of Baptism, the complete event recedes into the mystery of the Eternal that we are given in the Eucharist continual participation and renewal in that complete event. In both sacraments we are told that the Kingdom of God is amongst us not in Word only with suspended action, not in Spirit only, but in deed and in power, as real act in time, as Word-deed enacted in our flesh and blood and inserted into history. But precisely because it is both, it is at once a complete reality and an eschatologically reiterated event until Christ comes.

It is important to remember that both Baptism and Eucharist are sacraments of the Word made flesh. They do not have existence or reality independently of the Word. To make them self-sufficient and independent of the Word would be to take away their sacramental character, for it would deny to them their element of mystery, or infinite recession in the Word that is in the bosom of God and is God. That is why, following St. Augustine, the Reformers insisted that it is the Word which sacramentalizes, and apart from the Word sacraments cannot exist. Apart from the Word there is only an empty sign that is nothing but a ceremony. *Kerygma* and sign go together and cannot be sundered. In *kerygma* the *Word* is made flesh. In the sacraments the Word is made *flesh*. Baptism, *kerygma*, and Eucharist together form a whole, the sacramental life and action of the Church. "And Jesus came and spake unto them, saying, All power is given unto me in heaven and in earth. Go ye therefore, and teach all nations, baptizing them in the name of the Father, and of the Son, and of the Holy Spirit: teaching them to observe all things whatsoever I have commanded you: and lo, I am with you alway, even unto the end of the world." The emphasis here is upon *kerygma* and Baptism, but in the promise of the real presence *alway* we may surely understand the eucharistic communion.

II

The Eucharist of the Lord's Supper

Before we speak more precisely about the Eucharist we must be more precise about Baptism as the primary eschatological act of the Gospel, whereby we are ingrafted into the wholeness of Christ. The Baptism of John clearly had reference to the liturgical washing at the laver in preparation for the sacrifice of the lamb, a sign which pointed to a fullness in the Spirit that was yet to come. That Baptism had its counterpart doubtless in Jesus' cleansing of the Temple in preparation for His sacrifice as the Lamb of God whereby He was to make atonement for sin, a cleansing which pointed to the sanctification of the Church, cleansed with the washing of water by the Word, a glorious Church not having spot or wrinkle, but holy and without blemish. We cannot, however, speak about the Baptism of the disciples and of Jesus in univocal terms. Theirs was a Baptism of repentance and renewal even though the power of the resurrection was not fully released until Pentecost; Jesus' Baptism was substitutionary and was completed in His Baptism of blood on the Cross when He died for all men. In the profoundest sense all men are actually involved in that Baptism of Jesus, and it is that Baptism which turns John's Baptism into Christian Baptism. After the crucifixion and resurrection Baptism has much more than parabolic significance, for now the Word and act are one event, and it is because of that unity that *kerygma* and *baptisma* are always thought of together in the New Testament.

The Word in *kerygma* presses into physical enactment, creating the bodily Church—and that happens through Baptism. It is through the *kerygma*, however, that Baptism gains its particularity and is given power as concrete event. A purely substitutionary and objective Baptism would have little reference to the life which we live in history, even though after the crucifixion all history happens within and under the shadow of the Cross and the mighty act of God wrought out there. It is through the *kerygma*, through the ministry of the Church empowered by the Holy Spirit, that the Cross exerts its power over men and history. In the *kerygma* of the Church the living Word, Christ crucified and risen, lays hold of men in their sin and weakness. The Word demands decision and through men's obedience and disobedience it acts selectively upon them, calling the Church into being, a work which will be fully unveiled at the last day when the Word will complete its judgment. But already that Word is event, for through the *kerygma* the death and the resurrection of Jesus Christ break into the present, so that all who believe are given to participate in that death and resurrection and are inserted into the operational sphere of the Christ-event. Baptism is the fulfilment of that as the particular actualization of the Christ-event, so that through it the Church called out of the world becomes the Church which is the Body of Christ. There is only one Baptism, the Baptism of the Spirit at Pentecost which corresponds to the one Baptism of Christ, and into that each believer is incorporated through water-baptism.

Parallel to the hypostatic union between God and Man in Jesus Christ there is a sacramental union in Baptism between the divine action and the action of the Church, between its manward and its Godward action. Baptism is not in any sense an independent agency whose benefit is conferred *ex opere operato*; rather is it the action of the Church in obedience to the divine ordinance, which God uses to fulfil His holy Will. In other words, the mediation of the divine act is not through the element as such but in its particular use in the action of the Church. Baptism is, on the one hand, then, the breaking in of the Christ-event, so that it is not simply an historical event belonging to the past, but as a once-and-for-all historical event it is also precipitated into the present and is active with saving power here and now in the Church. Baptism indicates that the Church is the sphere and the medium in the world whereby the saving acts of Jesus Christ are at work, invading history and subjecting all things to Christ as King and Lord. Baptism is the outworking in time of the absolutely decisive event of the Cross and resurrection of Christ, and gathers to that event the corresponding life and action of the historical Church. The Church is not therefore merely an historical institution, but is a sacramental magnitude maintained in being upon foundations that are not laid with hands, rooted and grounded in the God-Manhood of Jesus Christ.

On the other hand, as in Baptism the Church binds believers to the *Heilsgeschichte*, pledges them to faith in Jesus Christ who died for them and rose again, and offers them to Him as Saviour and Lord, the Holy Spirit uses this Godward action of the Church as the means whereby He gives believers participation in the Baptism of Christ, inserts them into the Christ-event, incorporates them into His Body, ingrafts them into the New Creation, and makes them to sit in heavenly places. This means that something absolutely decisive is wrought in Baptism. Baptism in the Name of Jesus, in the name of the Holy Trinity, means that Christians are delivered from the power of darkness and translated into the Kingdom of the Son of God. A radical change has taken place which can only be described in terms of a complete change of Lordship. The Christian is no longer under the domination of the law or the elements of this world, but is dead to sin and alive to God through the Lordship of the Spirit, so that old things are passed away and all things are become new. Outwardly Baptism is no doubt incorporation into the earthly Church, initiation into the operational sphere of the salvation-event, and outwardly the Church on earth knows itself to be embroiled in the relativities of history and the sin of mankind, but behind all that and beyond, Baptism has a dimension in depth which is its eschatological *mystery*: "Ye are dead and your life is hid with Christ in God." The really significant event in Baptism is a hidden event; it recedes from sight in the ascension of Christ and waits to be revealed fully at the last day.

However, the Lord has not simply left His Church stricken with anguish and awe at the foot of the Cross, or standing looking up into heaven from Galilee. He has provided for the renewal and maintenance of its life and faith—in the Eucharist.

Through continual communion in the body and blood of the Saviour, the Church finds that Baptism is given its complement and recurring confirmation. After the Baptism of John, Jesus had called twelve disciples and formed them round Himself into one body, the reconstituted Israel of God. They were pledged to drink His cup and be baptized with His baptism, but the mystery of the Kingdom, the New Israel incorporate in the Messianic Saviour, baffled them. They understood indeed that they were called to cast in their lot unreservedly with Jesus and to share His life, but in the crucial moment they found themselves standing not with Jesus but with the crowd of sinners who were crucifying Him and for whom He was dying. They had all forsaken Him and fled.[1] At last the Messiah was left unutterably alone under the judgment of God upon the world's sin. He was their Lord and Master. He was their Representative and their very Life, but in the agony of substitution He was unutterably alone, the Lamb whom God had Himself provided for sacrifice.[2] The disciples could only stand afar off in sin and shame and fear, and broken-hearted that the bonds between Him and them were utterly severed. Then they remembered the Last Supper. That was why He had designed it, for He meant them to remember. And they realized that within that awful separation and in spite of it He had effectuated His oneness with them in a way that nothing could break, for He had given them in the Supper a sacramental counterpart to His atoning death. And then they knew that their baptismal incorporation into one Body with their Lord had come to its stark reality in the sacrificial death and its sacramental counterpart. They understood how in that wonderful Last Supper Jesus "had definitely consecrated them for inheritance in the Kingdom of God as those who, despite their brokenness so soon to be made visible, formed one body with Himself. He had given their lives a sacramental dependence on His own."[3] In the Lord's Supper and in the enactment on the Cross the mystery of their baptismal incorporation into Christ, and into the Israel of God, actually became materialized in flesh and blood.

[1] For this and what immediately follows see W. Manson, *Scottish Journal of Theology*, 1950, vol. 3.1, pp. 38 f.; and *The Way of the Cross*, 1958.
[2] Cf. O. Cullmann, *Christ and Time*, pp. 107 ff.
[3] W. Manson, *op. cit.*, p. 39.

After the resurrection and ascension the disciples understood why, again and again, Jesus had gathered the lost sheep of the House of Israel, the cultically unclean and those debarred from the Temple liturgy of sacrifice, and although it scandalized the priests He deliberately broke down the barriers erected by the cultus, and enacted in their midst a sign of the Messianic Meal, when many would come from the east and the west and sit down with Abraham, Isaac, and Jacob in the Kingdom of Heaven.[1] That eschatological meal was not an eating and drinking between holy priests and holy people, but the marriage-supper of the Lamb, who because He had come to bear their sin, gathered the poor and the outcast, the weary and the heavy laden, the publicans and sinners, and fed them with the bread of life and gave them living water to drink. The disciples remembered also the parables of the prodigal son and his feasting in the father's house, of the bridegroom and the wedding-feast, and the final judgment which would discover those who had given or not given food to the hungry and drink to the thirsty, and they understood their bearing upon the Lord's Supper as the great eschatological meal of the Kingdom of God through which that very Kingdom is realized here and now, as far as may be in the conditions of this passing world. The disciples recalled, too, those Galilean meals of fellowship with Jesus, the miraculous feeding of the multitudes by the Great Shepherd of the sheep, and the equally wonderful words He spoke about manna and water, about His flesh and blood, and the life-giving Spirit, and they knew that what had been parable and sign and miracle then had at last materialized in the Easter breaking of bread.

They saw in His death and resurrection such fulfilment of the Old Testament oracles as gave their teaching creative reinterpretation and threw a flood of light upon the mystery of the Cross. In that Jesus had died for them and risen again, He had inaugurated a new covenant within which they could sit down together and eat bread and drink wine, assured that they were one with their Lord, given to partake of His sacrifice, to share in the power of His resurrection and to be bound up with Him in the same bundle of life. The ends of the earth had already come upon them, for by this sacramental meal they tasted its powers and were given to stand with Christ on the other side of

[1] Cf. Lohmeyer, *Kultus und Evangelium*, pp. 36 f., 80, and 90 f.

the judgment, in the new creation. The incredible mystery of Baptism was become a visible reality, and the disciples continued in the breaking of bread to commune with their Lord and to proclaim His death as the power of God unto salvation.

In order to unfold more fully the significance of the Eucharist we must return to the event of the Upper Room. The apostolic records of that night make it clear that they saw converging in the institution of the Supper both the pascal and covenantal meals of the Old Testament and the messianic meals of the wilderness of Sinai and the hills of Galilee. It was charged through and through with eschatological significance. At the beginning of the meal Jesus must have followed the Jewish custom of passing round a cup of wine in token of thanksgiving to God; but before that was done, a piece of bread and a cup of wine were set aside for the Messiah in case He should suddenly come to His own in the midst of the feast. Then at the end of the meal, fully charged with pascal and covenantal significance, Jesus took the bread and wine set aside for the Messiah, and said, "This is my body broken for you. This is my blood which is shed for you." By breaking the bread and giving it to the disciples, by passing round the cup, He associated them with His sacrifice, giving their existence in relation to Himself a new form in the Kingdom of God, indeed constituting them as the Church concorporate with Himself. When the apostolic Church looked back upon that Last Supper they recalled that Jesus had bidden them do this repeatedly in remembrance of Him, proclaiming thus His death till He should come again to drink it anew with them in the Kingdom of God. St. John records, too, that the original Supper was set in the context of our Lord's high-priestly prayer in which He consecrated Himself and interceded for His Church.

There is a great deal here which we must discuss in order to elucidate its theological structure. We may begin by noting the two fundamental moments within which the Eucharist has its place: "the night on which He was betrayed", and "till He come", as St. Paul puts them. The Eucharist is therefore at once bound to history, and related to the advent of Christ at the end of history. It reaches into the past, to the death of Christ, and sets it in the present as reality operative here and now in the Church. On the other hand, the Eucharist reaches out beyond the present into the future, and becomes the means whereby the Church in the present is brought under the power of the advent of Christ. The Eucharist thus belongs to the very nature of the Church, rooting and grounding it in the historical Christ and His saving acts, and also bringing to the Church its own ultimate reality from beyond history. By the Eucharist that ultimate reality stands not only at the end of time but impinges creatively upon the Church throughout history, for it is both the *proton* and the *eschaton* of its existence. Through the Eucharist the Church becomes, so to speak, the great arch that spans history, supported by only two pillars, the Cross which stands on this side of time, and the coming of Christ in power which stands at the end of history. From age to age the Church is grounded upon these two supports by the Eucharist, so that its very being is bound up with the essential unity of the two events, the perfected event of the death and resurrection of Christ, and the future event of the *parousia*. It is because the Church receives its being ever anew, through the Eucharist, as the new creation which is yet to be revealed at the *parousia*, that it lives in dynamic tension here and now on the very frontiers of eternity.

Once again, we must return to the thought of the hypostatic union between God and Man in Jesus Christ, in order to understand this eucharistic reality clearly. We must think of that hypostatic union, however, not in the static categories of patristic thought, but in terms of biblical eschatology, that is, in dynamic categories. As the Captain of our salvation was made perfect through suffering, we must think of that holy union inserted into our flesh and blood at the virgin birth of Jesus as carried through our human life and death, through the contradictions of sin and the relativities of history, through the passion and agony of the crucifixion to its transcendent perfection in the resurrection of Jesus from the dead, so that He lives on for ever, our Mediator and Atonement, in whom all things cohere, and in whom all things in heaven and earth will be brought back to the fullness of God. It is by the Eucharist, following upon Baptism, that that union is inserted as an abiding union into the heart of our estrangement from God the Father, and into all the conflicts of history.[1] Here we are given the perfect union between the eternal and the temporal, between the divine and the human,

[1] Cf. Karl Heim, *Jesus the World's Perfecter.*

inserted into our flesh and blood, and it is that made flesh in the Eucharist which is the inner core of the Church's reality on earth. This has several implications which we must not pass over because of their bearing upon intercommunion.

(1) The enactment of this abiding union within the world's estrangement increases the tension between the new creation and the fallen world. Just as the union between God and Man became fact and reality for us once and for all through the desperate passion and agony of the crucifixion, so the Church bound to its Lord by this sacramental union can only follow Him by taking up His Cross daily. The world continues in its estrangement from God and its contradiction to Him, but that is surely why the Church is given the Sacrament of the Eucharist in addition to the Sacrament of Baptism. It is taught thereby that while in reconciliation and justification and sanctification the Church is already perfect in Christ Jesus, yet in the broken conditions of time, in the conflicts and divisions of history, so long as it waits for redemption of the purchased possession, it is unable to realize that perfection in its wholeness here and now. The Church must nevertheless reckon that it is dead to the old life and alive in the new, for that is what actually takes place in the Eucharist. That the Church is once and for all justified and perfected in Christ is enshrined in the Sacrament of Baptism, but that its justification and perfection are also prolonged in time is enshrined in the Eucharist. The perfection of the Church's union with Christ Jesus has to be carried through the conditions of time, and how it is straitened until that is accomplished! By means of the Eucharist, so to speak, the agony of Calvary is witnessed in the ages into which the Church goes out as the suffering servant in the mission of the world's redemption. And so it learns to fill up that which is eschatologically in arrears of the sufferings of Christ as it throws itself into the heart of the world's trouble and acts out there, however costly that may be, the reconciliation of the Cross.

The Church can do that only because in the heart of its life and worship there is set the Sacrament of Holy Communion in which it is united to Christ through His sacrifice, and in which also it is given to share in the triumph of the Saviour: "Be of good cheer, I have overcome the world." In the consummation of that triumph the Church will have no need of the

Eucharist,[1] but so long as it is still the Church Militant in this world, the Eucharist is both its agony and its supreme joy. Here there is the memory of the travail and agony of Calvary as well as expectation of resurrection and the new world beyond. But it is part of the Church's agony that here in the Eucharist the wholeness of its union in Christ is received only sacramentally in the brokenness of time, and the more that wholeness presses toward its complete unveiling at the *parousia* the more evident does it become that the forms of the Church's existence in this passing world are broken up in order that the abiding reality of the new creation may appear. The Sacrament of the Eucharist, then, is the form which our sacramental union with Christ takes within the brokenness and the divisions of history, and yet mediates the wholeness of that union as such an abiding reality that the brokenness and the divisions of history, in which the Church inevitably partakes, are revealed to be but the shell of the old life which passes away. The Eucharist is the sacrament which God has given to us as the counterpart of the ascension, for while He holds apart as yet the faith and sight of the Church until the *epiphaneia* or the *apocalypsis*, He also joins them to-gether, so that Christ makes Himself known in spite of the frac-tion of time. Here, as surely as the Church is given healing for its estrangement from God, it is given also healing for its divisions in history. The Eucharist speaks both of the fraction of the body on earth, evident even on the night of the Last Supper, and the "conversion" of the Church into the risen Body of Christ.

(2) The perfect union of God and Man which has broken into time in the virgin birth, and inserted into history at the Cross, is yet not held a prisoner to the relativities of time, be-cause of the resurrection. It entails a new creation which travels through time and history inasmuch as Jesus Christ lives on. Therefore, although we must communicate again and again in the real presence of this Christ-event through the Sacrament of Holy Communion, we cannot forget the reality of Baptism, that inasmuch as through Baptism the Church is once and for all in-corporated into the Body of Christ, it feeds uninterruptedly upon the flesh and blood of Christ through faith (John 6). As such the Church has eternal life abiding in it (John 15). That is

[1] Cf. Thomas Aquinas, *Summa Theol.*, III.q.61.4.

the reality which is so often misconstrued in terms of temporal repetition or continuity in the relativities of historical succession. To do so is to fall into the error of "sacramental occasionalism" and to by-pass the resurrection as the enduring reality in the heart of the Church. It is precisely because the Church lives on in the power of the resurrection that it must refuse to be imprisoned in the wrappings of by-gone history or of human systems and decisions. To give these absolute significance in its tradition means that the Church denies its ultimate reality as that which comes from beyond the relativities of history, and that it fails to realize the profound eschatological element in the Eucharist: that as often as the Church communicates in the body and blood of the crucified Saviour, it receives the judgments of the Cross upon the forms and fashions of this passing world in which the Church on earth, waiting for the redemption of the body, inevitably partakes.

The Church cannot participate in the Eucharist, and through it become the real Church, without placing itself under the impact of the *eschaton*. Whenever the Church denies that eschatological element in the Eucharist it becomes but a human Church, for then it denies that the Church transcends itself in the new creation, or rather is given to transcend its embroilment in the passing forms of this world. We must be quite clear, however, that it is because the Church is implicated through the Words and Sacraments in the ever-living continuity of the Christ-event travelling through and under the visible and historical continuities that the latter are disrupted, and will finally break up at the *parousia*.[1] The Church, which through Baptism

---

1 Cf. M. Schmaus, *Aus der Theologie der Zeit* (ed. by G. Söhngen), p. 78: "Was in der Eucharistie in der Weise des Mysteriums geschieht, wird im Leiden und im Sterben im Raume der Geschichte mächtig. Der ganze Verlauf der auf Christus folgenden Geschichte wird von ihrem Anfang und von ihrem Ende bestimmt. Am Anfang steht das Kreuz, das Zeichen des schöpferischen Untergangs. Am Ende steht der völlige Zusammenbruch der jetzigen Formen der Schöpfung sowie der neue Himmel und die neue Erde. Anfang und Ende wirken in jede Gegenwart herein. Vom Anfang und vom Ende empfängt jede Gegenwart immerfort Stösse, die ihr kein Leben in ungestörter Ruhe und Sicherheit gestatten. Unsicherheit und Ungeborgenheit gehören wesentlich zu der Welt, die im Zeichen des Kreuzes und im Zeichen des neuen Himmels und der neuen Erde steht. Die jetzigen Weltformen haben keine ewige Verheissung. Es ist vielmehr gesagt, dass sie einmal völlig zusammembrechen werden."

has been planted into the dying and rising of Jesus and initiated into the new order, must learn to put off the old as often as through the Eucharist it participates in its new being. That is partly why apocalyptic is an inner necessity for faith and the sacramental life of the Church, for apocalypse is the fulfilment of history against itself, and apocalyptic images indicate the contradiction between the form and order of the Kingdom of God and the form and order of all earthly institutions. The very fact that in the Eucharist the Church is confronted with its own ultimate reality breaking into history from beyond history, a reality inexpressible in terms of history alone, reveals to the Church that it is also an earthly institution, but that it cannot perpetuate this historical form and order as essentially divine or as belonging to the *esse* of the Church, without either denying altogether or presumptuously anticipating the ultimate eschatological judgment. Inasmuch as by His ascension Jesus Christ has withdrawn from history His visible face and form, the true face and the true form of the Church remain essentially a *mysterion*. To deny that is to deny the essentially sacramental character of the Church's ministry, and to resolve it into a mere worldly institution.

We must now turn to another aspect of the Lord's Supper which requires elucidation, that concerned in the words: "do this in remembrance of me", and "ye proclaim the Lord's death till he come". These words have received a great deal of discussion in recent literature which it is not possible to go into here. It would seem, however, that memory must be understood as *anamnesis* both before God and before man, and that *proclamation* is *objective proclamation* both before God and before man. These involve each other (cf. Mark 14: 9), though we shall have to discuss first one and then the other. The fundamental fact, however, that helps to clear up many difficulties is that memory and proclamation are here set in a sacramental context and must be interpreted accordingly if they are to elucidate the theology of the Eucharist. We are concerned here, then, with sacramental *memory* which, as Zwingli insisted, is more than "historical faith". It was at that Last Supper that Jesus also said: "The Comforter, who is the Holy Ghost, whom the Father will send in my name, he shall teach you all things, and bring all things to your remembrance, whatsoever I have said unto you." That helps us to understand. Memory that is sacramental has two sides to it (we recall again the Chalcedonian formula about the two natures of Christ) which cannot be fused or separated. It is at once the action of the historical Church for which Christ died, and the action of the eternal Spirit through whom Christ offered Himself without spot to God. The *anamnesis* is both historical and eternal, and in sacramental *anamnesis* they involve each other. The Church's memory of the historical death and resurrection of Christ in itself is merely memory of the historical past, but through the eternal Spirit by whom Christ offered Himself a sacrifice it becomes such *anamnesis* that the past is made a present reality. The eternal Spirit glorifies Christ, who died and rose again and now sits at the right hand of God, and so shows the Church things to come that He makes the Church to sit together with Christ in heavenly places. The Holy Spirit does not speak of Himself but listens to Christ who ever lives to make intercession for us, and what He hears He *echoes* in the *anamnesis* of the Church.

To the Church on earth, then, it is given in its eucharistic worship to *echo* the eternal intercession of Christ. The action of the Church is the *anamnesis* of an act that is once and for all, and enduring before the Face of the Heavenly Father; but it is no more than *anamnesis*, for it is not the act itself. It is the living echo of that act which Christ alone performs as Mediator and Saviour, "the splintered reflection on earth of Christ's presentation of His sacrifice in heaven".[1] In the sacramental *anamnesis* the Church is raised by the eternal Spirit to the throne of God, made unto Him a kingdom and a priesthood, saying, "Amen: Blessing and glory and wisdom and thanksgiving and honour and power and might be unto our God for ever and ever. Amen." The Eucharist is the *Amen*, the counterpart on earth, to the eternal oblation in heaven, and the eucharistic thanksgiving the counterpoint on earth to the new song, "Worthy is the Lamb", of the saints in the Church triumphant.

We must go on to add that the *anamnesis* of Christ's atoning death and its eternal power includes eucharistic intercession. How could the sacramental memory of His sacrifice be anything

---

[1] D. M. Mackinnon, *Report of the Sixth Anglo-Catholic Congress*, p. 134. I have borrowed from Prof. Mackinnon his use of the word *echo* in this context.

other than prayer, the prayer that has nothing to bring but clings to the Cross of Christ and holds it up before the Father, the prayer that has nothing to offer but pleads the merits of the Saviour's oblation, the prayer that knows not how to pray, but is energized by the eternal Spirit who Himself makes intercession for us with groanings that cannot be uttered? And what can His intercession be but the echoing in the Church of the intercession of the great High Priest? And so through the *anamnesis* the Church enters into the passion of the Redeemer, and in His name travails in prayer for all mankind. We know not what to pray for as we ought, but the Spirit helps our infirmities, and through the same eternal Spirit by whom Christ offered Himself to God, we may offer our intercessions, on the merits of His sacrifice alone. And where even two or three are thus gathered together in His name, the Lord is in the midst of them. When the veil is lifted, and the mystery of that intercession is revealed, we read: "An angel came and stood at the altar, having a golden censer; and there was given unto him much incense, that he should offer it with the prayers of all the saints upon the golden altar which was before the throne. And the smoke of the incense, which came with the prayers of the saints, ascended up before God out of the angel's hand." *Anamnesis* before God. And so the early Church prayed at the Eucharist: "Remember, Lord, Thy Church" (Did. 10: 5).[1]

When we turn to the eucharistic *proclamation* of the sacrificial death of Jesus, we find the same sacramental character that we found in the *anamnesis*. That was already apparent in the *kerygma*, where the missionary preaching of the Church was sacramentally contrapuntal to the continuing work of the risen Lord, but here we have the same *kerygma* as it is intertwined with the continuing being of the Church. Here it is *objective proclamation* in the life and action of the Church on earth, which corresponds sacramentally to the eternal action of the Lamb slain before the foundation of the world and to His eternal destination of the Church as the Bride for the future marriage-supper of the Lamb. It is more than parable; it is the actual *homoioma* of the Christ-event, in which the faith of the

[1] Cf. J. Jeremias, *The Journal of Theological Studies*, January–April 1949, p. 9.

Church has to do not only with its objective ground but with its *objective duration*.[1] This eucharistic proclamation enshrines therefore as its eternal *canto firmo* the Self-consecration of the Lamb of God, the Self-presentation of the Mediator before the face of the Father in His intercession for the Church, but that is the *mysterion* which is the dimension in infinite depth behind the action of the Church in the Lord's Supper.

The Church's proclamation is not itself identical with that mystery, but it cannot be separated from it. It is sacramentally and analogically derivative from it, but as such it is analogically different. There in heaven is the ascended Lamb Himself ever before the Face of the Father; here on earth is the waiting Church of sinners, with all saints, showing forth His death and pleading His sacrifice—"Lamb of God that takest away the sins of the world, have mercy upon us"—but both are united in the *koinonia* of the eternal Spirit, through whom Christ offered Himself to the Father, and through whom we are given to participate in that oblation made on our behalf. That is the profound mystery of Holy Communion, that the Church is given to participate (*koinonein*) in Christ's substitutionary Self-consecration ("For their sakes I sanctify myself that they also might be sanctified through the truth"), as it communicates in His body and blood, proclaiming His death until He come.

"Till He come", however, reminds us that participation in His substitutionary oblation is essentially eschatological. At last the eucharistic rite, with all its wonderful liturgy, will pass away with the passing form of this world, for it will be displaced by the marriage-supper of the Lamb. But in so far as that real presence of Christ in the Eucharist is the real presence of the *Eschatos*, that future Supper in the Kingdom of God interpenetrates the present action of the Church, so that here and now the Eucharist enshrines an essential displacement of the action of the Church by the action of Christ. It is the Risen Lord Himself who is the true Celebrant at the holy table, and unless that eschatological substitution, the *mirifica commutatio*, as Calvin called it,[2] is recognized, the eucharistic sacrifice becomes but a pagan ceremony. No doubt the Church's *re-actio* to the sacrificial

[1] Cf. Karl Barth, *Die christliche Lehre nach dem Heidelberger Katechismus*, p. 99.
[2] *Inst.* 4. 17. 2, 4.

actio of Christ itself partakes of sacrificial character, but if *re-actio* is identified with the *actio*, the Sacrament is destroyed, because its derivative sacramental and analogical nature is denied. Just as the once-and-for-all sacrifice of Christ entailed the rending of the veil and the ultimate destruction of the Temple, and the undermining of its liturgical validity, so the consummation of Christ's action in the marriage-supper of the Lamb sets aside the eucharistic liturgy in which now we see through a glass darkly, for then we shall see face to face. "And I saw no temple therein," said St. John of the New Jerusalem, "for the Lord God Almighty and the Lamb are the temple of it." But in so far as that future marriage-supper of the Lamb is already present eschatologically in the Eucharist, the liturgical *re-actio* of the Eucharist is displaced by the immediate *actio* of Christ Himself, as the reality which the liturgy had proclaimed. Thus there is a "point" in the celebration of every Eucharist in which the real presence of the *Eschatos* suspends the liturgical action, and makes it point beyond itself for validity and order. The Son of Man is Lord also of the Eucharist, and He dispenses it as He wills. In such an eschatological economy the sacrifice of the Church can only participate in the Sacrifice of Christ by *mirifica commutatio*, and all order and liturgy have validity and truth only in so far as they leave room for such eschatological substitution. Where that is not so the Lord insists on cleansing His Temple.

That is why the life and being of the Church are intertwined with eucharistic proclamation, for the presence of the living Lord in the Church, which is the very essence of the Church, is not a static presence, but is the living action appropriated by the Church in its continuous action of proclamation.[1] In such proclamation the Church declares that its anchor is cast within the veil, that its being is grounded beyond itself in the ascended Lord, that its real life is a divine gift, and by such proclamation it opens the door in the Church for the incoming of that ultimate reality from beyond ("If any man open the door I will come in and sup with him and he with me"). And so the proclamation includes the *Maranatha* as an essential element in its liturgical action.

It is clear, therefore, that the bringing of the Eucharist under

---

[1] This is brought out with great power in K. Barth's pamphlet, *Die Botschaft von der freien Gnade Gottes*.

the rubric of proclamation excludes the idea of its being a sacrifice in itself or in its own right. Not the actual and literal offering of the sacrifice, but an action proclaiming a sacrifice once offered and eternally valid before the Father is what the Eucharist effects. In other words, by such proclamation the Eucharist becomes the sacramental counterpart to the unique sacrifice of Christ, and therefore in its own way, inasmuch as it echoes that, and is derivative from it, a sacramental sacrifice. It is thus that in the Eucharist the Church continually sets before itself and appropriates, by the power of the Spirit, the atoning sacrifice of Christ "through the eternal Spirit", because through the Spirit the proclaiming activity of the living Lord stands behind the Church's proclamation, as His intercession stands behind its *anamnesis*, so that it is really Christ in the Eucharist who represents to the Church and makes effective for the Church His own atoning deed of sacrifice.

The eucharistic proclamation, then, points to the *divine action* as the heart of it all. We may bring our best to the sacrifice, as Abraham brought his beloved Isaac, but at last God Himself provides a sacrifice in the place of Isaac, in His only-begotten and well-beloved Son, for the atoning deed is His and His alone, though it is wrought on our behalf. That is the very heart of proclamation and atonement, and it is from there that the significance of eucharistic sacrifice is determined.[1] This crucial point is too often missed by theologians of the "Catholic" type, for again and again they are found using "sacrifice" and "offering" univocally of God and the Church. That is even true of de la Taille, although he can write nobly of this fact. "Our sacrifices and that of Christ do not exist as members of one and the same genus, in the strict sense, in which the word sacrifice, used of our sacrifices and of His, would be a univocal term, but they are only in the same order by way of analogy. His sacrifice being the principle, and ours being subordinate to it. . . . Just as Christ on earth absolutely and simply offered only one sacrifice, so the duality which exists between His sacrifice and ours must

[1] It is essentially false procedure therefore to interpret the atonement from the point of view of a theology of the Eucharist, which is itself drawn from an idea of sacrifice which has not been given creative reinterpretation in Christ, rather than to interpret the Eucharist from the point of view of a true and N.T. doctrine of atonement.

be made such as not to imply any repeated sacrificial offering made by Christ, but such as to subordinate immediately our own sacrificial activity to the offering of the sacrifice made by Christ in the past, which continues for ever by its own efficacy."[1] What is it then that differentiates Christ's unique sacrifice and puts such a holy distance between it and anything that we may do even in His name? Surely that Christ bore God's judgment upon man's sin, that He did that alone on our behalf, and further, that He wrought out that atonement not only as Man but as God-Man, as God in Man.

It belongs to the essence of atonement that Christ bore man's judgment, the judgment of God upon man's sin.[2] In the Cross, God identifies Himself with man just where he is farthest from Him, that is, just where he stands under the divine judgment. Such a deed of atonement whose essence is the bearing of divine judgment cannot be prolonged in a ceremonial cultus. It can only be proclaimed and celebrated. That which distinguishes Christ's atoning sacrifice from the Church's sacrifice is the bearing of judgment. We must distinguish, then, between the propitiatory sacrifice and the eucharistic sacrifice,[3] realizing that the heart of Christ's unique sacrifice, the bearing of judgment, cannot be repeated in the latter in any sense. Its value lies mainly in its being a sign pointing to the divine action of atonement, and in its being entirely subordinate to that.

The atonement, however, was more than the bearing of the divine judgment. It was the offering to God of a perfect holiness, a holiness corresponding to that of God Himself, the holiness of perfect obedience. Both in bearing the divine judgment and in offering a perfect obedience, Jesus Christ stood absolutely alone, acting on our behalf. What we could not do, He has done for us. It was a substitutionary atonement. As the sacramental counterpart to that, the eucharistic sacrifice has not to do ultimately with our offering, but with Christ's offering on our behalf, His putting of Himself in our place, and taking upon Himself our judgment. "All that constituted atonement was wrought in our place and in our stead; wrought verily in *our* place, that is,

1 *The Mystery of Faith* (English trans.), Vol. II, pp. 24 f.
2 The following is indebted to an Anglican theologian, the late Dr. F. W. Camfield. Cf. *Scottish Journal of Theology*, 1948, vol. I, I, pp. 282 ff.
3 Cf. John Calvin, *Institutes*, 4.18.12 f.

wrought *for* us and *as our act*."[1] The eucharistic sacrifice answers
to that *as our act*, and involves the acceptance of Him as the One
who has taken our place, the acceptance of His Self-offering as
our offering to God. But in the nature of the case the eucharistic
sacrifice must be entirely analogous in character to the substitutionary act of Christ, and involves its wondrous exchange.
It might be called the counter-sacrifice of the Church, but never
can it be said to be of the same genus as the unique sacrifice of
Christ Himself. By participation in His body and blood He gives
us to be associated with His sacrifice, but in such a way, as in the
Garden of Gethsemane, that He removes Himself to a holy
distance from us. We may indeed watch with Him, but in the
awful hour of His agony we know that He dies alone and we are
found among those who crucified Him.

What makes Christ's sacrifice absolutely unique is the identity
between the Offerer and the Offering and Him to whom the
Offering is made. In this connection the Reformers were fond of
citing the famous words of the great Augustine: "Since in a
sacrifice four things are considered, viz., to whom it is offered,
by whom, what and for whom, the same one true Mediator,
reconciling us to God by the sacrifice of peace, remains one with
Him to whom He offered, made Himself one with those for
whom He offered, is Himself the One who offered, and the one
thing which He offered."[2] It is that identity which sets His
sacrifice absolutely apart from anything else, and makes it quite
clear that the eucharistic sacrifice is only the *anamnesis* or *proclamation* of that lonely sacrifice, and does not involve any
identity between a sacrifice of our own and His.

It is quite certain, however, that such a unique sacrifice in-
vokes from us a corresponding sacrifice of thanksgiving and
praise, in which we turn our proclamation of Christ's death up-
wards to God, and not only plead the merits of Christ's sacrifice
alone, but offer Him all that we have and are. How can we
answer His grace except by offering ourselves up in obedience
and thanksgiving? We know that we are unworthy, and can
only offer Him our unworthiness, that He may make us worthy.
But the worthiness which He enjoins "consists especially in
faith, which places all things in Christ, nothing in ourselves, and

---

[1] F. W. Camfield, *op. cit.*, p. 292.
[2] *De Trinitate*, 4.24; cf. Calvin, *Inst.*, 4.18.10.

in love, love which, though imperfect, it may be sufficient to offer to God, that He may increase it since it cannot be fully rendered."[1] Thus all our sacrifices of praise, prayer and thanksgiving "depend on the greater sacrifice with which we dedicate ourselves, soul and body, to be a holy temple to the Lord. . . . We do not appear with our gifts in the presence of God without an intercessor. Christ is our Mediator, by whose intervention we offer ourselves and our all to the Father; He is our High Priest, who, having entered into the upper sanctuary, opens up an access for us: He the altar on which we lay our gifts, that whatever we do attempt, we may attempt in Him. He it is who 'hath made us kings and priests unto God and His Father'."[2]

There is a way, however, of speaking too easily about the bringing of our offerings in the Eucharist, about bringing the fruit of our labour as represented by the bread and wine, which savours rather much of the sacrifice of Cain. And then it is said that this offering and sacrifice of ours when laid on God's altar becomes identified with, and identical with, the sacrifice of Christ and we do verily offer Christ to God. Surely this *identity* involves an entire displacement of the centre of gravity, for after all, what the Eucharist proclaims is not our offering but Christ's offering on our behalf, which only in that derivative way becomes our offering. The denial of Christ's substitutionary act at this point for some doctrine of identity would mean an undermining of the atoning work of Christ. It is precisely this doctrine of identity between the bread and wine of the Eucharist with the glorified Body in the heavenly places, identity between the action of the Church on earth as it celebrates the sacrifice of Christ, and the perpetual Self-Offering of Christ Himself before the Face of the Father, which the theology of the Eucharist cannot allow, for that entails its destruction as a sacrament.[3]

Behind all this there is something deeper, an essentially Pelagian doctrine of the atonement, and certainly on a Pelagian view any substitutionary notion is impossible and abhorrent. How can Holy God allow one man to die for another, and judge the innocent man for the guilty? The doctrine of the atonement is impossible unless it is the doctrine of the divine action, of God

---

[1] Calvin, *Inst.*, 4.17.42.   [2] Calvin, *Inst.*, 4.18.16 f.
[3] Cf. Karl Barth, *Die christliche Lehre nach dem Heidelberger Katechismus*, p. 104.

Himself coming to intervene and to save. God indeed became man and translated divine action into terms of human action. "Thus the background of the atoning deed is not the Godhead *per se*, but the God-manhood of Christ. But if that be so, then the idea of substitution is inevitable, and is constitutive of the doctrine of Atonement. . . . What we could not accomplish Christ accomplished on our behalf. The infliction and judgment which we could not bear, He bore for us. He took our place and on behalf of us all He made satisfaction for our sins and for the sins of the whole world. It was not the Godhead *qua* Godhead that atoned; it was the God-manhood. And that means, not simply God *in* man, but God *as* man. The manhood was integral and essential and not merely instrumental. And that means in the acutest sense, substitution."[1]

There are, accordingly, false ways of speaking of the eucharistic sacrifice as that which invests the deed of Christ with its sacrificial nature or validity, or as that which continually presents the sacrifice of Christ to the Father. We have seen the element of truth that lies behind such views, but we must beware of stating this in such a way as to involve a Pelagian view of the atonement as though it were not altogether a divine act.[2] A great deal of the horror of the Reformers for the doctrine of the Mass was recoil from its faulty soteriology, and its Pelagian notion of man, even if he were the Man Jesus, appeasing God. Once it is clearly seen, however, that the atonement is God's act, and that He bears in Himself our judgment, that He does in Jesus what we cannot do, then the false doctrine of identity falls to the ground, and a true doctrine of eucharistic sacrifice can be enunciated, and a true doctrine of proclamation in which the Church can share in the atoning and victorious action of Christ.[3]

We must now turn to yet another aspect of the Lord's Supper, to the words "This is my body broken for you. This is my blood

[1] F. W. Camfield, *op. cit.*, p. 292.
[2] This was evidently in the mind of D. M. Mackinnon, *op. cit.*, p. 134, when he corrects his own statement: "We consecrate the death of Christ as a sacrifice, or rather, participate in the act whereby He consecrates His Passion as the recreation of the world in Him."
[3] A crude doctrine of identity can lead to terrible extremes, as when some people insist that in the Eucharist we must will the death that we have caused. That is to turn the eucharistic sacrifice into murder.

shed for you." There can be little doubt, as Calvin used to say,[1] that "almost the whole energy of the sacrament consists in these words". The impartial exegete cannot but conclude that it was upon these verbs that Jesus Himself laid the emphasis, that here it was intended not only that by these elements the crucifixion should evidently be set before our eyes, but that the stress should be laid upon the taking and eating and drinking, that is, in communicating in the body and blood of Christ. It is a sign of serious disorder in the Church's Eucharist when Jesus' own emphasis upon our communicating by eating and drinking His body and blood is overshadowed by a disproportionate emphasis upon the Church's sacrifice. The *Summa Theologica* of St. Thomas Aquinas is surely right when it gives the space for only one *Question* to the idea of sacrifice, and some twenty to communion in the real presence of Christ. Though the Last Supper was in point of historical time prior to the Cross, it was clearly designed, as the emphasis upon *broken* body and shed *blood* made clear, to take place as the meal following the completion of the perfect sacrifice once-and-for-all enacted on the Cross. No elaboration of exegesis upon the Old Testament can alter the fact that the sacrificial meals of the Old Testament did not repeat the act of oblation, but were the means by which the benefits of the sacrifice were conveyed.[2] The corresponding emphasis here in the eucharistic communion is the Church's thankful participation in so great salvation and its unrestrained joy (*agalliasis*) in the real presence of the risen Lord.

We can only look at the Lord's Supper through the eyes of the apostles who were eye-witnesses of the resurrection, and who recalled that again and again when they were breaking bread the risen Jesus chose suddenly to come into their midst. Those Easter meals gave them their understanding of the rite in the Upper Room. Recalling again the union between the deity and humanity of Christ, and the nature of the sacramental union grounded upon that, we must understand the Lord's Supper in similar terms. There is then, on the one hand, the historical enactment of the rite which the Church is commanded to repeat in accordance with our Lord's institution, handed on to us by the

---

[1] *Inst.*, 4.17.3.
[2] Cf. Markus Barth, *Das Abendmahl——Passamahl, Bundesmahl u. Messiasmahl*, p. 25.

Synoptic Gospels and St. Paul. On the other hand there are the resurrection events, such as that recorded by St. Luke of the two disciples at Emmaus to whom Jesus was made known in the breaking of bread, or that recorded in the Fourth Gospel, when "Jesus came and stood in the midst, and saith unto them, Peace be unto you. And when he had so said, he shewed unto them his hands and his side. Then were the disciples glad when they saw the Lord. Then said Jesus unto them again, Peace be unto you: as my Father hath sent me, so send I you. And when he had said this, he breathed on them, and saith unto them, Receive ye the Holy Ghost: whosoever sins ye remit, they are remitted unto them; and whosoever sins ye retain, they are retained."

The Last Supper and those resurrection appearances belong together in one sacramental whole. Though Jesus has withdrawn His visible presence from us, there is such an intervention by the risen Lord as the invisible reality behind each celebration of the Lord's Supper. Jesus Christ is as really present in the Eucharist as He was on that Easter day to His disciples. As surely as in the Eucharist we handle bread and wine, we put our fingers into His wounds and He breathes upon us His peace and forgiveness in answer to the prayer: "Lamb of God who takest away the sins of the world, grant us thy peace." The Eucharist then is the sacramental enactment of the real presence of Christ. It is the historical action of the Church in which the historical passion of the Saviour is vividly exhibited before our eyes, but we must go on to say, with Calvin, that "what the minister figures and attests by outward action, God performs inwardly".[1]

When we say, however, that the Eucharist is the sacramental enactment of the real presence of Christ, we must make clear that it is the real presence of the God-Man. No doubt it is through the eternal Spirit, through an act issuing from the Godhead, but it is the divine enactment of the Incarnate Presence in the Church. Our Lord was not only the bearer of the divine Word of forgiveness, but He enacted that Word in our flesh and blood, the flesh and blood which He had made His own from the Virgin Mary. We may go on to say that on the ground of that supreme action, the mystery of the incarnation and the crucifixion is sacramentally "re-enacted" in those who have been baptized into Christ. When we turn to our Lord's teaching

[1] *Inst.*, 4.14.17.

as recorded in the Fourth Gospel, in His discourse on the bread of life, we find that there is an eating of the flesh and a drinking of the blood of Christ before eucharistic participation. But how could it be otherwise inasmuch as the Word was made flesh, for His words are Spirit and Life? The union of the baptized with Christ through the Word involves also a continual feeding upon the flesh and blood of Christ.[1] He who is sacramentally incorporated into the body of Christ is already participant in sacramental communion. We must allow ourselves to be reminded therefore that the Eucharist presupposes baptismal incorporation, presupposes the Church as the Body of Christ and that faith brings to the Eucharist a continuous feeding upon the body and blood of Christ. What are we then to say of eucharistic communion? Surely, as Calvin has made so clear in the Reformed Church, that while we can only eat and drink the body and blood of Christ through faith, yet, by the power of the eternal Spirit, the Church is given through the Eucharist a *relation in being* to Christ, beyond its relation to Him through faith.

Calvin was fond of discussing this matter with reference to the words of the Epistle to the Ephesians: "That Christ may dwell in your hearts by faith, that ye being rooted and grounded in love may be able to comprehend with all saints what is the breadth, and length, and depth, and height; and to know the love of Christ, which passeth knowledge, that ye might be filled with all the fullness of God" (3: 17 f.). Christ dwells in our hearts by faith, but His dwelling in our hearts is an ontological relation not identical with faith, though through faith. So we may say that in the Eucharist believing and actual communication through the bread and wine are not one and the same thing.[2] There can be no doubt that as yet we walk by faith and not by sight, nevertheless the significance of eucharistic communion lies in the fact that by the act of the eternal Spirit the believing Church is given to step over the eschatological boundary, and to partake of the divine

---

[1] Calvin's *Commentary on John*, 6.35, 53; *Inst.*, 4.17.5. Cf. 4.17.30: "A perpetual connection with Christ could not exist unless He dwells in us *corporeally*, independently of the use of the Supper."

[2] See, for example, *Inst.* 4.17.5. Cf. W. Niesel, *Calvins Lehre vom Abendmahl*, p. 38.

nature. As faith and hope pass away, while love endures as the eternal reality, so here already through the Eucharist relation in being in the love of God follows from faith and hope.[1]

We must pause to say that there is an infinite mystery here which completely transcends the ability of our minds to grasp, a mystery that is more to be adored than discussed. Wise indeed were the Chalcedonian fathers who formulated the *unio hypostatica* only in negatives, and wise are they who likewise are content to adore the mystery in the Eucharist without explanations of how the *unio sacramentalis* actually takes place. The Reformed Church standing upon the Chalcedonian Christology repudiates both Nestorianism and Eutychianism in its doctrine of the sacramental union, denying that there is either separation or fusion between the elements of bread and wine and the reality of the body and blood of Christ.[2] Just as the humanity of Christ remains true humanity even after the resurrection and ascension and is no docetic phantasm, so the bread and wine remain true bread and wine and are no mere species,[3] though by consecration they are converted into instruments of the real presence.[4] Through the consecrated elements the Church partakes of the very body and blood of Christ, and there is enacted a *true and substantial union*,[5] an ontological union, between Christ and His Church. Christ has become bone of our bone and flesh of our flesh, but in the Eucharist we become bone of His bone and flesh of His flesh. No union, save that of the Persons of the Holy

[1] Cf. W. Niesel, *op. cit.*, p. 95: "Die eschatologische Grenze wird durch die Tat des heiligen Geistes überschritten, und aus dem Glauben folgt ein Sein in Christus." Cf. also E. Walter, *Das Kommen des Herrn*, Vol. I, pp. 38 ff.

[2] This was the position taken up by Zwingli against Luther, by Calvin against both Romanists and extreme Lutherans, and by Peter Martyr in his notable controversy with the Bishop of Winchester at Oxford. It passed into Anglican theology and became a feature of the Caroline divines.

[3] Calvin argued that the doctrine of transubstantiation involved docetic heresy, for it undermined the analogy between the elements and the reality which they figured. "The analogy between the sign and the thing signified cannot be destroyed without destroying the truth of the sacrament." *Inst.*, 4.

[4] For a clear statement on the conversion of the elements see *The Mystery of the Lord's Supper, Sermons on the Sacrament* by Robert Bruce (edit., 1958), pp. 114 f. Cf. Calvin, *Inst.*, 4.17.14.

[5] This was Calvin's usual way of stating the nature of the union.

Trinity, could be closer, without passing into absolute identity, than that between Christ and His Church as enacted in the Holy Eucharist.

It is in the Eucharist, then, that the Church really becomes the Church, both as the ontological and eschatological reality and as the extension into history of the visible sacramental fact which is the Church's existence on earth. It is both the filling of the Church with its divine mystery, and the manifestation of that mystery within history without its ceasing to be mystery. In no sense can the Church be said to be an extension of the incarnation, though here we have to do with the re-enactment by the Word of its becoming flesh. The Eucharist, therefore, together with Baptism, involves the mystery of the incarnation, the virgin birth and the resurrection of Christ. The virgin birth and the resurrection were the miraculous signs through which the divine Word both entered history in Self-revelation, and yet ever remained identical with Himself. Parallel to that, Baptism and the Eucharist are the miraculous signs through which the divine Word enters into the Church it has called out of the world, in Self-impartation, and yet ever remains identical with Himself. Baptism and Eucharist as one Sacrament are analogically related in the Holy Spirit to the virgin birth and the resurrection as the one act of divine Self-revelation. Virgin birth and resurrection, however, involved more than Self-revelation; they involved the actual descent of the Son of God into our humanity, and the actual ascent of the Son of God in ascension bearing with Him our humanity. Likewise in the Eucharist there takes place an actual *katabasis* of the living Lord, and an actual *anabasis* in which He bears the Church up with Him to the throne of God—whether "in the body or out of the body", who can tell? But it is an eschatological anticipation both of the Advent of the Son of Man and the rapture of the Church. The Eucharist involves at its very heart the *sursum corda*, for our union with Christ in history and yet out of history is a reality that utterly transcends all our categories of space and time.

The incomprehensible fact is that God begins eternally with Himself. The Son is begotten, not made. And the ineffable mystery of the Eucharist is that in it God begins with Himself in the continuity of the Church's action in the creaturely world, but independent of it.[1] That has supreme importance for what follows in our next section, for it means that the Church through its ministry can no more exercise its authority over the Eucharist than Joseph could exercise his authority over the virgin birth. As Joseph could only stand aside at the miracle of the incarnation, so the ministry of the Church can only stand aside even in the Eucharist where it is ordained to serve. The Church can never manage the Eucharist or exercise any lordship over it unless it wishes to be like the kings of the Gentiles that exercise lordship and authority over them and are called benefactors. At the Last Supper Jesus took pains to make that clear, enacting a vivid parable before the disciples in washing their feet that they might learn to forswear all lordship. The Kingdom appointed to the Church and its ministry at the Eucharist is grounded on the abasement of Christ unto death, and is one of service (*diakonia*). The Church is joined to its Lord at the Eucharist only as a body is joined to its head. The Eucharist means the enactment of the authority of Christ the Head over the Church and over its ministry. *Ecce ancilla Domini.* Inasmuch as the mystery of the virgin birth is sacramentally present in the Eucharist, it belongs to the Church in the Eucharist humbly to *receive* (*Take ye, eat ye*) the eternal Word as the ground of the Church's being, and to be entirely subordinate to Him as Word.[2]

Further, inasmuch as the mystery of the Resurrection is sacramentally present in the Eucharist, it belongs to the Church in the Eucharist to acknowledge that its outward historical form which partakes of the fashion of this passing world is made the empty tomb out of which the new creation is raised up to enter the Kingdom of God. This means that at every true Eucharist, where there is a sacramental enactment of the mystery of the virgin birth and the resurrection of the body, there is involved an eschatological suspension of historical continuity and the order and authority which that involves.

[1] See the superb discussion by Karl Barth, *Dogmatik*, I, 2. pp. 187 ff., *Das Wunder der Weinacht*, to which I am much indebted. (E. T. pp. 172 ff.)

[2] Cf. Edmund Schlink, *The Student World*, 1950, I, p. 48: "The Church is the place, the creation and the instrument of the Lord's Supper but never its Lord. On the other hand, we find degeneration where the Church departs from its function as receiver and server of the Lord's Supper and makes itself lord of the Lord's Supper."

III

Intercommunion and Order

We must now draw the foregoing discussion to a close by working out its implications in regard to intercommunion. We may begin by recalling an incident which all three Synoptic Gospels record, the objection by the priests and scribes to our Lord's cleansing of the Temple (or reformation of the Church), and to His practice of teaching in the Temple against the priestly order. They came to Jesus and asked Him: "By what authority doest thou these things? And who gave thee this authority to do these things?" Our Lord answered first by reference to Baptism and then by a telling parable which the priests and scribes recognized as directed against the priestly and legal mind. Jesus was undoubtedly referring to cleansing before sacrifice, and to the eschatological preaching of John that the axe is laid to the root of the tree. He indicated further that one cannot ask questions about the highest authority, for that is to misconceive it—and it is upon that misconception that all rigid doctrine of orders is based.

But may we not allow His words to remind us of something else, that the authority for Reformation and the administration of the Eucharist, even against the priestly and legal notion of validity in the idea of episcopal succession, is derived from Holy Baptism? If Baptism means actual incorporation into the Body of Christ, and already means through the Word a continuous feeding upon the flesh and blood of Christ, as our Lord stated so clearly in the Fourth Gospel, who are we to deny those so baptized renewal of their incorporation in the Body of Christ, provided that they are sincere? Baptism reminds us that Christ dwells in us corporeally, independently of the Supper, for otherwise absolute continuity there could not be. Baptism reminds us that the real continuity of the Body of Christ is not to be sought on the plane of historical relativity but in the continuous act of God, which in the Resurrection is continuous temporal fact. Therefore to refuse the Eucharist to those baptized into Christ Jesus and incorporated into His resurrection-body amounts either to a denial of the transcendent reality of holy Baptism or to attempted schism within the Body of Christ. How can we hold apart the Body of Christ from the Body of Christ? How can we hold apart the once-and-for-all incorporation into that Body and its continual renewal in the Holy Eucharist? Surely a clear and high doctrine of Holy Baptism forbids us to allow any wedge to be driven between Baptism and Eucharist. If Baptism is of the living God, then who can deny those baptized the right to partake of the Eucharist? If Baptism is of men, then we disinherit the masses of common people.

We must turn to another incident, however, to see more clearly into this question of authority—to the encounter between our Lord and the Pharisees over the Sabbath-breaking of the disciples, also recorded by all the Synoptic Gospels. It is the incident in which Jesus declared: "The sabbath is made for man, and not man for the sabbath; therefore the Son of Man is Lord also of the sabbath." The context speaks about Jesus' eating and drinking with publicans and sinners, which as we have seen was an enactment of the messianic meal; then it speaks about the coming and going of the Bridegroom, the new wine of the Kingdom of God which always breaks old bottles when poured into them, and the action of Abiathar who did not refuse to give to outcast David and his hungering friends the holy bread that was reserved by sacred law for priests alone. It is in such a significant context that these words about the authority of the Son of Man are recorded. In the presence of the Son of Man the barriers to intercommunion are thrown down, the new wine of the Kingdom breaks the old bottles, the sacred bread from the altar is distributed to the hungry, and publicans and sinners are freely invited to eat and drink with the Lord. The Son of Man is therefore Lord of the Sabbath and all that it stands for, the Lord of the cult, the Lord of the sacred bread.

It is in entire keeping for us in the Christian age to say, following our Lord: "The Eucharist was made for man, and not man for the Eucharist. Therefore the Son of Man is Lord also of the Eucharist." That is to say, the Son of Man reserves the right to dispense His own Supper to whom He will, and to distribute the holy bread to the outcasts and the hungry, in spite of all priestly protestations. In the presence of the eschatological Christ, the Son of Man, all barriers to intercommunion are broken down. So it will certainly be when the Bridegroom comes, and the marriage-supper of the Lamb takes place. But in as much as there is the real presence of the *Eschatos*, of the Son of Man, in the Eucharist, the new wine which we drink in the Kingdom of God breaks down the old vessels and spills over freely to all who hunger and thirst after righteousness. So soon as we realize that the Eucharist is charged with the real presence of the Son of Man, to whom all judgment has been committed, we realize that it is the Lord's Supper (*Kyriakon deipnon*) and not our own (*idion deipnon*) and that we cannot send any Church or any sincere baptized believer away, without sinning against the majesty and grace of the Son of Man.

That does not mean that the Church is prohibited from "fencing the Table", by excluding from participation in the Eucharist the lapsed who have denied their Baptism or the impenitent and insincere, but it does mean that the Church must exercise its discipline *with the authority of the Son of Man,* and not with the authority of priests and scribes and Pharisees. It is by the Word that the Son of Man exercises His authority, and by the Word that He judges and divides between men. "Lord, how wilt thou manifest thyself unto us and not unto the world? Jesus answered and said, If a man love me he will keep my word and my Father will love him, and we will come unto him and make our abode with Him." "If any man hear my voice and open the door I will come in and sup with him and he with me." On the other hand, Jesus says also: "If any man hear my words and believe not, I judge him not: for I came not to judge the world but to save the world. He that rejecteth me and receiveth not my words, hath one that judgeth him: the word that I have spoken, the same shall judge him in the last day." It is with just such judgment, said St. Paul, that the discernment of the Lord's Body in the Eucharist is concerned. In other words, the real fencing of the holy Table is lodged in the prophetic ministry through which the holy Majesty and Grace of the Son of Man are brought to bear upon the Church. It is when the Son of Man, Christ crucified and Christ to come, is proclaimed with power in all His saving grace and judgment, that the Table is kept holy and undefiled; and it is then when His Word and authority are glorified that it is indeed the Lord's Table and the Lord's Supper, and not a private supper owned and administered on exclusive principles by the Church. It cannot be said too plainly that whenever the prophetic ministry decays,

13—C.A.C.

whenever the Church refuses to give priority to the ministry of the Word over the ministry of Tables, the priestly authority gets out of hand, and inevitably falls under the judgment of the Son of Man.

There is another aspect of this matter to which we must give full recognition, for it is of the utmost importance—the place of order in the Church. "The spirits of the prophets are subject to the prophets; for God is not the author of confusion but of peace, as in all the Churches of the saints" (1 Cor. 14 :32 f.). That means that the Church and its ministry cannot be indifferent to church order. There is a subjection even in the realm of spiritual gifts and *charismata*. On the other hand, St. Paul says quite plainly that "the Lord is the Spirit, and where the Spirit of the Lord is, there is liberty" (2 Cor. 3: 17). There cannot be any absolute fixity of order in the charismatic ministry of the Church. How are we to understand this order in which there is both freedom and control? That was one of the crucial problems facing St. Paul in the Corinthian Church, and the answer he gave is taken straight out of the Eucharist, though it is closely linked with Baptism.[1]

We may fill out St. Paul's thought with other New Testament teaching, and put the matter in the following way. In Baptism the Church is incorporated into the Body of Christ and puts on Christ. That is to say, the Church partakes of the form of Christ's Body. The conformity of the Church to Christ, which is once-and-for-all in Baptism, is not static, but dynamic, for it is bound up with the Church's obedience as it carries out the ordinance of the Lord to proclaim His death till He come. That concerns both missionary *kerygma* and the eucharistic proclamation, though it is above all in the Eucharist where the Church knows Christ in the fellowship of His sufferings and the power of His Resurrection that it becomes conformable unto Him. There the Church is crucified unto the world, and is transformed by the renewing of its mind into the image or form of Jesus Christ. It is in the Eucharist, too, that the Church becomes visible as the Body of Christ in history, for it is there that it becomes a membered Body under the Headship of Christ. "We being many are one body, for we all partake of the one bread." That

[1] Cf. especially for the following, E. Käsemann, *Evangelische Theologie*, 1948, 9–10; and H. Dobert, *Evangelische Theologie*, 1949, 11.

membering or ordering of the Church is the new order or the
new covenant of the Kingdom, into which the Church
is initiated at Baptism, but which now materializes in visible
bodily fashion. It is the constitution of the Church in Jesus
Christ.

Christ is Prophet, Priest, and King. Therefore the Church,
which in Baptism puts on Christ and in the Eucharist becomes
one Body with Him, is given to participate in that *triplex munus*.
As His Body the Church manifests the form of that Body as it
exercises in obedience to Him, a prophetic, priestly, and kingly
ministry. We have to remember, however, that the Church is
only joined to Christ as a body is joined to its head, and its
ministry as Body is not the same as the ministry of the Head. To
take priesthood, for example, with which we are mostly concerned at this point in our discussion: Christ's Priesthood and
the Church's priesthood cannot be spoken of in univocal terms
any more than Christ's sacrifice and the eucharistic sacrifice.
They are not of the same genus. Once that is understood clearly
a great deal of the confusion resulting from the ambiguous use
of the word "priesthood" can be swept away. It should be perfectly clear right away, therefore, that the Church's priesthood
cannot be thought of as having in any way control over Christ,
any more than the body can control the head.[1]

Two further facts about the ministry of the Church must be
noted:

(a) The Form of Christ in the Eucharist remains a mystery,
and is not to be fully discerned. We see Christ by faith, only
through a glass darkly, for He is veiled behind the elements as
well as unveiled or revealed through them. That means that the
whole question of the Church's order and ministry is bound up
with the Self-revelation of Christ, and because of that the
Church's order cannot come under its ultimate control. It belongs to the nature of Revelation to take concrete form as
human word, human form, human ordinance. Revelation
therefore conceals Christ behind word, sacrament, ordinance,
as well as reveals Him. A direct reading off of the Church's
form and order from the Eucharist is impossible. It belongs to
the nature of the Church to bear witness in definite orders to the
Form of the Body of Christ and so to manifest that Form in

[1] See *Royal Priesthood, S.J.T. Occasional Paper* no. 3, 1955, ch. IV.

historical conditions, but because that Form is the content of
Revelation the Church cannot transcribe it into the conditions
of time and history in any perfect or indelible or fixed structure.
Every time it partakes of the Eucharist it allows its order or
historical structure to be called in question by that which here
comes from beyond history and is not expressible in terms of
history alone. It is only in such a way that we can think of the
order or the orders of the Church.

(b) In this situation it is the function of the Church's ministry
to build or edify the Church on earth by Word and Sacrament,
so that the form and order of the Church in history may correspond sacramentally to the true form and order that are yet to
be revealed. This means that we must think of the priesthood
of the Church as having an essentially sacramental character.
Through Baptism and the Lord's Supper the Church is formed
into a corporate priesthood, a royal priesthood,[1] but that priesthood remains essentially a mystery, and only becomes visible in
a historical and membered priesthood which points to a fullness
beyond itself. That is why St. Paul speaks of this membered
priesthood not in terms of priesthood but in terms of *charismata*.
We may distinguish then between the Church's priesthood and
charismata, by saying that the priesthood is essentially corporate,
is a whole, and cannot be broken up into parts. *Charismata* are
the gifts of the ascended Lord, and are essentially fragmented.
Not all are prophets, not all are apostles, or teachers or workers
of miracles. There are diversities of gifts and administrations
and operations, but it is the same Spirit, the same Lord, and the
same God who worketh all in all, and behind all this diversity of
gifts and members there is one body in Christ. The diverse
charismata have no value in themselves, but only as they minister
together to the edification of the whole body.

The Church in history, then, is related to its ascended Lord
by means of these diverse *charismata*, which partake indeed of
historical fragmentation and which shall therefore pass away
before the ultimate reality which is the oneness of the Church to
Christ in love (1 Cor. 13),[2] but which here and now are the

---

[1] Cf. 1 Peter 2: 5, 9; Rev. 1: 6; Luke 22: 29; 1 Cor. 11: 25; 2 Cor. 3: 6.
The Church in the New Covenant is appointed at once a Kingdom and a
priesthood or a ministry.

[2] Cf. E. Walter, *Das Kommen des Herrn*, I, pp. 38 f., 90 ff.

historical means that God uses to build up the Church on earth. In this situation it is the function of the ministry to edify the Church by Word and Sacrament, that its form and order may more and more approximate to and partake of the one Body of Christ. That takes place above all in the Lord's Supper, where the *charismata* are to be regarded as the signs pointing to the new divine order which is ever breaking through the eucharistic participation and being realized afresh in the Church on earth. That new divine order is only visible in orders that serve it truly and never in orders that obscure it or seek to manage it. It is the function of orders to make room in the Church and to keep that room open for the actual intervention of the ascended Lord in Word and Sacrament.

Here in the Eucharist, therefore, we are given our deepest insight into the meaning of order under the Lordship of Christ, as order which is sacramentally and eschatologically conditioned. The actual ordering of the Church partakes of the form and fashion of this passing world, and as such it can never be identified in its historical structure with the essential form of the Church or be allowed to anticipate the order yet to be fully disclosed in the *eschaton*. It can only point beyond itself. The Church that is truly ordered will possess its orders as if it possessed them not, coveting earnestly the more excellent way which abides for ever, the way of love, when all orders, however necessary and sacramental they are within history, will pass away. Such a Church will watch and pray for its Lord, waiting for His coming, when it will put off the image of the earthly, the compromised ecclesiastical shell that marks its continuing historical existence, and put on the image of the heavenly.

From all this, three conclusions follow which are important for our discussion of intercommunion.

(1) The Eucharist cannot be subordinated to any conception of order. If the Church really becomes the Church in the Eucharist, how can it bring order to the Eucharist if it is there that it receives its order with its true being? It is only because there are repeated celebrations of the Eucharist that the Church can bring order to the Eucharist, but the very repetition of the Eucharist means the relativization of that prior order and its reordering in the presence of the Church's Lord. As often as we

celebrate the Lord's Supper we proclaim His death till He come, we receive anew His death and resurrection into the existence of the Church, and so bear about the dying of the Lord Jesus in the body of the Church that the life also of Jesus may be made manifest in that body. Through the Eucharist, therefore, death worketh in the Church and its members and orders. If through the Eucharist the Spirit of Christ is in the Church, then its "body" is dead, mortified by the death of Christ—that is to say, its "body" understood as its implication in the forms of this world. It is only when through the eucharistic enactment the judgment inherent in the death of Christ is allowed to break up the hardened forms of the Church's liturgy, into which eschatology is continually being transmuted, that the Church can truly serve the Lord it worships, and at the same time hold out life to the world.

It is sometimes argued that the Eucharist does not stand alone, but is embedded in the historical continuity or the institutional continuity of the Church, including its structure of faith and order, which is part of the significance of its continual repetition in the action of the Church. Undoubtedly the celebration of the Eucharist is so embedded in the institutional continuity of the Church, but the Eucharist by its very nature, in as much as it enshrines the real presence of the Son of Man, the Lord of the Eucharist, stands above the institutional continuity of the Church and *can never be made relative to it*, for that would make the Church the master of the Son of Man and not His servant.[1] This is the crucial point in ecumenical discussion on intercommunion, for it is here that the ultimate difficulty lies, in the difference between Churches which take biblical eschatology seriously and those who are retrenched in a fixity of orders within which they involve the *Lord's* Supper as though it were their own. As Professor Manson has said so well (in the same article): "The sacrament is a catholic ordinance for catholic approach. It proclaims not the Church in the Lord but the Lord in the Church." It is one of the extraordinary facts about the ecumenical fellowship that to-day the younger Churches are everywhere feeling the pressure of the coming

---

[1] For a remarkably clear discussion of this fact, to which I am much indebted, see W. Manson, "Church and Intercommunion", *Scottish Journal of Theology*, 1950, vol. 4.1, pp. 4 f.

Kingdom upon them and bear evidence of a truly charismatic ministry—that is nowhere more in evidence than in the Church of South India—but some of the older Churches show, on the contrary, evidence of a marked hardening of their orders, which can only be interpreted as a sign of the last times.

(2) The Eucharist cannot be subordinated to history. The enactment of the eucharistic presence into the flesh and blood of history means that the Church can never be allowed to forget its involvement in history. We do not stand before the Son of Man as we shall do when He comes again, for His suspension of final judgment until the last day gives history its course. The Church stands to-day and all through history where the Lord's Supper takes place, between the Resurrection of Jesus Christ and His Second Advent, that is, in the midst of history. The Revelation, which calls the Church into being and recreates it from age to age, takes place within history, and it is there that the living Lord gives Himself to be known to us, within the actual ongoing historical Church and nowhere else. On the other hand, the eucharistic presence involves the power of the Resurrection, which breaks the fetters of history and tells us that the risen Lord cannot be holden in the fixity of the past.

In other words, the Eucharist means the enactment of the real presence of the living Christ to-day, and every day it is celebrated. But if we have to do with the real presence of Christ *to-day*, we may not bind that to the embodiment of Christ in His Church in the passing forms of another day—that would be to perpetuate a dead Christ and to by-pass the resurrection from the dead. If Christ had not ascended and we had continuous visible contact with Him to-day, that would doubtless mean that the historical events of His birth, ministry in Judaea and Galilee, and death under Pontius Pilate, would be relegated to the incidents of past history and perhaps forgotten, but His ascension tells us that to know Jesus Christ and make contact with Him we must concentrate upon those historical events of His birth, life, and death; that is to say, we must concentrate upon the historical foundation of the Church's faith. "I have received of the Lord that which also I delivered unto you. As often as ye do this ye proclaim the Lord's death till He come." At the same time the withdrawal of Christ by ascension from visible implication in ongoing history, and His promise to come again as the Lord and Judge of History, tells us that all historical existence is made relative to His immediate presence. It is that real presence which breaks into history in the Eucharist, from beyond history, which cannot be construed in terms of history alone, and which cannot be imprisoned in history, either in the history of a particular period such as the Catholic ages or the Reformation, or in the long sweep of Church history. The Eucharist therefore cannot be made subordinate to history, for it is creative of history.

Nor can we forget the fact that every time in the Eucharist we eat the broken body and partake of the blood of Christ we are communicating in the death of Christ, partaking of the judgment which that death involved, in order that we may also partake of the power of His resurrection. To participate in the Eucharist and its proclamation of the death of Christ until He come is to involve the Church in the final judgment upon the forms of history in order that its new life may appear. The repeated celebrations of the Eucharist do not mean that the Church is growing old with tradition and ancient glory, for its glory is yet to be revealed in the manifestation of the Son of Man, but it means that the Church is ever growing younger and younger, until at last it arrives at the great day when as a Bride it shall be presented to the Bridegroom for the consummation of its joy in the marriage-supper of the Lamb. In as much as the Eucharist is an anticipation of that day, it stands above history, and can never be subordinated to it or made relative to the fixity of its passing forms.

(3) If the Eucharist cannot be subordinated to history or to any particular conception of order, but is the transcendent manifestation of the Son of Man within history until He come in the fullness of His glory, then the Eucharist is above all the divinely given means of unity in the Church. "We being many are one body, for we all partake of the one bread." That is a fact that can never be made relative to anything outside of it, if it is not to be dwarfed and domesticated into a private rite. The very place of the Eucharist between the two Advents of Christ, in the very midst of history with all its divisions and heart-rending failures, means that it is designed to be such a means of unity

within diversity that in spite of diversity and division that unity is continually recreated in conditions of time until its full reality is disclosed in the Kingdom to come. We are unable to trace the lineaments of the Kingdom in the fragmented patterns of history so that we can say: lo here is the *Una Sancta*, or, lo there is the *Una Sancta*. But we know that we have been baptized into one Body, and that there is one Lord, one Faith, one Baptism. Supervening upon that we have been given the Holy Eucharist as the sacrament of unity in diversity to tell us that our oneness with the Lord does not depend upon our success or failure in loyalty to Him, but on His Will to be one with us and to make us all one in Him. That belongs to the heart of Christ's high-priestly intercession, and we cannot hold that the Eucharist is in any sense the counterpart on earth to that (not merely in some pious mystic hope, but in actual enactment of the mystery of our unity in flesh and blood) without believing that it is through participation in the Eucharist that we are meant *more and more* (as Calvin put it) *to coalesce in one body with Him and so with each other*.

If the Sacrament only proclaimed that unity in word and did not also serve to enact it, it would not be the Sacrament that the Church holds it to be. Here the corporeal Self-communication of Christ to the Church through the one bread and the one cup, actually enacts in flesh and blood the unity of the one Lord, and constrains us to concrete corporeal obedience in the one Body of the Lord. The refusal of intercommunion entails a failure to discern the Body of the Lord and an unworthy participation in His body and blood. St. Paul told the Corinthians quite explicitly that for groups to meet for communion separately is not to hold the *Lord's* Supper, but to turn it into a private supper, and indeed to create schism in the Church. It is for that cause that so many are weak and sickly in the Church. There can be no doubt, therefore, that Churches ought to sit down together before the presence of the Son of Man, and together eat and drink the judgment of the death of Christ upon their sinful divisions and compromised histories, in order that together they may be given anew the power of the resurrection to rise above the trammels of the past and to realize the very unity of the one Body into which they have been baptized.

This means that intercommunion should come early in the

14—C.A.C.

approach of the Churches toward full unity in the ecumenical fellowship, for that unity can never be reached so long as the separated Churches refuse to give each other the divine medicine for their healing. The Holy Eucharist cannot be celebrated without the breaking of the bread and the pouring out of the wine. Let it be celebrated, then, within the fraction of the Church, wherever the Church is sincere enough to resist unto blood everything that stands between it and its Lord. Let the Church that gives communion to another remember the words of the Lord: "In as much as ye have done it unto one of the least of these my brethren, ye have done it unto me." And let the Church that refuses to give communion to another remember also those other words of the same Lord which will be spoken at the final judgment: "I was an hungered and ye gave me no meat: I was thirsty and ye gave me no drink." "Lord, when saw we thee an hungered or athirst, and did not minister unto thee?" Then shall he answer them, "In as much as ye did it not unto one of the least of these, ye did it not unto me." Those are solemn words which have direct bearing upon intercommunion.[1]

It is certain that at the last day all the barriers of liturgy and cult and order that have been erected in history around the Holy Table of the Lord will be torn down, for in that great day "The Spirit and the Bride say, Come. And let him that heareth say, Come. And let him that is athirst come. And whosoever will, let him take of the water of life freely." And St. John adds, if any man shall take away these words from the Book of Prophecy, God shall take away his part out of the Book of Life, and out of the Holy City. We cannot afford to wait until the *eschaton* to hear those words. The Eucharist is given to us here and now as an anticipation within history of the marriage-supper of the Lamb. In every true Eucharist, therefore, the Church, as the Bride of Christ, will join the Spirit, saying, *Come. Whosoever will, let him take the water of life freely.* Only when that happens can it be an eschatologically valid Eucharist.

[1] See further *Essays in Anglican Self-Criticism*, edit. by D. M. Paton, pp. 202 f.

INDEX

I. *Biblical References*

INDEX

II. Names

à LASCO John, 142
Aquinas, Thomas, 156, 173, 185
Askew, E., 11
Augustine, 32, 56, 141, 156, 164, 182

BAILLIE, D. M., 6, 54
Bardy, G., 154
Barth, Karl, 28, 161, 178 f., 190
Barth, Markus, 185
Baumstark, A., 154
Brownlee, W. H., 105
Bruce, Robert, 188
Brunner, Emil, 158
Bucer, Martin, 142
Bultmann, R., 126 f.

CABROL, A., 154
Calvin, John, 51 f., 55, 64, 66, 138 ff.,
    148 ff., 161, 178, 181 ff., 186 ff., 201
Camfield, F. W., 181 f., 184
Casel, O., 154
Clement of Alexandria, 60, 85
Cullmann, Oscar, 69, 168

DAUBE, D., 40, 42 f.
de la Taille, M., 154, 180
Dobert, H., 194
Dodd, C. H., 58 ff.

EHRHARDT, A., 39

GARDINER, Stephen, Bishop of Win-
    chester, 188
Gaugler, E., 161
Guardini, R., 154

HEBERT, G., 75, 78
Heim, Karl, 171
Héris, P., 154
Hippolytus, 118

IRENAEUS, 118

JAMES I, 11
Jeremias, J., 177
Josephus, Flavius, 108
Jülicher, A., 59, 61
Jungmann, J. A., 154

KÄSEMANN, E., 194
Kierkegaard, S., 69
Kirkpatrick, J. M., 12
Kittel, G., 63, 74
Knox, John, 55 f., 138, 148 ff.

LEVISON, N., 97, 99
Lohmeyer, E., 169
Luther, Martin, 139, 188

MACKINNON, D. M., 176, 184
Manson, T. W., 63
Manson, William, 168, 198
Marsh, John, 6, 154
Martyr, Peter Vermigli, 142, 156, 188
Marx, K., 126
Masure, E., 154
Melito of Sardis, 114

NIESEL, W., 187 f.
Nygren, Anders, 4

OSIANDER, Andreas, 143

PATON, D. M., 202
Pelagius, 137, 183 f.
Pius IV, 150

REID, J. K. S., 69

SCHLEIERMACHER, F. D. E., 125 ff.
Schlink, Edmund, 4, 190
Schmaus, M., 154, 174
Schmidt, K. L., 61, 63
Servetus, Michael, 143
Söhngen, G., 154, 174

TERTULLIAN, 118

VONIER, A., 154

WALLACE, R. S., 59
Walter, E., 188, 196
Warnach, V., 154
Weidlé, V., 156
Weiser, A., 74
Wotherspoon, J. H., 12

ZWINGLI, Ulrich, 140, 175

INDEX

III. Subjects